BATTLESCAPES

Scene from a Napoleonic battlefield sur le Nemen, 1807.

BATTLESCAPES

The Impact of Terrain on Military Strategy

Ian D. Rotherham

Pen & Sword
MILITARY
AN IMPRINT OF PEN & SWORD BOOKS LTD.
YORKSHIRE – PHILADELPHIA

First published in Great Britain in 2024 by
Pen & Sword History
An imprint of
Pen & Sword Books Ltd
Yorkshire – Philadelphia

ISBN 9781399066112

A CIP catalogue record for this book is available from the British Library.

Set in Aldine 401 13/16.75
Printed and bound in the UK on paper from a sustainable source by CPI Group (UK) Ltd., Croydon, CR0 4YY

Pen & Sword Books Limited incorporates the imprints of After the Battle, Archaeology, Atlas, Aviation, Battleground, Discovery, Family History, History, Maritime, Military, Politics, Select, Transport, True Crime, Fiction, Frontline Books, Leo Cooper, Praetorian Press, Seaforth Publishing, Wharncliffe and White Owl.

For a complete list of Pen & Sword titles please contact
PEN & SWORD BOOKS LIMITED
George House, Beevor Street, Off Pontefract Road, Hoyle Mill, Barnsley, South Yorkshire, England, S71 1HN
E-mail: enquiries@pen-and-sword.co.uk
Website: www.pen-and-sword.co.uk
Or
PEN AND SWORD BOOKS
1950 Lawrence Rd, Havertown, PA 19083, US
E-mail: Uspen-and-sword@casematepublishers.com
Website: www.penandswordbooks.com

MIX
Paper | Supporting responsible forestry
FSC® C013604

A Russian gun battery in trouble in the Russo-Japanese War.

Contents

The spectre of European war, 28 July 1914–11 November 1918.

Foreword

In *Battlescapes* Ian Rotherham takes students and friends on walks around beloved landscapes across Britain and around the world. Through its pages we reconsider the evolution of human impacts on an astonishing variety of landscapes and waterscapes, especially as they have been shaped – and often degraded – by mass conflicts covering more than two millennia.

His richly observed descriptions of those terrains and dramas are informed by a career's scholarly knowledge of a wide variety of landscapes and waterscapes, the ways entire societies and natural systems have shaped each other, and their capacity for resilience. Uniting environmental, social, and military history, he presents as the book's distinctive message that 'the contestation of landscape becomes more sharply defined in times of conflict as established protocols and rules of management and exploitation breakdown'.

Professor Rotherham's work is deeply rooted in the long tradition of military geography, expressing his intimate knowledge of the evolution of military technology through history. But it is much more than that. *Battlescapes* is an outstanding integration of civilian and military disciplines with ecological studies.

He presents ten main factors in this integrative view of history, lucidly and systematically illustrating them with many case studies across the globe, from the Scottish highlands, across Eurasia, Africa, and to the Americas.

These stories depict mass social dislocations, but adaptation and resilience as well. This theme is sensitive to both warriors and civilians, as they manipulate their terrain and manage to survive. They include not only formal conflict, but also guerilla warfare and mass refugee movements, including both emigration and immigration as populations struggle from one homeland to another.

An especially innovative chapter discusses the landscape consequences of cultural and religious differences, as dominant groups attempt to control dissention and non-conformity, through fratricidal wars across Europe and elsewhere. On a broad canvas, these conflicts are dimensions of Europe's global empires and the struggles of other cultures in response.

For anyone concerned with the environmental health or degradation of the world we live in today, *Battlescapes* gives a fine baseline for anchoring their consideration of the place of mass conflict in environmental history.

A striking feature of the book is its lavish use of illustrations, an education in itself. Equally significant, the book applies its perspective on human and natural history to

Above: Modern-day view across Holland Fen near Chapel Hill, Lincolnshire. (Johanthan Thacker)

Below: Scottish Highlands. (needpix.com)

the author's team's present-day work for healing and rewilding human and natural communities in Sheffield and beyond. As their UKEconet website asserts, their work addresses:

'... wilder, more connected futures to halt declines of species and environmental quality yet recognising the cultural nature and heritage value of many landscapes. This programme emerges from 30+ years of seminars and conferences organised by our team and partners. With major challenges of future climate change, land-use, biodiversity, heritage, economy, and community, we bring together a unique group of experts, academics, researchers, the public, and practitioners to debate the issues'.

In summary, *Battlescapes* is a richly rewarding tour guide across history and ecosystems. It belongs in classrooms, bookstores, and homes across the continents.

Richard P. Tucker
(Former Adjunct Professor University of Michigan, Professor Emeritus Oakland University)

British sentry in Flanders during the First World War.

PREAMBLE

WARFARE and conflict, from minor skirmishes to full-blown battles or campaigns, are often determined by knowledge of terrain and other environmental factors. This principle has applied throughout history and continues to hold true in contemporary conflicts. For communities facing threats, a deep understanding of local terrain is often essential, and goes hand in hand with their strong connection to the landscape and 'possession of place'. Invaders are almost always outsiders and will inherently possess less knowledge about the contested locales. Indeed, for both defenders and aggressors, terrain knowledge can be the key to success, but the crucial step lies in the application of insights about the local environment on the theatre of conflict. In the case of civil wars, local terrain knowledge may be less immediately significant, as both sides are often familiar with the locale.

Throughout history, kings, princes, emperors, and military commanders, such

Monument to Second World War tanks in Lviv, Ukraine, from the 1950s.

Firing a massive French railway cannon during the First World War, 1918.

as generals, marshals, and warlords, have faced the same or similar challenges. To achieve success, they must outmanoeuvre their enemies, accumulate necessary resources, and exploit their vulnerabilities by attacking the opposition's weak points. Moreover, a military leader must strive to avoid becoming trapped and must be capable of capitalizing on the opportunities of victory while trying to mitigate, whenever possible, the potential impacts of defeat. While methods and equipment in warfare have evolved over the centuries, the fundamental principles remain largely unchanged. Additionally, individual battles and conflicts do not occur in isolation; they are part of historical timelines. The ambitions of rulers, politicians, tribes, nation-states, and the failure of diplomacy, along with competition for scarce or valuable resources, are all factors that trigger or contribute to conflicts. Individual confrontations can result from specific events or long-standing disputes that have spanned decades or even centuries. Consequently, the context, strategies, and consequences vary significantly. Within all these scenarios, the significance of geography, terrain, and topography often plays a pivotal role, and throughout history, military tacticians have sought to exploit nature and adapt to its constraints.

Charging from the trenches during the First World War.

Yet, the roles of landscape in the theatre of war and in the fostering of dissension or nonconformity are often underappreciated. This lack of insight is intriguing since the nature of countryside and landscape has consistently influenced the tactics of warfare and determined the outcomes of conflicts throughout history. From the medieval English fenland riots to the twentieth-century Marsh Arab landscapes in Iraq, the countryside has encouraged resistance, nonconformity, and dissent. Societies under threat from aggressive neighbours or rival cultures have harnessed and utilized the landscape to influence their defence strategies. Wetlands, rivers, expansive forests or jungles, deserts, and mountain ranges have all played significant, albeit often underappreciated, roles in human conflicts. For instance, the Florida Everglades provided the setting for a prolonged American campaign against the few remaining Native Americans holding out there in the nineteenth century. This conflict was called the US's first Vietnam; it was a conflict in which knowledge of the wetland terrain and conditions allowed a vastly outnumbered and outgunned population to resist an aggressive external force for many years.

Similarly, terrain and local knowledge played a significant role in the Franco-Prussian War of the late 1800s, where French generals used the wetland landscape to

Massive French railway cannon, First World War, 1918.

Osceola or Billy Bowlegs, resistance leader of the Seminoles in the Florida Everglades.

devastating effect. In the Second World War, the Dutch flooded the drained polders to halt the Nazi advance into Holland, and the Germans retaliated by flooding Dutch farmland. Guerrilla warfare in the mountains of former Yugoslavia during the Second World War, or in the hills of Afghanistan in the late twentieth and early twenty-first centuries, are other examples of terrain aiding resistance. The role of landscape in Scottish conflicts is also prominent, from apocryphal stories of Roman legions dispatched by Pictish tribes emerging from trackless forests, to the Scots defeating the English at Bannockburn by luring the heavy cavalry into wetlands. These are just a few examples of a widespread but under-researched subject. Mountains, wetlands, deserts, and vast forests have all played major strategic roles in conflicts, ranging from warfare to civil unrest and religious strife. The importance continues in the conflict in Ukraine, where armoured columns and troops quickly become mired in mud and wetlands, and supply chains come under stress. In Taiwan, the straits act as a clear barrier to mainland Chinese expansionist aspirations, and the island itself

Battlefield of Woerth in the Franco-Prussian War of 1870.

includes mountainous and forested countryside that favours indigenous resistance.

This volume applies aspects of current research to neglected fields, such as landscapes and heritage of past conflicts, like the airfields of the First and Second World Wars, defensive and offensive structures, and much more. The book does not aim to be comprehensive in its coverage of the issues but intends to provide a broad narrative spanning from prehistory to the present day. Marine conflicts and aerial battles are not considered in detail since this would broaden the scope too much for effective coverage. Similarly, fighting in complex island archipelagos is not discussed in detail. Furthermore, the examples

German body armour during the First World War.

German convoy stuck in the mud in 1942.

German soldiers in off-road vehicles during the muddy season in 1941.

of battles, wars, and other conflicts are selected as exemplars for reasons related to landscape and are not comprehensive in any sense. Some conflicts and battles are discussed in more than one chapter because they demonstrate aspects of different environments or habitats. Individual chapters explore aspects of warfare and nature, or landscape, while others address issues habitat by habitat.

One major objective of this volume is to consider the significance of location, landscape (topography and terrain), and to some extent, associated climate and weather, in determining the outcomes of military conflicts throughout history. The analysis process involves balancing the advantages or disadvantages for combatants in various landscapes or geographical settings. Furthermore, there are lessons to be learned about the costs and benefits in conflicts and the often futility of war when landscape can make a significant difference in the inevitable toll on lives and resources.

Additionally, warfare has a profound impact on both society and the landscape,

German soldiers advancing with a flamethrower during the First World War.

and the interactions are two-way. Wars and individual battles may be considered together and separately. Knowledge or understanding of landscape, terrain, and topography influences tactics at both levels. Political conflicts generally revolve around control of territory and/or resources; sadly, warfare often becomes the result and may be the resolution. Understanding landscape and the terrain of conflict is therefore significant in determining the tactics of both aggressors and the victims of aggression. The type of conflict and its causes and aims are incredibly significant in terms of their interactions with nature and landscape and their relationships with

King George V visiting the trenches of the First World War, outside a captured German dugout.

Dutch soldiers hide in a peat barge, Breda, 1590.

The challenges of warfare in a bog, source unknown, possibly from the Franco-Prussian War.

strategy and tactics, whether it's a single, unconnected battle or a broader, longer-term war. The aims of aggression, from a border raid to a full invasion and occupation of territory, also affect and influence the mode of engagement. Hit-and-run raids from one territory into another, such as the medieval Scottish reivers into Northumbria or along a coastal zone like the Viking raids on the east coast of England, may primarily aim to acquire possessions. These goods could range from valuables to livestock and slaves. However, sporadic raids sometimes evolve into territorial grabs and occupation. The latter can vary in nature. In some cases, like the Roman invasion of Britain, the process involves the displacement or Romanization of the ruling elite, resulting in cultural absorption. The peasantry and other workers often remained but with different rulers. In other examples, like

The swampy landscape of Flanders and Belgian victory over the Germans at the Yser Canal in April 1918.

Warfare in a wetland during the First World War, with the caption reading: "— these — rations."

the Saxon invasion of post-Roman England, there was a much deeper shift of the indigenous populations out of their occupied territories. The Britons were squeezed out from eastern and southern England and retreated west into southwest England, known as West Wales, and into Wales, Cumbria, and north into Strathclyde in southern Scotland, where they became the Strathclyde Welsh. The later Viking invasions of the British Isles were launched from Scandinavia around the Scottish and Irish coasts, particularly, and from Denmark and adjacent lands along the east and southeast of England. Like the Anglo-Saxon approaches, these incursions began as hit-and-run raiding parties that later established permanent settlements. While there was some interaction with and absorption of the indigenous communities of the time in all these cases, the Anglo-Saxons and Vikings also displaced and slaughtered entire

The last Viking King of York, the infamous Eric Bloodaxe.

social groups and seized territory and resources. In many cases, the genetic consequences of this overlaying of invaders in a particular geographic region has left evidence in the modern DNA of resident populations. With these differing motives underpinning conflicts and warfare, the importance of terrain and topography of the countryside for both attackers and defenders can be vastly different. The associated tactics and strategies that play out in the landscape accordingly vary.

The King's Hussars, British cavalry in the 1800s.

The Regiment of Horse, a British cavalry troop in the 1800s.

The English city of York has, since Roman times, been defended with walls of one form or another. To this day, substantial portions of the walls remain, and York has more miles of intact wall than any other city in England. (Tom Blackwell)

British Expeditionary Force in Flanders 1917.

CHAPTER 1
Introduction to landscapes of resistance

Conflicts such as warfare are geographical phenomena, and they are not random or uniform in their occurrence. A mix of human and physical geography underpins any understanding of conflict and landscape as the theatre of warfare. Relevant factors in triggering and determining the outcomes of conflicts include location, land and associated mineral resources, human population issues, travel, and transport infrastructure, and military technology. The latter are constantly evolving to include new methods of human slaughter, such as computer-guided drones, which totally change approaches to conflict.

Geopolitical influences underpin aspects of the geography of battles as local, regional, tribal, national, and global imperialist interests compete for control. Macro-geography and history help inform spatial and geographic matters of strategy and deployment. Conflicts are often associated with competition for territorial influence between

Bodies floating in floodwater on the Yser near Calais during the First World War.

rulers of nation states, or at a more parochial level, tribal interests. Some wars result from such competition, but others are the consequence of internal discontent and the desire to overthrow an established order. In evaluating these processes, it is important to consider the influence of power balances between revolutionaries, governments, and rival regimes. Through this lens, situational advantages and disadvantages, spatial location and the associated terrain and climate, and human influences are all important in understanding conflicts.

Battlescapes

Consideration of the geo-spatial aspects and histories of individual battles and battlefields is important in helping draw broader conclusions about the factors involved in wider conflicts. This further enables an understanding of the specific characteristics of violent political disputes. Essentially, wars and individual battles can be categorized according to the historic period in which they occur, and by where they take place: deserts, forests, woodlands, grasslands such as plains or savannah, mountains and hill-country, swamps and other wetlands, farmland, or in urban settings. The numbers of combatants and the types of weaponry involved are significant alongside the politics of any conflicts. No single criterion can explain or categorize the relationships between violent disputes and the landscapes in which they take place.

Furthermore, there are obvious historical issues such as the development of technologies like specific weaponry or the evolution of tactics that change the nature of warfare. These everchanging factors alter the interaction between fighting and terrain or wider landscape implications. Such historical factors can be used to distinguish, among other things, modern and ancient ground battles. We need only look at the advent of breech-loading rifles in the 1850s which increased the range of engagement. The development of modern railway systems, and then rapid road

British Redcoats in the late 1800s.

transport, coincided with this to extend the scope of conflicts and battles beyond the limits of an individual soldier's line of sight. Prior to this change a soldier, or warrior, was engaged in killing their opponents at distances of less than a hundred metres; face-to-face action was intimately embedded in the local terrain. In such circumstances, leadership was more a matter of tactics than broader strategy.

In ancient battles, a general used the lie of the land and his tactical nous to achieve success, or not. In modern warfare, there is far more dependence on stratagems and influences beyond the immediate landscape. This can be understood by considering the historical transformations in conflicts; such changes are not merely technological but socio-political too. Clearly, there are huge differences between conflicts where the key protagonists lead 'from the front' and will be engaged eyeball to eyeball, and modern warfare where leaders direct operations from a safe distance. We see this transformation through the 1800s and early 1900s in the colonial wars between traditional warriors and professional soldiers of modern Western armies. Other innovations which transformed conflicts include both naval and aerial adaptations and technologies; and as noted earlier, these are on-going. Modern remote sensing transforms reconnaissance and information gathering and has evolved from balloons to light aircraft and satellite imagery, and emerging artificial intelligence applications are part of the shifting sands of modern warfare.

Overall, competition and discontent may have multiple causes and complex spatial manifestations. It is widely accepted that revolutionary political change, operating through geographic and historical forces, is fundamental in conflict and in determining its outcomes. Indeed, the setting for wars and battles is a matter of place and time that helps focus multiple, seemingly random, historical events into more-

Ancient European Battlefield.

or-less structured outcomes that may in part be predictable. The results of conflicts over competition for power are thus in part determined, or at least influenced, by environmental circumstances and situations.

Landscape and warfare

For participants, soldiers or partisans, landscape and geography offer barriers and opportunities relevant to violent conflict. These facets include plains and savannahs, forests and woods, hills and mountains, rivers, streams and lakes, farmland and associated buildings, and roads of other infrastructure. Such features offer concealment, routes for movement, observation points, sightlines, killing fields, and firing platforms or positions. The same principles apply whether in rural or urban situations, though the balance of natural and built components varies between the two. Climate and associated weather also have a significant bearing on the soldier's ability to move through a landscape, to be concealed and to aim, shoot, and fire. Examples of the impacts of seasonal extreme weather are the effects of monsoon rains in tropical zones where the movement of vehicles, men, and especially of heavy armour, becomes virtually impossible. Similarly, the fields, meadows, and grasslands of summer may become impassable snowfields in winter.

Artillery bogged down on the Flanders Front in November 1917.

Close-quarters combat in the snowy First World War trenches, April 1915.

All these factors affect the conflict itself as well as inward supply lines, and the removal of the wounded.

Many wetlands, mountains, forests, deserts, and plains are contested landscapes and have been so for millennia. Continuing up to the twentieth-century removal of the Marsh Arabs by Saddam Hussein, water and wetlands for example have been central to regional conflicts and cultural tensions. These issues are important in understanding many inter-regional conflicts, military campaigns generally, and numerous long-standing cultural interactions. Yet, as noted for wetlands in the book 'War & Peat', the environmental histories of these spaces with respect to human conflicts remain

Chasseurs D'Alpin attacking Germans in the Vosges.

largely neglected topics. Terrain may obstruct incursions and invasions on the one hand but facilitate easy mobility and even conquest on the other. Understanding how best to utilize, or where appropriate to minimize, adverse effects of these factors may be critical in determining the outcomes of conflicts large and small. In terms of military tactics, the natural environment, often experienced as landscape, is perhaps most significant through its wetness or dryness, its temperature, and through its relief (topography).

For soldiers on the ground, the landscape factors which are of the most importance are sightlines and distance, that is, how far you can see and shoot. This of course is influenced by terrain and topography, and by the technology available to you. Human artefacts such as hedges, plantation woods, buildings, and crops may also be important. How easy it is to move personnel and vehicles, or other equipment, is influenced by the availability of roads, railway lines, canals, and rivers, and by the firmness of the ground, slope, vegetation type and density, as well as seasonal influences. It is these factors which need to be considered in terms of conflicts, battles, and wars. Landscape can then be assessed in terms of wetness, dryness, ruggedness, flatness, variety or

Norwegian skirmishing party March 1894.

uniformity. Predictability and reliability of conditions is also important.

Communities, countryside, and conflicts

This book addresses issues of people, conflict, landscape, and ecology. It does so by considering ten main interactions and influencing factors supported by pertinent illustrative examples:

1. Environmental influences on war and conflict through topography and nature are frequently critical of military strategy and conflict outcome.
2. Terrain and topography influence the outcomes of warfare and military or tribal aggression through knowledge and strategy of both aggressors and defenders.
3. For potential invaders, incursions into foreign lands may bring immediate success. However, the ability to hold the territorial gains may hinge on the nature of that landscape and, for example, the effectiveness of supply lines. Extensive wetlands, forests, mountains, or deserts, provide refuges for resistance and defence. The long-term success of a military campaign may flounder in the face of stern local opposition by deeply embedded forces being able to melt away into a countryside they know well. In such situations disparities in military technology can be outweighed by local knowledge and local resistance.
4. From early times up to the present, countryside and ecology have influenced war and conflict through topography and nature, often being of critical significance to strategy and outcome.
5. From medieval times to the modern period, heaths, and moors particularly, were often used as military training grounds.
6. In England, especially during the Second World War when they were brought

into use as airfields and similar facilities, heaths, and reclaimed wetlands, such as former fens, were used as wartime bases.

7. In Britain and Europe bogs, moors, and other peatlands played unplanned passive roles in warfare, such as being the last resting places for stricken or lost bombers of both sides during the Second World War. The European countryside provided materials of immense value to wartime efforts. For peatlands, especially bogs and fens, this included the supply of horse litter, sphagnum moss, alder buckthorn, or peat fuel. Woods and forests supplied food, construction wood and timber, fuel, and more.
8. Conflicts, socio-economic stresses, or extreme weather, all influenced fuel use and the competition and therefore exploitation of mineral coal, wood, peat, and other fuels. Such usage often changed landscapes to form the modern countryside we experience today.
9. Mountains, fens and bogs, deserts, and islands especially, have been places of sanctuary, of non-conformism, and independence, and so were extensive forests, and jungles.

Cutting down trees in the wood of Boulogne, the defence of Paris 1870, Franco-Prussian War.

Sardinians cutting down trees Alessandria, 1859, the Italian War.

Turkish soldiers felling trees on Mount Karaula, Herzeg War, 1875.

10. Finally, historical embeddedness and 'ownership' of the turf become central and critical to the outcomes of many conflicts. Being historically rooted in a particular locale and its terrain may combine with a backs-to-the-wall response to being under threat in your own backyard. In this respect, as seen with twenty-first century Ukraine, an indigenous population facing the overwhelming odds of an aggressive invader will have huge incentive to defend its place and an invaluable advantage of intrinsic knowledge of terrain and topography.

The central argument of this book is that landscape and countryside of varying sorts have been hugely important to people in times of conflict or stress. Furthermore, the resulting interactions have had major impacts on the ecology and landscapes we see today. In addition, it is suggested that most of these complex phenomena have been largely overlooked, or at least forgotten. Moreover, the role of landscape through terrain and topography has been influential, and sometimes key to the outcomes of conflicts. For both defenders and invaders, knowledge and effective adaptation, or use of the countryside, can be the key to success or failure.

The countryside, with its vital resources, is a hotly contested space; it was so in the past and it remains so today. However, the contestation of landscape becomes more sharply defined in times of conflict as established protocols and rules of management and exploitation breakdown. Furthermore, opportunities to 'land grab' or 'resource

Japanese assault on the Russian centre at Liao-Yang 1904.

Emergency felling of trees for fuel with armed guards, Irish Land War, 1887.

grab' may be increasingly present during wars and other unsettled times.

The relationships of people and landscapes, of economies and conflicts, and ecology and history, are complex and multi-faceted. These interactions were considered in detail in previous work for peatlands (including bogs, fens, moors, and heaths), in terms of people and nature in relation to history and conflicts with outcomes both significant and surprising. This idea of '*War & Peat*' (2013) for example, emerged from long-term studies of peatland, such as fens, bogs, heaths, and moors, regarding their histories of utilization and the impacts of conflicts on ecologies. The present volume takes the arguments much further to include woods, forests, mountains, deserts, and more. With deeper research it became clear that conflicts and strife, such as war, political and economic unrest, or extreme weather, had great impacts on the ecology of the countryside.

Russian cavalry crossing an icy river March 1904.

Landscapes of various sorts had not only affected regional economics but had been hugely influential in the theatre of war itself and in the progression and outcomes of conflicts. Throughout history these areas of countryside have been contested landscapes and resources with conflicts not restricted to actual warfare and military campaigns but including more subtle social and economic interplays. For the wider countryside, the 'battles' include those such as the Peat Campaign of the 1980s and 1990s in England, to save the last remaining lowland raised mires, as one example. Without this campaign, sites like South Yorkshire's Thorne Moors and Humberhead Levels would now be landfill, mineral extraction landscapes, or perhaps intensive farming.

The French at the Somme, August 1916.

Pre-First World War soldier in trench coat in Columbus Ohio.

However, the wider ramifications run deep. In the Scottish Highlands, the traditional clans were largely excluded from the landscape by the Highland Clearances. Whereas across England the process of rural depopulation occurred with parliamentary enclosures of the commons during the 1700s and 1800s. Essentially, through socioeconomic and political manoeuvring, the peasants' commons were taken away and whole populations were displaced from the land. Their fate was to become either urban wage slaves in the emerging industries, or itinerant labourers in the countryside, or to emigrate as pioneers around the world. Nevertheless, a conflict of sorts persisted, and ultimately, in response to the twin pressures of demand for legitimate access to former common lands, and escape from the now grossly polluted and overpopulated industrial cities, the emerging working classes campaigned for access to open lands like moors. So, from the 1920s and 1930s, access campaigns grew in cities like Sheffield and Manchester, to claim back access rights to moors and bogs lost under the enclosures. By the early millennium, access to the wider countryside in England was finally given back as a legal right: a battle won. Conflict over landscapes can occur between social classes as well as between nations, and some of this involves violence.

Topography as battlescape

The peat-based British landscapes such as moors, heaths, bogs, and fens exemplify the broad range of influences of topography on conflict and human contestation over space and resources. Additionally, the landscapes have themselves been radically affected by human history and human unitization. Important to realize too, is that the single major effect of historic usage of landscapes by people has been a reduction in extent of these habitats. This is to such an extent that it is almost beyond contemporary imagination. To understand more fully the roles of specific habitats, such as fens and other peatlands, during conflicts or other stresses, you must first appreciate just how widespread they were at that time. Additionally, the nature and condition of the pre-

The Mud Bath 1914, the First World War Western Front.

The new hovercraft designed to beat the swamps tested at Imphal Barracks, York, March 1961.

industrial countryside was dramatically different from the sites that remain today. For instance, fens and bogs were wetter, deeper, and more contiguous in the landscape, and so their influences on people were much greater. The same logic applies to woods, forests, chases, heaths, and commons in the countryside.

Importantly, extensive forests along with major rivers, mountain ranges, and even extensive deserts, can form natural national or tribal strategic boundaries. Wetlands can also be important territorial markers. Natural features delineate occupancy or ownership and may have significance in times of conflict as both symbolic and actual boundaries. They are not only striking as visual markers in the landscape but can be hard to cross or navigate over, through or around. Because of this, terrain and topography often form significant boundaries that demarcate areas and may remain contested spaces with critical edges oscillating over time.

Furthermore, the landscape can present obstacles and markers which assume symbolic significance along with physical difficulties. For ancient Rome, the crossing of the Rubicon River in Italy for example was highly significant, and in the northern parts of its realm, the Rhine River assumed importance in demarcating the Roman Empire from the lands beyond. In some cases, a natural barrier might be marked by a built structure such as the Antonine Wall and Hadrian's Wall in Scotland. In the northern Sahara in North Africa, there are similar constructed boundaries which mark out the southern

Firing a French gun, First World War.

boundary of the Roman Empire of that time. These built markers were sometimes defensive but, more importantly perhaps, they were symbolic. The gateways were portals for trade routes and the walls or gates showed where the rules of Imperial Rome began and where the world beyond the empire started. The Great Wall of China, also both defensive and symbolic, enhanced natural contours and topography to separate civilization on one side, and the 'other' world beyond.

Adapting technology for conflict in difficult landscapes

Patrol Air Cushion Vehicle (PACV)

Topography and environment play major roles in contemporary conflicts. In the Vietnam War, from around 1956 to 1975, for instance, the wet, tropical forest and swamps proved pivotal in the way the war was conducted. United States tanks and armoured vehicles were effective on dry land but not in swamp, forest, or mountain. This meant that technological superiority did not easily equate to military advantage since difficult landscapes can be great levellers.

Faced with major challenges of terrain the American army tried innovations such as the Patrol Air Cushion Vehicle (PACV), also known as the Air Cushion Vehicle (ACV), in army and coast guard service; this was a United States hovercraft used as

British Hovercraft Corporation BH7, 1970s.

a patrol boat in marshy and riverine areas between 1966 and 1970. The PACV was based on the Bell Aerosystems Bell SK-5 hovercraft which was a licensed version of the British Saunders-Roe (later re-named the British Hovercraft Corporation) SR.N5 hovercraft. In 1965, the SK-5 was adapted for American military use with three purchased by the US Navy for operations in the developing Vietnam War. Design of the Army PACVs began in 1966 and was completed the same year with training of PACV crews undertaken in the waters off Coronado, California near San Diego.

Six hovercraft of two different designs were built, three for the army and three for the navy. The navy's more closely resembled the civilian SK-5s on which they based, but the army craft had more extensive modifications. Each hovercraft was 38ft 10ins (11.84m) long and 23ft 9ins (7.24m) wide. They were 16ft 6ins (5.03m) high when floating on the air cushion. Weighing 15,660lb (7.10 tonnes) fully loaded the PACVs had crews of four with a driver, radar operator, and gunner, and carried up to twelve troops. These mostly rode the vehicle on the outside.

The craft were powered by a General Electric 7LM100-PJ102 gas turbine engine with a 304-gallon (1,150-litre) fuel tank, an auxiliary power unit, and Westland

Griffon 2000 TD Landing Craft Air Cushion.

Military BH7.

transmission all located amidships. The engine powered the three-blade variable-pitch propeller for thrust and the 7-foot (2.1-metre) diameter centrifugal fan for lift, making the PACV very fast compared with contemporary watercraft. They were capable of speeds of up to 60 knots (110km/h or 69mph) with a range of 165 nautical miles (306km/190mi) and endurance of up to seven hours. The PACV was developed because its lack of draft meant that it was operational in shallow and reed-choked waters, widespread in South Vietnam. This was particularly the case in the contested areas of the Mekong Delta and Plain of Reeds. The PACV was also found to be valuable because of its unusual height; it was faster than other watercraft in the conflict. However, it faced major drawbacks which included high manufacture costs – around $1 million (equivalent to thirteen river patrol boats) – and unreliability. In the depths of the Vietnam wetlands, the

Ancient 'Roman' catapult used in the British trenches for lobbing bombs, First World War.

supply chain for spare parts, essential for maintenance, was problematic.

The hovercraft, with jaws and eyes painted on the raised front of the vehicles, was an intimating sight, but the noise meant their approach was obvious. Military helicopters scouted ahead to guide the craft toward their targets. Lightweight construction also meant that neither the machine nor the troops were protected from incoming fire. During their use in the conflict they were successful in pursuing Viet Cong fighters overland and into the swamps, but two army hovercraft were destroyed. The PACVs in Vietnam were considered unsuccessful because of the cost and maintenance and they were withdrawn in 1970. Following this service, the navy PACVs returned to the United States where they were used by the coast guard; one sank in an accident. The Vietnam War hovercraft illustrate some of the difficulties intrinsic in warfare undertaken in extensive wetlands. Similar vehicles were employed in the Iraq War of the early 2000s.

Terrain, tactics, and technology

Approaches, tactics, and responses to warfare vary over time, and armies have adapted techniques to suit specific circumstances. For instance, in open and exposed landscapes artificial earthworks and trenches have been employed to provide protection and cover against incoming fire and assault. However, there is a clear difference between an earthwork bank and ditch for example, and a trench. The Romans effectively invented the metal spade as a tool their soldiers carried, which could be used to rapidly dig earthworks for either offensive or defensive purposes. The Boers in South Africa during the Boer Wars with Great Britain (First Boer War: 20 December 1880–23 March 1881; Second Boer War: 11 October 1899–31 May 1902) used foxholes (a type of defensive strategic position using a small pit as cover for one or two fighter and constructed so the occupants can effectively fire from

Port Arthur, Russo-Japanese War.

it) dug in the open ground to provide cover for soldiers in camouflage colours. This was a highly effective tactic when compared to the British approach of ordered ranks in red uniforms. However, none of this was trench warfare as such. The 'invention' of trench warfare is attributed to the Russians and the Japanese in the early twentieth century.

Russia and Japan came into direct conflict in 1904, and the Russo-Japanese War ensued over rival territorial claims in Manchuria and Korea. Japanese troops laid siege to the Russians in Port Arthur (Lüshunkou, eastern China); after failing to break the siege in September the Russians were defeated at the Battle of Liaoyang. Their army retreated northward to the Sha Ho River which is south of Mukden (Shenyang) and there the two rival forces dug in to trenches around ninety miles long (145 kilometres). In January, the Japanese force took Port Arthur, and those troops joined the battle at Mukden. Aware that the Russians might call in far greater reinforcements, the Japanese were anxious to immediately drive home their advantage. The Japanese General Oyama Iwao had around 207,000 troops whereas the Russians, under General Alexei Kuropatkin, had approximately 290,000.

Japanese Marines attacking Chinese Shanghai, 1932.

The Battle of Nanshan fought across the narrowest part of the Liáodōng Peninsula during the Russo-Japanese War 1904 with a catastrophic loss for the Russians.

A Cossack party surprised by Japanese scouts and struggling to cross a river; Russo-Japanese War 1904.

Underground hand-to-hand fighting with sappers at Port Arthur, Russo-Japanese War, 1904.

The Battle for Port Arthur, Russo-Japanese War 1904.

Russian artillery with transport problems in Manchuria, Russo-Japanese War 1904.

Japanese soldiers bringing in winter fuel, March 1905.

Japanese soldiers practising catching carrier pigeons with hawks, March 1905.

Russian graveyard near the front, First World War.

At the time, this was the biggest single battle ever fought; in cold, icy conditions with snow blizzards the Japanese broke the Russian line with frontal assaults. Despite sustaining high casualties, through direct assault across open ground against entrenched positions, the Japanese forced the Russian army to retreat in disarray. The troops fired from trenches with rapid-fire rifles and machine guns dug in behind barbed wire, supported by artillery fire with high-explosive shelling from behind. The latter were hitting targets well beyond sightlines; forward observers with telephones guided the artillery barrage. The Japanese had superior technology and double the number of machine guns. The nature of this trench warfare, and the way the campaign was conducted, was a forerunner to the catastrophic battles of the First World War.

In the Battle of Mukden, the Japanese lost around 70,000 men but won the day. Observers mistakenly attributed this victory to superior fighting spirit and that highly motivated infantry could effectively overpower machine guns and artillery. This 'lesson' misunderstood the technological and tactical superiority of the Japanese and their willingness to ship huge casualties if that was the cost of victory. This misinterpretation had tragic implications on the Western Front of the First World War; the tactical approaches of the generals on both sides was foreshadowed by Mukden.

Trenches are still visible today at Sanctuary Wood Hill 62 near Ypres, 1980s.

The Russo-Japanese War showcased technical innovations and tactical approaches to frontal warfare on extensive fronts and across open ground. This conflict sowed the idea of trenches to hold ground and from which to coordinate and launch attacks.

Battlescapes as landscapes of resistance

To consider this subject one must examine the integrated whole, in terms of landscape and people, and the component elements, separately. This allows the separation of the individual stories from the whole, but then brings together the overall context and description of the wider relationships between conflict and countryside. The reasons why there is so little known about this aspect of ecological history is that, for the most part, ecologists understand little of history, and most historians know little about ecology. It is this deep-seated disciplinary separation that has, it seems, limited interest and research into such a potentially important topic.

In addressing these issues, this book explores broad matters of battlescapes as landscapes of resistance and draws general conclusions with exemplar case studies. The specific issues are then examined in greater depth with examples often drawn from Great Britain and Europe, but elsewhere too. As we consider examples throughout history and around the world, there are themes and conclusions that emerge regarding tactics and approaches of rival generals on the battlefield, or between invaders and indigenous peoples in the landscape. Terrain, topography, and ecology are frequently the deciding factors and tipping points in many conflicts.

To better understand the interrelationships between combatants and nature or landscapes, it is also necessary to have a clear concept of 'strategy' and 'tactics'. The former is the coordination of battles and resources to achieve political objectives. The latter involves the deployments of specific actions to influence the tide of battle. The context of these is that until the nineteenth century, individual battles or skirmishes mostly took place within the visual sightlines of a commanding officer. Soldiers were guided by and responded to orders and directions relayed from the commander by various forms of signal, from shouts, to gestures, whistles, drums, flags, and trumpets or bugles. Those in command controlled as far as possible the deployment of combatants, the use of weapons, and the military ploys appropriate to the spatial or geographical setting to win the day. The tactics applied were then mechanisms used to kill, immobilize, or otherwise destroy enough of the enemy and their infrastructure to cause annihilation, surrender, or flight and secession of disputed territory. Skirmishes and battles often take place in the wider context of a war of varying duration and tactics are applied within the strategic framework of the overall conflict. In both these situations whether strategic or tactical, a decision must be made whether to attack or defend. Taking the initiative to attack means assuming a spatial action and incurring associated risks of movement in the landscape and commitment of personnel and resources to the undertaking.

In terms of geospatial placement, a defender will often have an advantage unless an attacker is able to take their enemy totally unaware. With landscape and terrain giving advantage to the defender, an attacker will need superior numbers or weaponry, or surprise. The defensive position will normally be assumed such that it enhances the firepower of combatants and weapons in the face of an assault. Mobility plays a potentially significant role in such circumstances and brings into play both aggression and defence as necessary; assault means a commitment to forward direction which may be irreversible. Furthermore, a successful leader may deploy tactics that force the enemy into a decision of whether to attack or retreat, or to hold their ground. Such deployments by both sides take place in the context of landscape – terrain and topography. Tactical choices to defend may mean making a stand in a strategic position or actively retreating. Static defence tries to create a barrier which proves impenetrable to an assault, and which keeps necessary lines open for both essential supplies and for potential retreat or withdrawal. Mobile defences involve an organized withdrawal from the field and might be used to tempt an attacker to a

War by Edwin Landseer c. 1870 illustrates the horror of the battlescape.

position where forces are dissipated, and lines (including supplies) are stretched too far. Such defence may then be turned into an attack as vulnerable flanks and lines of supply and communication become exposed. Terrain may be central to the success of such strategic manoeuvres; disorderly retreat can easily become a route.

Commitment to attack involves a decision to mobilize troops and resources usually to break through the defence or else to encircle the location to assault the flanks or rear of the defenders. Ploys may include false or disguised movements to confuse defenders and to try and reveal weakness in the defensive line or position. From such insight the assailants will try to apply sufficient force to overwhelm defensive positions either totally or else a little at a time.

For an army on the move, be it large or small, and throughout recorded history, it has been standard practice to send ahead scouts to check terrain and potential enemy forces, and to have an advanced troop or vanguard, and a baggage train behind with supplies and followers. Today, information is gleaned by spy-planes, drones, and satellites.

Finally, although sections of the book address the issues though the broad types of landscape and countryside and hence their topography and terrain, some features

Obtaining basic necessities such as food becomes problematic during wartime; this is a horsemeat shop in London.

clearly occur embedded within others. For instance, forest and mountains or hills may be juxtaposed, as may forest and wetland, or mountain ranges with lakes, rivers, and bogs; in such cases, the countryside and habitats may be referred to differently under the broader headings. The other issue is that the impact of landscape on conflicts has been noted, as has the converse: that of conflicts on landscape, as it is important to consider the militarization of landscapes. In the twentieth century in particular, extensive areas of rural land were set aside for the exclusive purpose of military training, this impacted greatly on their nature and their condition. Examples in England include the training areas of Sherwood Forest, Salisbury Plain, and numerous barracks and airfields across eastern England especially. The city of York is an example of a settlement which grew up on its military locational significance, and in the Second World War its countryside was important as a base in the aerial conflicts in both England and on the continent. Across Europe, with the aftermath of two twentieth-century world wars, and then the Cold War, and now war in Ukraine, large areas of both east and west bear the scars and the remnants of built infrastructure from these conflicts.

Loading a British trench mortar during the First World War.

Chapter 2
Nature, natural resources, and conflict

This chapter provides an overview of aspects of natural resources and warfare. It gives a broad insight into the interactions between conflicts and resource demands and uses, and the roles of competition for resources in triggering wars. We then consider some impacts of wars and battles on resource use and supply. Detailed examples of wetland resources and warfare are described from England and Ireland, and with reference to energy supplies, from North America. Competition for usage of different fuels may be shifted by conflicts and other causes of potential shortage. Various examples of relationships between war and natural resources are described in the other chapters too.

Resources and conflicts

Historically, access to and possession of, natural resources were central concerns of

Clearing up a First World War battlefield.

French motor-mounted, anti-aircraft gun with camouflage. 1917.

German soldiers gathering camouflage greenery.

French railway-mounted artillery, 1918.

French frontline observation post, 1915.

people, civilizations, tribes, and countries. Ancient boundaries delineated territories established around necessary resources and were often marked by natural features or barriers. Once such lands were established as a recognized area for a tribe or nation, peacetime access to resources for utilization was largely restricted to that region. This might be subsequently enhanced or supplemented by trade with near neighbours or, if necessary and expedient, by theft through conquest or stealth. As early civilizations and nations around the world emerged, grew, and waned, access to useable resources, particularly forests for timber, minerals for metals, and foods such as grain, were key drivers. Long-term shortages of timber for ship building or fortifications could lead to the inevitable collapse of nations. Furthermore, competition with neighbouring countries for things like timber could stretch supply lines beyond a point of sustainability.

Throughout history, conflicts arose from the need or desire to control natural resources, from timber (early Mediterranean civilizations), to grain (Russia and Ukraine in the 1930s), and minerals such as metal ores. People were also a natural resource to be captured, controlled, and used (e.g. the Middle Ages Scandinavian Viking cultures or perhaps the Arabic cultures of the same era). Acquisition of resources was not just the prerogative of the rich and powerful, but also a focus for those lacking essential material wealth. The Scottish peoples throughout history often looked southward to raiding across the border into the more affluent lands of northern England, not for conquest or control, but simply for the acquisition of resources like cattle, money, and occasionally people.

Connected to the possession of natural resources is the ownership and control of territory. Central to the control of territory is the role of topography and terrain in the definition of a region and its identity. There is then the matter of the extent to which a defined area can be identified, demarcated, and then defended. Access to important natural resources could then be critical in the rise to power of a tribe, nation, or civilization such as the early Celts in central Europe, where the exploitation of mineral salt mines was a trigger for their emergence as a superpower. Coal and iron helped propel Great Britain to global superpower status in the 1700s and 1800s, and freely available peat-fuel kick-started the 'golden age' of the Dutch economy in the 1500s.

In modern times, the Western interventions in Middle Eastern conflicts have been driven by a desire to control vital supplies of crude oil now essential to the global economy. While there may be claims that interventions are motivated by benign aspirations to support democracies and freedom, autocracies are conveniently overlooked if they have important oil supplies to trade. Less fortunate are countries lacking such obvious mineral wealth such as Tibet. Its repression is allowed by the international community because it does not have oil or some other commodity of global significance that is considered worthy of intervention. The message from this, is that access to natural resources is the key consideration in both aggression and defence.

French soldier wearing waders because of the quagmire, July 1915.

During the Second World War, Norway was subject to brutal invasion and abuse by Nazi Germany, but its neighbour Sweden remained unoccupied and neutral. There were several reasons for this; until around fifty years previously the two had been a single united nation. Firstly, Sweden was bigger and more heavily populated, and secondly (but like Norway) was physically rugged and defendable terrain. However, the third and key issue was the role of Sweden in terms of mineral resources and primary production; it was a steel manufacturing country. The Nazi war machine needed Sweden's steel and invasion would undoubtedly have halted manufacture and supply with a crippling impact on the German production of vital weapons and machines. The Germans did however take control of the main port for steel exports, located in Norway.

We can track the progress of wars and conflicts around the globe and by civilizations great and small over thousands of years; the control and acquisition of natural resources is a key driver of conflict. The search for gold by the European Spanish Conquistadors led directly to the annihilation of the Central American Aztecs and Incas. Over subsequent centuries, the pursuit of extensive 'free' farmland by settlers in places like North America, Australia, and South Africa displaced, or entirely removed, local indigenous peoples from vast areas of terrain.

However, while the need to control resources was often a major motivator for conflict and conquest, the over-exploitation and subsequent shortage of natural resources might be catastrophic. In Europe, during the 1500s and 1600s, dwindling supplies of wood and timber in countries such as Spain and England compromised

A wartime carrier pigeon and mobile loft in France, October 1916.

those nations' abilities to construct ships for naval operations. In the absence of sufficient ships, trade links and empires could not be maintained or defended. Nevertheless, the situations were complex because wood was also required for the building of defensive structures such as castles and other fortifications, and even more critically, for making charcoal to smelt metal to make armour, weaponry, cannon, and cannonballs. Without any of these a European country, on a constantly feuding continent of the sixteenth and seventeenth centuries, was exceedingly vulnerable. Pushed toward over-exploitation of natural resources such as trees from forests and the wider countryside, the environmental costs of grandiose adventuring, such as the construction of the Spanish Armada, defined countries' longer-term fates in subsequent centuries.

Triggering conflicts

Natural resources trigger and fuel conflicts. However, wars often destroy or exhaust vital natural resources with dramatic long-term implications for countries and civilizations. Natural catastrophes can also tip competitive balances between cultures, communities, and nations, triggering collapse, invasions, and conquests. Exhaustion of natural resources may lead to a gradual or even abrupt decline, or expansion, to absorb and exploit those from neighbouring territories.

Wartime carrier pigeons were used in many different situations; these are released from a stricken plane, December 1917.

Of course, in many cases, remote location and difficult terrain may place communities out of reach from aggressive neighbours with expansionist ideas. Again, topography and environmental factors may mean a region has limited economic activity which makes a territory less inviting to an invader. In this case, communities and societies may remain relatively intact, more harmonized with their local nature, and less homogenized by being peripheral and perhaps remote. In a passive sense, a community living in mountains, in wetlands, or in arid lands, may be protected by its landscape. This may change if the lands have mineral wealth and resources that might draw unwanted attention from would-be aggressors. The other exception to this general observation is perhaps when there are over-riding cultural or political reasons for conquest and subjugation as seen with China and Tibet. The latter being a predominantly peaceful population living in a remote high-mountain region with very limited resources, conquest is for other reasons. A final aspect of terrain and topography is where land or sea connect places of strategic importance and thus become the target of foreign aggression. This has been a key driver for many conflicts throughout history, from the role of Stirling as the gateway to the highlands of Scotland in medieval times, to the Russian invasion of Crimea in the twenty-first century.

The control of natural resources has been a source of dispute and conflict throughout

German artillery observation post in a haystack in 1914.

history. However, the actual roles of nature and wildlife, or indeed domestic animals, have also been a major factor, ranging from Celtic war-dogs to Hannibal's elephants, or the modern use of trained dolphins in maritime engagements. One often forgotten use of domesticated animals was that of carrier pigeons during both world wars. The First World War use of pigeons at the Battle of Verdun in France was especially important.

Verdun in France

In February 1916, Erich von Falkenhayn, the German Chief of Staff, decided to try and take the fortress city of Verdun in eastern France. With the artillery normally protecting the city forts mostly withdrawn for deployment elsewhere, it was felt this could be done and would be of strategic benefit. Furthermore, the defensive trenches in this zone were badly constructed and undermanned. Rather slow to respond to the offensive, the French defences were outnumbered by around two to one and were receiving significant artillery bombardment. However, somewhat late in the day, the French government decided that Verdun must be held at all costs. This defensive task was assigned to General Philippe Pétain. By the summer, the Germans were close to overwhelming the city when many of their forces were transferred to counter Allied attacks on the Eastern Front, and west on the Somme. There followed offensives and counter-offensives resulting in neither side gaining significant ground, but at a cost of around 700,000 French and German casualties.

Both sides used heavy artillery bombardment before each attack, and the Germans used specially trained stormtroopers armed with hand-grenades and flamethrowers to clear the French trenches. The French retaliated with what was called a creeping barrage of artillery fire just ahead of their advancing troops. Taking this approach deeper into enemy territory became difficult because of basic problems in communication and a landscape increasingly shrouded in smoke from explosives. Aerial reconnaissance was gradually becoming more feasible.

The French at Verdun, August 1916.

German soldiers dragging guns and ammunition through heavy mud during the Russian campaign, 1942.

The French lines at Verdun, August 1917.

One hero to emerge from the Verdun conflict was the carrier pigeon. In many situations these were the most reliable and sometimes the only method of communication as they flew to mobile pigeon lofts with messages attached to their legs. The flight 'home' might take them through shellfire and poison gas. Sometimes pigeons were used with cameras attached so that the recipient could 'see' the state of enemy lines and other infrastructure. At Verdun, with French troops trapped inside one of the forts in a desperate conflict with invading German troops, and unable to communicate with the outside world, it was the pigeons that carried messages to the relief force outside. One pigeon was even granted the wartime decoration of the *Légion d'honneur* as a mark of respect and gratitude for its service.

For the German command, the aim of the Verdun focus was to bleed their opponent white by attacking a point of relatively low tactical significance but one they were not prepared to lose and thus would pour in men and resources for its defence. This proved to be the costly consequence for both sides in what became indescribable mayhem.

The draining of the English Fens

The causes of the English Civil War of the 1600s were varied and complex. However, access to, and control, resources were a major part of the reason for conflict. A key issue and problem for the English Crown in the late Middle Ages and early modern period was raising monies and controlling income-generating businesses and innovations. This was particularly problematic during the reign of King Charles I because of his dismal relationship with Parliament and the fact that the latter controlled the king's access to finance. This was one of the main drivers behind the king's interest in the draining of 'drowned lands' like Hatfield Chase in South Yorkshire and the Fenland's Great Level in Cambridgeshire. Parliamentarians suggested that the king's interest in these reclamation schemes was purely to fill his royal coffers without having to resort to parliamentary sanction. Furthermore, Oliver Cromwell, member for Huntingdon, and others of a like mind, suggested that these schemes were for the king's personal gain and not the betterment of the kingdom or the needs of the commoners.

In this way, the parliamentarians were able to fan the flames of discontent across the Fens and the other low-lying wetlands. While there was truth in the fact that these were intended as major moneymaking schemes, the claim regarding the interests of the commoners was perhaps unfair. Charles and the Crown had often supported the interests of the commoners in maintaining their rights against incursions by the greater aristocracy, and the lesser gentry. Indeed, it was probably this support that caused much of the underlying discontent among these increasingly politically influential groups. Cromwell himself used this opportunity to rise from relative obscurity and to campaign vigorously against the undertaking across the region. The predictable result was that Cromwell suddenly found himself increasingly popular across the Fenland counties and a champion of the cause of the commoners. In fact, he was soon described as the most popular man in the region and hailed by fenmen as 'The Lord of the Fens', as he went from meeting to meeting, stirring up resentment and protest. Forster, in the *Lives of Eminent British Statesmen* (1837) says:

'From that instant the scheme became thoroughly hopeless. With such desperate determination he followed up his purpose – so actively traversed the district, and inflamed the people everywhere – so passionately described the greedy claims of royalty, the gross extractions of the commission, nay, the questionable character of the improvement itself, even could it have gone on unaccompanied by incidents of tyranny – to the small proprietors insisting that their poor claims would be merely scorned in the new distribution of the property reclaimed – to the labouring peasants that all profit and amusement they had derived from commoning in those extensive wastes were about to be snatched for ever from them – that, before his almost individual energy, King, commissioners, noblemen-projectors, all were forced to retire, and the great project, even in the state it was, fell to the ground.'

The success of the Cambridgeshire fenmen reverberated around the kingdom and encouraged others to resist such changes. Those in the northerly regions once again saw the possibility of getting rid of their own 'improvers' and 'drainers'. The Earl of Lindsey had succeeded in the enclosure and drainage of around 35,000 acres of the Lindsey Level, completed in 1636 at considerable expense. Part of the project involved inducing farmers to take up residence and to cultivate the reclaimed lands. However, problems arose when the fenmen burst upon them and destroyed houses and property, killed their cattle, and let the floodwaters back onto the reclaimed land. Similarly, in West and Wildmore Fens between Tattershall and Boston, there had been some progress by adventurers in reclaiming areas. They had been relatively successful in draining and then cultivating an extensive area of now richly productive land. However, with the atmosphere of almost open revolt now pervading the area, the fenmen gathered to deliver a body blow to the reclaimers.

Apparently, under the pretext of gathering for a traditional football match, they rampaged across the countryside and were violent in the extreme. During the match they burst over the enclosures, burnt the corn and the houses, and killed both people and cattle. They then turned to the drainage works themselves, breaking the embankments and blocking the drains. When they left, the reclaimed lands were once again under water. Therefore, following a few years of prolonged insurrection, the Levels were once again a vast waterbody and the drains to the sea were again silting up and failing to discharge. However, despite these problems, a grant was subsequently made to the same adventurers to drain 72,000 acres of Fenland from the River Glen to Lincoln and the River Trent, and in recompense for the outlay, the undertakers received 14,000 acres of new lands.

In 1641, the Earl of Bedford applied to the Long Parliament for permission to continue and resurrect the engineering works. However, the general civil unrest across the region prevented any real action. The Earl died soon after, his considerable wealth vastly reduced by his involvement in this so-far unsuccessful undertaking. Surprisingly, with all the unrest and resentment, the Dutch drainage engineer Vermuyden, invited by King Charles, remained on the scene, pursuing the idea of reclaiming this vast wetland. His political situation, as a close associate of Charles must have been difficult, but his eldest son, also called Cornelius, was a colonel in the parliamentary army under Fairfax in the build-up to the Battle of Naseby. Cromwell wrote to Fairfax on 4 June 1645, 'The party under Vermuyden waits the King's army and is about Deeping; has a command to join with Sir John Gell, if he commands him'. However, the younger Cornelius Vermuyden resigned his commission a few days prior to the Battle of Naseby, having suddenly found his presence required beyond the seas. It appears that he did not return to England until after the Restoration, in but 1665, he was once again a member of the Corporation of the Bedford Level.

Vermuyden senior was probably too focused on his drainage projects to be diverted into the political turmoil, at least more than could be avoided. He must surely have held allegiance to the Crown, as both Charles I, and his father James I, had been his staunch advocates. With civil war still raging, Vermuyden wrote his *Discourse on the Drainage of the Fens*. In this tract, he pointed out the works still necessary to bring about the drainage and reclamation of the 400,000 acres of the Great Level. With much lobbying and pamphleteering over many years, there were petitions to Parliament to resolve the means of perfecting the drainage of the Great Level. Finally, in 1649, authority was granted to William Earl of Bedford to complete the work begun by his late father. Once again, a Dutch drainage engineer, Westerdyke, was summoned to criticize the works and plans of Vermuyden, but Vermuyden won the day and was appointed to oversee the drainage. Dutch workers were gathered to begin this new phase of the endeavour, but after a promising start, the project gradually stopped because of lack of money and failing confidence.

Bearing in mind the costs and failings of the earlier attempts this failure was perhaps not surprising. Some of the adventurers sold their shares to reduce any further risk of liabilities. Others continued but under severe financial duress. However, despite the setbacks, work carried on, this time utilizing a supply of cheap labour with Scottish prisoners of war taken at the Battle of Dunbar on 3 September 1650. This was a battle of the Third English Civil War at which the English parliamentarian forces under Oliver Cromwell defeated a Scottish army commanded by David Leslie, loyal to the future King Charles II. Charles II had been proclaimed King of the Scots on 5 February 1649. So, on 23 June 1650, he landed in Scotland at Garmouth in Moray. On his arrival he signed the 1638 Covenant and the 1643 Solemn League and Covenant and was proclaimed King of the Scots. However, with resignations from the army and political anger over the Scots' actions, Cromwell took leadership of the parliamentarian forces and marched north. Despite initially meeting stubborn Scottish resistance and facing almost certain disaster on the outskirts of Dunbar, Cromwell turned the tables following a Scottish tactical blunder. He won the day, and the Scottish army fled the field with the slaughter of the Scottish soldiers, described by Cromwell as 'executions', extending over around eight miles.

Finally, at the Battle of Worcester on 3 September 1651, Cromwell defeated Charles II who fled to mainland Europe. Cromwell became virtual dictator of England,

German soldiers cutting peat fuel 1942.

Scotland and Ireland; Charles spent the next nine years in exile in France, the United Provinces, and the Spanish Netherlands. Following the death of Cromwell in 1658, political crisis led to the restoration of the monarchy, with Charles returning triumphant as king. On 29 May 1660, his thirtieth birthday, he arrived in London to widespread public acclaim. All legal documents were modified and dated as if Charles II had succeeded his father as king in 1649.

It is suggested that the Fenland riots, the drainage of the wet landscape, and competition for land and resources all combined to trigger the English Civil War. Some of the conflict was played out in the fenland regions themselves, and the individual battles and skirmishes often took place on open heaths, moors, and similar landscapes. Furthermore, as discussed later, the political fallout from this long and cataclysmic conflict led to the demise and wasting of many woods, parks, and forests for their timber and wood resources. This broad overview demonstrates many of the deep-seated interactions between landscapes, politics, people, and conflicts. Cromwell came to power on the back of opposition to the king's drainage schemes which were driven by a need to raise finance for the royal coffers. Once the king was displaced, and beheaded, Cromwell sanctioned the drainage anyway.

Fuel from the countryside in times of peace and war

Energy is central to people and to the development and functioning of societies. In this context, sources of energy vary from sunlight to water and wind power, through to stored solar energy captured in fossil fuels or in biological resources like peat and wood. Over centuries of societal evolution and sophistication, communities have tended toward fuels with higher calorific values. With revolutions in agriculture and industry, modern societies have increasingly depended on cheap fossil fuels from coal and oil. However, pre-industrial revolution societies and often rural communities, generally turned to locally available and less sophisticated fuels, especially peat (or turf) and wood. Other materials such as bracken, gorse, and even animal dung, were also burnt. An often-neglected topic is the impact of social unrest, economic issues and resource shortages, extreme weather, and conflict on the uses of fuels and the competition between different ones.

Sometimes, war or extreme weather might trigger a move from the utilization of coal, back to peat, a resource either not used or used historically. This shift was described for farmers in the south Lancashire Pennines, apparently as a response to bad winters and coal not being available. They reverted to using the long-abandoned local peat turbaries. However, this raises issues of preparation since the peat fuel needs careful harvesting and drying to be useful. In a bad winter, the peat may not solve the immediate problem since you must plan six to nine months ahead. In this case, it seems more reasonable that the farmers reverted to peat use during the wartime period or the 1920s 'Depression' as a response to economic pressures and energy shortages. If it is done at short notice, drying can take as much energy as it gives out on burning. Traditional harvesting of peat turf involved weeks of drying and turning in windrows.

Energy and conflict in North America

Nevertheless, this phenomenon of shift in fuel sources can be seen around the

Japanese soldiers cooking with charcoal, May 1905.

German troops 1914, Western Front.

world, especially in North America. In the 1870s, the potential of peat and turf for domestic fuel supply in Minnesota was considered as was the importance of competition with more sought-after fuels, and the impacts of their scarcity was stressed. Peat fuel might be viable if an area was remote from forests for wood-fuel, and away from coal transportation routes. By the 1890s, the origin, distribution, and commercial value of peat deposits for the US were investigated noting the relationship between peat use and the lack of available fuel wood. In northern Europe the greatest use of peat fuel was during the eighteenth century when forests had been cleared but mineral coal was not in widespread use. The latter was because transport to rural areas was difficult. Shaler asserted that most of the rural population of northern Germany, Scandinavia, Russia, France, and the British Isles, except for the wealthier classes, depended on peat and turf for household fuel.

The descendants of Native Americans in the town of Gay Head were described as among the last to use peat fuel in that part of the US. Indeed, by the late 1800s, the availability of cheap anthracite coal led a move away from peat fuel. The decline in peat use, a free resource except for the cost of collecting and processing, was driven by the availability and low price of coal. One shift was from community local peat turf harvesting to commercial extraction and processing of peat fuel. The first such commercial peat processing in the US was in 1902, when a strike of the Pennsylvania miners caused a fuel crisis: civil unrest and shortage.

However, in the US during the First World War, there was considerable interest in a move from coal and wood to peat or turf as domestic fuel. In 1916, it was reported that little machine-processed peat fuel would be extracted in the US in 1915, but by 1917, there would be a resumption of operations. In 1918, there was difficulty in obtaining an adequate and cheap fuel supply in Canada. The reasons included a labour shortage in the US that restricted coal imports to Canadian provinces. The situation was considered very grave in that fuel could be reduced or even cut off completely. The report argued for urgent attention to developing peat fuel as 'an excellent substitute for coal' and finishes with a plea for 'the establishment of a peat industry on a sound basis in Canada, and thus insure the people against a possible shortage of fuel and the suffering it would entail'. In 1917, the value of peat fuel for industrial steam generation was described; a key issue was price competition with coal. As coal prices rose peat would become competitive. The wartime coal shortages in the US in 1917 and 1918 showed that peat fuel could be extracted and priced competitively if coal was scarce and expensive. This observation was evidenced by subsequent activities and supported by numerous governmental and scientific reports.

A mix of war and domestic strife affected interest in and viability of peat as fuel

Hurrying up the coal mines of US and Canada November 1906, when the countries turned to peat fuel in place of coal.

Peat harvest at Langenmor, Schleswig-Holstein, 1937, during a time of economic hardship.

in both the US and Canada. Competition between different fuels led to price and availability issues and usage might shift from a high energy-intensive fuel like mineral coal to a lower-grade but more widely available source like peat.

Irish bogs and peat fuel during times of conflict

Traditional peat cutting has been of huge importance to the Irish people; use for domestic fuel causing the greatest decline in northern Ireland's peatlands. During the seventeenth and eighteenth centuries, with the demise of native woodlands, peat became the major source of fuel in Ireland. Rights to cut peat, known as turbary rights, were allocated to landowners often on small plots of land. Traditionally, peat was cut by hand using a special turf-spade known as a sleán or slane. Interestingly, hand-cut turf production in Ireland reached its peak in 1926 when over six million tonnes of turf was cut. This followed the First World War and the Irish Troubles, with the Great Depression and its resultant civil unrest starting to simmer. The economy of that time was in a very bad state. However, over subsequent years, the amount of turf cut declined steadily until the Second World War, when peat again became a vital domestic fuel. At that time, imports of coal from Great Britain almost ceased because of the conflict and energy was in short supply. The result was that deep peat in Irish raised bogs and extensive areas of blanket bogs were cut.

In Ireland, the use of fen peat as a source of fuel, known as mud turf, was less common because the peat is very shallow and cannot be cut with a spade. Instead, mud turf is gathered by digging a hole and mixing water with the peat, then tramping or 'puddling' it with bare feet, shovelling it onto the bank, and finally moulding it into blocks by hand. This was a very labour-intensive process and was only practised in a few areas, such as Brackagh Moss in County Armagh. After the time of the Second World War, the low price of coal and oil kept domestic peat cutting to a relative minimum, and by the 1970s, annual production of peat fuel was reduced to about a million tonnes, mostly from the blanket bogs in the west. However, the introduction of tractor-drawn auger machines during the 1980s increased the amount of peat cut again. Since then, mechanized peat extraction has become the norm in Northern Ireland and the tradition of hand-cutting turf has almost disappeared. In the Republic of Ireland, the government energy body Bord na Móna was established in 1946 by the Turf Development Act 1946 to oversee peat mining for fuel and for horticultural exports.

The wartime impact began a process of industrial exploitation which continued almost unabated to the present day, which has totally changed many Irish landscapes, and is only ending in the 2020s.

The consequences of the above impacts have been massive destruction, now contributing to climate change through carbon release. In Northern Ireland, nearly eighty per cent of raised bogs have been cut over for fuel. Most of this peat cutting was ostensibly for domestic purposes, but the relatively limited commercial extraction for fuel here has had important local effects. Commercial extraction needs planning consent, but the complexity of land ownership and turbary rights sometimes makes the distinction between commercial and domestic cutting difficult to determine. The situation in Ireland demonstrates the impacts of utilization, the variety of approaches, and the potential effects of war and other socio-economic stresses.

The intensive manual cutting began with the First World War and the mechanized boom followed the Second World War. The inherent absence of alternative fuel sources in Ireland, and the early loss of woodland, combined with conflict to trigger long-term catastrophic environmental destruction. Over many centuries, the effects of on-going conflicts with England's colonial ambitions, the resulting poverty, and widespread consequent environmental degradation, combined with global conflicts in the twentieth century to shape the modern Irish countryside.

Then, in the nineteenth century, conflict, absentee landlords, poverty, and starvation triggered a mass exodus of Irish communities to countries around the world. Moreover, as with the emigres from the Scottish Highlands and Islands, these people were skilled in draining bogs and cutting peat. These traditions and skills were taken with them around the globe to transform landscapes wherever they settled.

Peat press at Oganowo in southwest Poland showing wartime fuel use in July 1944.

The Second World War and the fate of the English Fens

The impacts of the Fens on the English Civil War, and of warfare on the Fens, were discussed earlier. However, as with Irish peat bogs, this interrelationship continued up to and during the First World War and through to the Second World War. This final phase of wartime impacts is worthy of more detailed consideration.

The outbreak of the Second World War triggered serious food shortage across Great Britain. Because of the crisis, British government interest in farming improvement and its associated drainage was piqued. In the Fenlands, as described in *The Lost Fens*, land at Priory Farm immediately around Wicken Fen in Cambridgeshire was acquired by pioneering horticulturalist, Alan Bloom. By the spring of 1940, Bloom was considering ambitious plans to reclaim the fen for farming. He stated that, 'There were other more or less waterlogged and inaccessible parts of the Fens, and why should I not try to get a few people together with money to invest, and make a big thing of this reclamation job?' At first his scheme did not get much support, but it was at least a hint of things to come. By June 1940, he had invested in a caterpillar tractor (freshly imported American technology) to facilitate access onto wet and difficult land. He described how, in his view, Priory Farm was effectively a battlefield on which the forces of dereliction were paused in their encroachment on farmed land.

Bloom felt that for years the advantage had been with the 'wilderness' and nobody could farm against water. However, the tables were now turned, with the plough on the offensive. On the one side, 'swamp' was deliberately encouraged because it gave sanctuary to wildlife, but on the other, Bloom's side, there was farmland with its aim of food production. The level of water in the dykes, which divided the two, determined which would prevail. Indeed, with flat land on both sides of the drain, there was no possibility of compromise. In this situation, Bloom's main adversary was the fledgling National Trust and he felt that he had to 'fight … the local governing Committee … men with mainly academic interests. They could not see things in the same light as those whose interests were agricultural'. In this contested countryside, the final stage was to be determined by the war effort and the supposed potential to bring into cultivation around fifteen acres of the flooded lands at the request of the War Agricultural Committee.

However, things quickly changed when the War Department decided that nearby Adventurers' Fen would be used as a bombing target. Both Bloom for Priory Farm, and the National Trust for the nature reserve, received government requisition notices. Nevertheless, the situation then altered abruptly with the requisitions cancelled because of a strategically important and rare plant, Alder Buckthorn (*Rhamnus frangula* or *R. catharticus*). This shrub can be harvested and used to make fine-grade charcoal needed for explosives. In August 1941, the Biology War Committee presented a memorandum on *R. frangula as a source of charcoal for munitions*, to the Joint Committee of Government Research Organisations. With maritime blockades halting overseas supplies, there was a shortage, and this had become a matter of national security. Because of the report, a survey into the distribution of the species had been commissioned in November 1941, and it was found on Adventurers' Fen.

The discovery brought a temporary stop to the reclamation work of Bloom and other farmers. In the meantime, they were paid to clear scrub and selectively harvest the Alder Buckthorn. The work involved cutting or coppicing the Buckthorn; any re-growth was expected to take at least three years. However, the Buckthorn was soon all cut out and the War Agricultural Committee was fretting over the state of the Fen. The National Trust was paid for the harvest taken from their land, but the War Committee was anxious to bring the area into cultivation for food. The revised proposal was for the entire two hundred and eighty-six acres of Adventurers' Fen to be 'improved'. In this minor war within the War, the rules of engagement had changed, 'the Catchment Board engineers and officials, the overseers and their men – were of the opinion that Adventurers' Fen could be and would be drained'.

Nevertheless, it seems that some local farmers were still against the scheme saying it would be a colossal waste of money and would not work. However, the War Agricultural Committee had already begun work on reclaiming the southern part of Adventurers' Fen prior to March 1941, and the hope was that farmers would be cropping the whole site by the summer of that year. Apparently, the Catchment Board men had already deepened the drain to the immediate north of Rothschild's Thirty Acres, a nature reserve, and the impact in lowering the water-table was seen to be considerable for some distance inside the reserve. From Bloom's perspective this was a good sign of improvements to come.

In establishing and managing the nature reserve, the National Trust had been effective in making a swamp in the now drained and desiccated fenland; the wider fen being dry because of historic drainage schemes. Not a drop of water was allowed to run into the drainage system from the re-wetted reserve. The water could only drain away very slowly and so the site was exceedingly wet which was good for conservation but a major hindrance to farmers wishing to dry Burwell Fen and surrounding lands. Therefore, the first job for the farmers was to dig out and clear the dyke outfalls into the 'interline' and the old main drain. The aim was to drain off the surface water and facilitate ploughing on lands adjacent. Major new drains, 'new dykes – in long straight gashes' were cut across the ancient landscape to release the pent-up water. Bloom wrote, 'It was sheer delight to watch that water running full pelt from seven or eight points along the boundary of the Fen out of those grips we had been digging'. After a few days of a drying breeze, they could begin burning off the surface vegetation; the end of an era was closing in on Adventurers' Fen. This was in effect the closing stages of a process begun during the English Civil War.

Finally, the clearance was completed by lighting just a small pile of sedge litter, the flames burst up as if the land was doused in paraffin. Bloom described how, 'The flames crackled and licked the lower growth, and ran up the bare, hard reed stems to consume first what plumes remained over winter, leaving them twisted and burnt like spent match sticks. All beyond became hidden in smoke, mounting, swirling higher and higher, black at first but turning a rusty-white against the background of blue sky. Out of the smoke bushes came into view, blistered and gaunt as the flames swept on … the smoke … seemed to be hundreds of feet up in a billowing cloud'.

The result was apparent within less than thirty minutes, with the Fen changed completely in appearance, the dull buff-grey turned to black. Except for occasional reeds persisting in damp turf pits, the charred bushes and smouldering sedge hassocks were all that remained. Bloom and his companions grinned through their blackened, sweaty faces as they surveyed their victory over ancient nature. The cultivation costs were grant aided at £2 an acre plus the cost of ploughing. Half of the grant was to cover the costs of the work and half went to the landowner or farmer. The tenancy on this land was to run for three years after the end of the war to coincide with the powers of the War Agricultural Committee.

However, despite the fanfare, this whole exercise was to a large degree a publicity stunt to promote the war effort and boost public morale. The fenland countryside was the victim of human efforts that cost a fortune and produced very little return. Bloom admitted that it was clear by late 1942 that the costs of the work had been significantly under-estimated. But as he said 'there was nothing I could do about it. We had our work cut out to get the two hundred and eighty-six acres cropped by 1943, let alone 1942'. This outcome was despite a colossal investment of public money and huge effort by Bloom and his colleagues. Shortly after this, King George and Queen Elizabeth, the Minister of Agriculture, the Duke of Norfolk, and Mr Tom Williams MP, visited the area with a huge number of pressmen to inspect the efforts to feed the landlocked British Isles. They were doubtless impressed by the battlefield of the fens, since this was just the sort of stirring stuff that the country needed.

Nevertheless, despite the wartime rhetoric the reality was very different and in fact the work had triggered a major ecological disaster. By February 1943, the area was losing massive amounts of topsoil, with losses getting progressively worse through March. Despite this, the land was soon sown with oats and barley, beet and potatoes, but dry weather brought the ironic spectre of drought. The solution to water shortage was to get permission from the Catchment Board to abstract from Wicken Lode which drew down the water-table on the remaining nature reserve fen even further. In May, the area experienced a bad gale which swirled up great black clouds of dust over Swaffham, Waterbeach, Soham, and Isleham, giving the sky 'a queer, dark tinge for hours'. This was apparently the worst 'blow' for years and a result of the War Agricultural Committee's efforts. This process of fenland soil erosion continues today, and it is estimated that there are fewer than thirty-five harvests remaining in some fenland bread-basket landscapes.

Dust settled over a wide area and was reported more than twenty miles away in Bury St Edmunds. The ancient fenland, robbed of its water, was now just blowing away on the wind. A further complication of the wind-blown soil was that when deposited it infilled the drainage dykes which then needed to be re-dug. Some crops needed to be replanted two to three times. Nevertheless, they harvested wheat, barley, and sugar beet with the best crops off Rothschild's Thirty Acres former nature reserve. By late 1943, Alan Bloom's initial work was done, and the land was moving toward intensive, industrial agriculture. As he says: 'Adventurers' Fen and Priory Farm had proved that crops equal to any other black fens – and better than some – could be grown. Those ideas and hopes, that for so long I'd been pushing back into the pigeon-holes of my mind, could now begin to emerge. More complete fertility, extended mechanization, more and better buildings, a thorough livestock policy, alternative leys to give some of the much-cropped land a rest in turn'.

Bloom went on to consider how the improvement of these three hundred acres had cost the nation so much. It was, he felt, the country's fault for neglecting the land in the first place. The intensive two years made up for time lost twenty or thirty years before. But he now looked forward to the permanent recovery of agriculture in Britain and an end of neglection. He observed signs that 'the welfare of the land must in future run parallel with that of the nation', so that 'cheap food, abundant in quantity and variety, is the only thing that matters'.

This vision held by Bloom was a premonition of post-Second World War farming land-use in Britain through to the late twentieth century. Along with cheap food, the response to the wartime agricultural revolution also brought floods, droughts, carbon release, climate change and biodiversity loss on an unprecedented scale. There has also been the massive unsustainable loss of fenland topsoil. Much of this dramatic change was driven by the wartime spectre of an island under siege and desperately short of food. Indeed, we could state with some conviction that the demise of biodiversity and nature across much of rural Britain in the late twentieth century was driven by the 'island under siege' mentality created by two world wars. Perhaps greed also played its part.

Bloom's account describes the final demise of the ancient southern fenland, but little did he realize how rapidly the post-war zeal for mechanization, agri-industrial development, and food self-sufficiency would totally transform both landscape and communities. Subsidized by public funds and petrochemicals the war effort re-shaped the Fens.

Fenland naturalist and BBC presenter James Wentworth-Day presented a different perspective, and in his *Fenland Adventure*, wrote, 'They drained the fen with a great clamour of bureaucratic self-praise. The waters went away and the fish died by the cartload. The reeds stood rustling and dry above the black mud. Then they set fire to the reeds, and for a day or more my secret fen roared and crackled in a tawny yellow, red-hot sea of flame. Great billowing clouds of black smoke rose up and polluted the blue skies and swept away on the wind until dust, ashes, and smoke fell like a grey pall on the roofs and the green heath of Newmarket, away on its windy upland'. The duck rose up and were away, and the moorhens, rails, bitterns, warblers and others too. When the wind blew the dust, smoke, and ashes away, all that was left of the secret fen was 'burnt and black and scorched. An insult to the high fen skies. An altar of burned beauty. A sacrifice to man's neglect of pre-war farming, a burnt offering to humanity's failure to live together in harmony. And thus, in a funeral pyre vanished the last and loveliest remnant of what had been a recreation in all its wild glory of the ancient Fens of Eastern England'. He had bought the fen 'to preserve it, to save for all time the essential Englishness of it, to love and enjoy the sight of birds and clouds, the wind in the reeds, herons fishing in summer shallows, gulls wheeling against May skies, the sting of winter sleet'.

Now however, it was no more. Wentworth-Day questioned the wisdom of the transformations:

'Is the world any better for this change in my fen, or in the ten thousand acres of other fens which they have drained, burned, grubbed up, and cultivated during the War? Materially, yes. Spiritually, no. Economically, again no. Those are the answers in a nutshell. On my fen they spent thousands of pounds in expensive drainage, in constructing concrete roads which will probably crack, sink, and become derelict in a few years. The bill for our County Agricultural Executive Committees is estimated to be in the neighbourhood of £25,000,000 a year. Do the Committees grow £25,000,000 worth of food each year? The answer, I think, is no.'

There had been a brief respite from total destruction because the ministry wanted to harvest the vital Alder Buckthorn. However, the fate of the fens was ultimately sealed by the military conflict. In the wider landscape, arable production from the old fens rivals the best in the world, but it depends on massive inputs of petrochemical fertilizers and fuels, and so, despite the claims, is not actually self-sufficient. Furthermore, as the topsoil blows away or simply breaks down into carbon dioxide gas it is debateable how much the wartime 'improvement' of the relict fens produced. Dependent on substantial financial investment, the results were certainly not sustainable in the broader sense. Eighty years on, the short-term, industrialized farming that was pioneered to support the war effort has proved disastrous. For ecology, the environment, and ultimately to both the economy and local communities, the transformed fenland is just not sustainable.

Natural resources and human conflicts

Some key issues in the complex interactions between natural resources and human conflicts have been outlined. Other examples, with further case-studies are presented in later chapters throughout the book. However, there are some core issues to emerge from the discussion so far in terms of the specific instances presented. Conflicts, both military and civil, can disrupt energy and fuel supplies and usage and cause

Making wickerwork fencing for the First World War trenches.

major impacts on landscape, resources, and people. This is seen time and again with mineral coal, peat turf, and wood. In the current European conflict in Ukraine, the energy supplies are proving a pivotal weapon. In previous decades, war in the Middle East was influenced by issues of access to oil supplies and the oil itself was used as an economic force within global conflicts.

Access to global resources such as grain production, again as exemplified by Ukraine today and in the Second World War, proves significant in international disputes. In arid zones, and particularly with climate change, access to water resources can be a political lever and very contentious. Lack of water can soon prove catastrophic to a population, but in the case of disputes between Bangladesh and India for example, a threat to the former is too much water as controlled by the latter. In Africa, along the length of the Nile River, different states vie for the right to extract and use the precious resource.

Trees and forest resources have been important in conflicts from supplying timber for fortresses, stockades, castles, and ships, to providing boarding for trenches, and fuel for fires. Indeed, in the early Mediterranean civilizations the loss of forests to supply these essentials, and the stretching of supply lines to new forest areas, proved the undoing of many communities and empires. In medieval England, there was tension between charcoal manufacture from woods and forests for the smelting of

Making charcoal for the trenches in a French forest during the First World War, 1918.

British forces moving guns through the quagmire of the Western Front, December 1916.

British tank attacking German lines during the First World War.

iron, vital for armour and munitions, and the use of the resource to provide timbers for the navy.

Clearly too, in the face of warfare, desperate communities may cause major damage to natural resources which would otherwise be carefully managed and protected. This is in part because systems of administration break down and because people are desperate but also because armies may simply take what they need. Long-term resource management and conservation for sustainable usage fall victim to short-term exigency.

Use of coppice wood in First World War German trenches.

Military honour for wartime carrier pigeons during the battle for Verdun in France 1916

British infantry at Flanders October–November 1914.

Chapter 3

Landscapes and resources, twin elements of war

As discussed, landscapes and their resources provide settings for warfare, and materials and products are demanded by combatants and communities. Furthermore, conflicts large and small impact the countryside and its resources. In many cases, it is the countryside and its associated resources that constitute the primary objective of aggression. Taking the logic developed so far, we can see the countryside having two main elements in conflicts. Firstly, the countryside is made up of landscape which comprises elements of terrain and topography. Secondly, the land produces and holds natural resources which support social development and the creation of economic wealth. Such resources are then important for the sustainability of communities. They could provide a platform for political power and aggressive ambitions toward neighbours and are something to be protected from outsiders. Resources underpin much socio-economic development and cultural identity.

A park for British tanks, 1918.

French tracked off-road military vehicle, First World War.

German Mk 1 Panzer Tank, Second World War.

Terrain, topography, and territory

Howitzer on caterpillar wheels copes with muddy battlescapes during the First World War.

Terrain and topography of the countryside are critical to social identity and sense of place. Furthermore, they often provide natural barriers which resonate with the same. These factors combine to generate distinctive cultures, peoples, and nations. For indigenous communities, terrain and topography may be their own landscapes of resistance in the event of invasion or other external threats. If subject to military incursions, people may retreat into defensive terrain where natural conditions are inherently difficult for an invader and where local knowledge is advantageous to a defender. Wetlands, mountains, forests, and deserts all provide landscapes into which resistance movements can retreat and even negate overwhelming military superiority. Furthermore, such refugia for indigenous resistance may grow over the

A British anti-aircraft gun near Frezenburg, Belgium, October 1917.

A British night attack on the German trenches on the First World War Western Front.

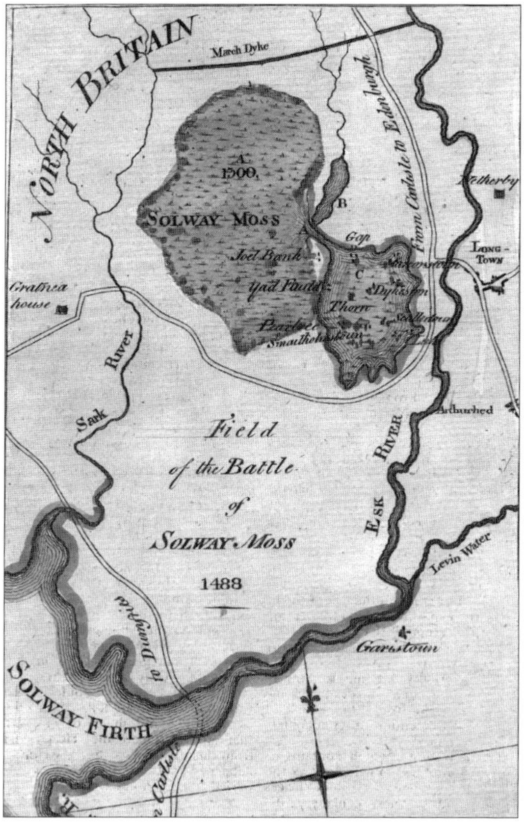

Battle of Solway Moss, November 1542, with 15,000–18,000 Scots routed by 3,000 English.

Night bombing and strafe, 1916, showing the impact of nighttime on the battlescape terrain.

longer-term to provide serious troubles for an occupying force. When occupation of a foreign territory becomes long-term, one outcome may be the displacement of the original native people to more remote and peripheral areas of the landscape or otherwise subjugated. In core areas, the result may be a hierarchal society of resource owners with an underclass of native workers.

Rivers and wetlands

In conflicts throughout history, topography and terrain have proved critical in the outcomes of conflicts both large and small. Wetlands for example were significant for the outcomes of the Norman invasion of England and the cataclysmic battles of that period, such as Hastings, Fulford Bridge, and Stamford Bridge. In Scotland, during the Anglo-Scots wars, Flanders Moss and the Forth River had major influences over the outcomes of battles such as Stirling Bridge and Bannockburn. As the gateway between the highlands and lowland Scotland with the seats of political influence,

French troops near Verdun, January 1917; this illustrates the topography and the impact of the battle on the countryside.

the control of Stirling, and the river crossing, was the key to effective power in the country. Rivers often marked out territorial boundaries and hindered troops travelling by land; they also offered speedy and sometimes safe passage for those in boats. Travel up-river by invading forces also had the potential advantage of a speedy retreat if events made that necessary. This was certainly the case with the strategic significance of York as the one-time capital of the kingdom of Northumbria and a gateway to the control of northern England.

Conflicts in the Anglo-Scottish wars also included battles such as Flodden Field in northeast England, and Solway Moss in the northwest, in both cases the outcome decided on the impacts of a peat bog. In the former, the better-trained and well-equipped Scottish troops marched across a hill-slope bog and became mired down. In the latter example, the Scots, spooked at night by the English vanguard, ran headlong into the vast morass of the Solway Mosses from which many never returned.

More modern conflicts influenced by wetlands include both defence and offence in the European Low Countries when dykes were breached to flood the countryside in order to halt the German advance. The Germans retaliated with their own flooding of farmland to destroy Dutch crops. In the 1960s, the Vietnam War involved extensive

British troops under fire as they bring in a captured German battery on the Western Front during the First World War.

Sea floods in Holland triggered by German and Allied bombs breaching the dykes.

Breaking the ice to cross the frozen Yellow River, China, late 1800s.

wetlands and humid forests, as did the earlier Seminole War in the US's Florida Everglades. In the period from the early 1800s to the middle of that century, described as America's 'first Vietnam War', this demonstrated how wet forest and local adaptation to conditions can outfox a superior military force.

Woods, forests, and mountains

Extensive forests in Germany and in northern Britain proved troublesome to Roman ambitions of extending the boundaries and influence of their empire. In Scotland, the apparent loss of an entire Roman legion, though disputed by some historians, was largely attributed to vast areas of mountain forest in which the Picts could hide and launch guerrilla attacks to decimate the legion. The somewhat apocryphal legend of the 'Great Forest of Caledon' was probably an excuse for an embarrassing military defeat. While the terrain of the Scottish Highlands and the Cairngorms was clearly very difficult to negotiate and navigate, the all-encompassing forest simply did not exist; it was a myth. Even the loss of the York-based legion may itself have been misinformation as there is some evidence of the legion's recall to Rome for service in the eastern Mediterranean.

Where they occur, mountain ranges have always provided sanctuary for indigenous resistance when a territory come under attack. The physicality of mountains presents serious barriers for insurgent force, and indigenous people are likely to benefit from their knowledge and adaptation to local conditions and geography, and their experience of living in this extreme terrain. Invaders find mountains difficult environments to penetrate or traverse and may lack the survival experience and necessary equipment or clothing for the conditions. Extensive mountain ranges may give indigenous fighters safe and remote sanctuary so that invading forces are unable to prise them out to open conflict. Throughout history mountains have been used to great strategic

Chillon Castle, near Montreux, Switzerland in the 1980s.

benefit: German tribes in the north of the Roman Empire, Gauls in the west, Picts in northern Scotland, fourteenth-century Welshmen against the English, and Afghans resisting various invasions from the eighteenth century to the modern day. Other examples of such resistance include Yugoslavia subject to German invasion during the Second World War, and the guerrilla campaigns of Native American Apache leader Geronimo in the Indian-United States conflict of the late 1800s and early 1900s. Mountains, arid lands, and cold lands, offer sanctuary to those playing hide and seek with superior military forces.

Weather and warfare

Bad weather can have a big influence on the outcome of a conflict such as in the Anglo-French wars (the Hundred Years' War of 1337–1453) and particularly the Battle of Crécy in 1346. This conflict pitched the extremely powerful but slow French crossbow against the English longbow with disastrous consequences. With the French army around twice the size of the English, including 5,000 Genoese crossbowmen, Philip VI of France ordered an immediate assault on the English lines. However, heavy rain had rendered the crossbow strings very wet which

Tracks for carrying German concrete to a dugout, First World War.

American slit trench 1943.

hampered their use. The firing was slow, and the range much reduced, with the result that they suffered heavy losses under English fire. Somewhat impetuously the French cavalry now joined the melee, but they became mired down in the sodden battlefield, entangled with the struggling crossbowmen already caught in the deep mud. The mounting numbers of dead bodies further confused the situation and after fifteen or more failed charges, deep into the night, the French king abandoned his colours and fled the field. He left around 2,000 French dead; the victims of bad weather, difficult terrain, poor tactics, and inept leadership.

Agincourt, France, 1415.

Agincourt: the morning of the battle.

Women working in a forage reserve depot First World War, Britain.

An eight-year truce in the long conflict between England and France ended in 1355. At this time, Edward III of England attacked northern France; his son, Edward the Black Prince, took an army of 8,000 soldiers, including 2,500 longbowmen, to raid deep into central France. King John II of France took his own force across the Loire River to meet the English east of Poitiers. With their army outnumbered by the French, the English force assembled on a narrow front protected to the flanks by both a stream and a marsh. The French cavalry assaults failed to break the line and were driven back under fire from the longbows. In retreat, the French knights were forced into hand-to-hand combat and following a surprise assault from the English fell back in disarray with many knights, and King John himself, captured. This clever use of stream, marsh, and superior tactics led to a treaty that gave more strength to the English stronghold within France.

We also see the potential impact of terrain at the decisive battle of Agincourt on 25 October 1415. In this case, the result was an English victory over the French when the English army led by King Henry V famously defeated their numerically superior, and more heavily armoured, opponents. The English longbow was clearly a major factor but so too was the English understanding of the terrain; the effects of heavy rainfall on already boggy grassland proved decisive as the armoured French knights

British military camp at Wiseton Park, North Nottinghamshire, early 1900s as an example of military use of the countryside, even in peacetime.

Military trench shelter with sandbags and timbers, First World War Allied troops.

were massacred by the lighter-moving English foot-soldiers. Drawn down the hill onto an obviously weaker foe the French cavalry were effectively lured into a marshy killing field. As the English had discovered at Bannockburn and Stirling Bridge, medieval heavy armour and marshes are a poor mix.

When Suleiman became the Ottoman sultan in 1520 his attention turned to the European kingdom of Hungary at a time of major political and military upheavals across much of Europe. France was in conflict with the Habsburg Empire and the Holy Roman Emperor, and disunity and disruption was rife within Hungary itself. Although weakened by internal conflicts, the Hungarian king assembled a force of around 30,000 troops and fifty cannon on the swamplands of the plain near the town of Mohács. The Ottomans brought somewhere between 50,000 and 70,000 soldiers and two hundred cannon. While the initial attack by the Hungarian cavalry made serious inroads into Suleiman's force, they were decimated by intense cannon-fire and ultimately annihilated by the quick-moving light cavalry of the Ottomans which coped better with the wet conditions. This was a catastrophic defeat for Hungary and opened the gates for the Turkish armies to advance across Europe and ultimately to Vienna.

These examples provide insight into the varied ways in which countryside and conflict interact and play out. Ambitions to expand empires and control territories trigger invasions and annexations. The goals of conquest and expansion may be the extension of interests and control, and access to key resources especially people, minerals, and farmland or forest. However, success may be swayed by topography and terrain, and the effective adaptation to local conditions, including landscape and weather.

British troops storming a village at the Somme.

Chapter 4
Terrains of conflict, assault, and defence

As discussed in terms of tactics and strategy, landscape as countryside can be turned to the advantage of both attacker and defender. Military commanders may be able to use topography and terrain to enhance a defensive position or to support a particular assault tactic. How effectively a military force utilizes terrain in these ways depends on their knowledge of the local and regional countryside and its inhabitants – and on their leader's understanding of tactics in the specific circumstances of the locale.

The Romans in Gaul

In the Gallic Wars of Julius Caesar (58 to 52BCE), terrain and clever military strategy, combined with novel military technology, combined to bring about Roman victory. After a series of Gallic uprisings and punitive suppressions by the Romans,

A British battery crossing rain-sodden ground near Ypres while under fire, 1917.

resistance gathered around a young chieftain named Vercingetorix. Caesar's tactics hinged on the innovation of the metal spade which legionnaires carried. This enabled the rapid construction of earthen banks and ditches for either offence or defence and had already been used to overcome the Gallic capital, Avaricum. However, Vercingetorix succeeded in drawing Caesar into a trap as he attempted a further siege which went badly wrong with losses of a thousand or more dead; the Romans barely escaped. With the prospect of the legions retreating to southern France, the Gauls decided to try the same tactic on a grander scale and assembled their forces on the massive Alesia promontory. The ruse backfired when the relief force of around 250,000 Gauls was delayed by bad weather and Vercingetorix found himself surrounded on the fortified hilltop. Caesar had his troops swiftly construct two encircling banks and ditches with walls: the inner one to keep Vercingetorix and his warriors inside and the second one to keep the relief force out. This meant coordination between the two Gallic forces was problematic and while the relief force suffered thousands of casualties those on the great plateau were dying of thirst and hunger. Vercingetorix surrendered and the Gallic uprisings were quashed. Terrain and topography, together with access to vital natural resources, like water, can prove decisive in conflicts.

Landscape as the theatre of war

Along with providing vital resources and thus becoming disputed territory, countryside was frequently the arena for conflicts, from minor skirmishes to full-blown battles and prolonged wars. The nature of countryside, through its landscape and resources, becomes central to many conflicts throughout history and particularly to their outcomes. Landscape may hinder, or facilitate access and transit, and may connect or separate areas which are more-or-less favourable from a military perspective. The

A heroic depiction of First World War British cavalry in action entitled 'Across the enemy's destroyed trenches'. In reality the terrain is totally unsuitable.

Crawling to the German trenches under fire in the First World War.

A First World War Western Front battle scene.

Crossing no-man's land, Western Front, First World War.

Attack by the Ulster Division, July 1916 at the Somme.

impacts and implications of landscape in a region vary throughout history as land-use and land 'improvement' alter the nature of the terrain, for example converting fenland to drained farmland, or forest to pasture. Furthermore, the uses of terrain and topography also vary with evolution of warfare and the military machine. In Second World War England for instance, there was a great need for level ground in the lowlands from which to launch RAF fighters and bombers. Many of the sites chosen for airfields would have been extensive wetlands two or three hundred years previously. In some instances, as in sites around York, the legacy of wetlands rendered them totally unsuitable.

To better understand the impacts and implications of countryside for warfare or other conflicts, it is essential to have a good understanding of landscape change over the period in question. The possible strategies and actions of, say, the Battle of Hastings in 1066 in southern England are only sensible when the terrain is 'rewetted' to the condition it was in at the time. Certain routes become impassable and positions for defence and assault begin to make more sense when the field of battle is seen more-or-less as it *was* and not as it is today.

The geographical location of countryside and its landscapes are also significant. Control of resources has already been noted, but the importance of trade routes and supply lines also comes to the fore. A key part of strategy is in identifying nature's strengths and weaknesses, from the perspective of both defender and assailant,

Flooding on the Somme after German dynamiting of the canals, 1917.

Beaumaris Castle, Anglesey, in the 1970s showing the defensive position on the edge of wetland and covering the strategic Menai Strait.

and utilizing these to best effect with enhancement where necessary. We see major boundaries and defensive constructions such as the Great Wall of China or Hadrian's Wall in Northumbria, England, following the natural contours of the land to maximize impact. The location of Hadrian's Wall exaggerates natural defensive positions and enhances sightlines from and along the wall. This enables lookouts to see friend or foe in plenty of time, and to communicate the sighting to either side via the regular mile-forts and beacons. Enhanced location means the constructed wall tops precipitous and often rocky escarpments; the whole defensive alignment is further supported by deeply cut ditches and banks beyond the wall itself. Strategically placed beacons were first used in Britain by the Romans; their use continued to the Tudor dynasty of the Middle Ages.

Defensive locations

Strategic position and natural defences are used similarly in significant fortifications, from prehistoric to the modern era. Carl Wark and Mam Tor are Iron Age hilltop enclosures in the English Peak District that make full use of topography in their imposing situations; Carl Wark has the added advantage of a massive gritstone boulder slope and craggy escarpment. Likewise, Maiden Castle in Dorset utilizes the hilly terrain and steep ground to maximum effect. Fast forward to the Peak District's medieval period and to Peveril Castle at Castleton that has two defensive sides provided by precipitous rocky slopes. Where natural defences occur in the topography, it was widespread practice to both utilize and enhance them. This was famously the case with major medieval castles such as Edinburgh and Stirling in Scotland, where the ramparts sit atop massive cliffs standing high over the surrounding landscape. Conisbrough Castle in South Yorkshire similarly stands high and proud over the Don Valley Gorge overlooking the vast medieval wetlands of the Humberhead Levels. It reinstates a strategic defensive significance extending back to prehistory.

Fortifications were also surrounded by moats that might mix man-made structures and naturally occurring wetlands. The defences of York for instance made full use of the floodland associated with its rivers, and in North Wales the huge Beaumaris Castle on Anglesey had extensive natural marshland intrinsic to its defences. However, as noted earlier, understanding landscape change is important. Also, in North Wales the magnificent Harlech Castle was one of the Norman-English fortresses built to subdue Welsh rebellion, but the functioning of the site is unclear when viewed in the twenty-first century. Today the castle is on a high cliff but well back from the sea, yet in the fourteenth and fifteenth centuries ships and boats could approach almost up to the foot of the site to re-provision the garrison.

Danes Dyke, East Yorkshire, sometime around 1906.

Topography was clearly important in prehistoric times with headlands around the British coastline utilized for both settlement and defence. Flamborough Head in East Yorkshire was occupied from a very early date; to the seaward the cliffs provided excellent protection. This meant that the landward exposed flank could be made secure by the enhancement of a natural feature, Danes Dyke, which runs four kilometres across the headland. A wooden palisade may have topped the massive bank and ditch to further enhance the defensive function. While called Danes Dyke, the original structure was probably Iron Age rather than Viking and was perhaps re-used at later dates. Just north of this is the location of medieval Scarborough Castle, again situated on high sea cliffs with excellent views and defences in all directions and with a protective function for the important harbour below. The archaeology of the site confirms prehistoric occupation with a significant Roman signal station too.

Indeed, around the English coastline similar histories emerge on varying scales. South of Coverack in Cornwall a coastal path follows the line of Chynhalls Cliff and leads to Chynhalls Cliff Castle on the point of the same name. The defensive structure is formed by two large earth-and-stone banks built across the promontory with a ditch between them. This is one, albeit striking, example of an Iron Age cliff castle. They date from the mid-Iron Age around 500BCE. Close by there is Lankidden Cliff Castle with a hundred-metre-long rampart up to four-metres high

Chynhalls Cliff Castle, Cornwall.

and a ditch today about half-a-metre deep. Significant parts of the site have been lost to erosion. All around this coastline there is evidence of similar structures going back to a prehistoric landscape that was well populated and the centres of important metal production and trading.

Territorial markers

In terms of the wider countryside and its topography and terrain, similar approaches can be widely seen. Across the northern part of the English midlands for instance a territorial, and perhaps defensive line, ran eastwards from the high ground of the Pennine hills across South Yorkshire. This is known as the Roman Rig but is clearly pre-Roman as much of it marks out the high ground of the Iron Age Brigantes tribe to the north. As the structure runs across the countryside, parts of the area were protected by the extensive wetlands of the time; to the east from the Don Gorge across the great Humberhead wetlands the territory was protected by impenetrable peat bog and fen. It is likely that smaller kingdoms and tribal areas would be demarcated by long-since obliterated networks of banks and ditches to identify boundaries and defensive lines. On high ground west of the Roman Rig is the Bar Dyke in Bradfield, South Yorkshire. This is a well-preserved example of such an earthwork probably constructed as a frontier defence either during the prehistoric or

Scarborough Castle, Lighthouse, and boats pictured in the early 1800s in strategic locations: towering cliffs, the site of defensive settlements from a Roman signal station, and a medieval fortress.

post-Roman periods. Understanding such features becomes particularly important to our knowledge of ancient regional boundary alignments and the wider context of the Dark Ages kingdoms of Northumbria and Mercia. Bar Dyke is an example of a 'cross dyke': substantial linear earthworks generally between a kilometre and two kilometres in length made up of one or more ditches arranged parallel to one or more banks.

Strategic and defensive linear features in the countryside are found widely and from diverse dates, from the late Neolithic to the medieval period. These major structures are mostly found in upland landscapes running across ridges and spurs; today they are recognized as earthworks, as cropmarks on aerial photographs, or both. Many cross dykes originated in the Middle Bronze Age, but others are known to have been utilized in the Middle Ages, reused – or with new ones constructed – during the medieval period. These features were boundary markers most likely indicating some form of land allotment, but they were also used as trackways, cattle droveways, and defensive earthworks.

Another very well-known linear boundary is Offa's Dyke on the England-Wales border. This is a linear earthwork that roughly follows the Welsh-English boundary and consists of a constructed ditch and rampart with the ditch on the Welsh-facing side. The huge earthwork is carefully aligned to present an unobstructed view into Wales from along its entire length. This is an immense structure and would originally have been around twenty-seven-metres wide and eight metres from the bank top to the ditch bottom. The history and origins of the dyke have long been considered one of the great mysteries of the period. The first known reference to it was by Asser, the biographer of King Alfred, who wrote, about 100 years later that 'a certain vigorous king called Offa … had a great dyke built between Wales and Mercia from sea to sea'.

It seems that the dyke was built as a response to events in the border region involving the princes of Powys in Wales. Whether it was an agreed boundary, a defensive structure with long-lost additional fortifications, or fulfilled some other use, is still debated. Construction began about AD785; this significant undertaking must have taken several years to build. However, despite the great effort expended, the ninth-century history of the region indicates that the dyke was only important for a relatively short time and was then abandoned.

The presence of defensive structures and settlements on significant topographic locations may also inform our understanding of landscape at that time when a site was occupied. In Ecclesall Woods in Sheffield, a now well-wooded site, there is a large Bronze Age hilltop enclosure situated on the top of a west-facing steep escarpment which drops down to the Dark Ages kingdom boundary in the valley below. On the flanks of the hill, the site is overlaid by a substantial Romano-British field system. The kingdom boundary between the Anglo-Saxon kingdoms of Northumbria and Mercia is the Limb Brook. Woodland and deer-park banks and ditches are found on both the Mercian and Northumbrian sides of the stream and follow the older boundary.

The importance of location

Further east in Sheffield, overlooking the now-industrial Lower Don Valley and situated at the western end of the great Roman Rig across South Yorkshire, is a major Iron Age hillfort at Wincobank Hill. Today the site is covered with ancient multi-stemmed coppice oak trees. The strategic and defensive nature of these prehistoric settlements is unmistakable evidence that these hill slopes were cleared of tree cover very early in their history. Without trees, both locations present long-distance views across and into neighbouring territories; an essential prerequisite of a prehistoric settlement.

Finally, it is a general observation that ancient settlement sites often occupy the higher ground, especially where the location permits distant views and where these are afforded a full 360-degree circle. In England for example, if you find a hilltop with good visual properties you will often find evidence of early human settlement; this holds for many other places around the world too. Roundball Hill, just south of Honiton in Devon and on former common land with an ancient wood on its shoulder, is a classic example. This small but neatly rounded hill has wide vistas across former wetlands and either wooded or marshy valleys, encircling its crown is an obvious earthwork marking prehistoric settlement. Visibility was important for communication between and within tribal groups, this was often by signal fires on hilltops; it was also vital to see and have warning of visitations from neighbours who may or may not have friendly intentions.

Location within a landscape context has always been significant in terms of establishing defensive positions and therefore influencing later settlements. York for example, was founded in AD71 when Quintus Cerialis constructed a military fortress (*castra*) on flat ground above the floodland of the Ouse River close to the confluence with the lesser Foss River. In this situation the town was well supplied with water, had good river-based transport and natural protection by both the rivers and associated wetlands. The significance of this location proved important as York grew to be a capital city and a centre of both military power and of ecclesiastical learning. A consequence of these attributes was that over the centuries York was a primary location to either capture or to hold; some of the associated events are described in later chapters. Nottingham Castle was similarly placed above the great Trent River and on top of a massive, sheer cliff overlooking the extensive floodplains and meadows of the river.

Topography and settlement choice does not only apply to defensive functions but to religious ones too. For example, older Christian parish churches are almost invariably on high ground. Combined with their tall spires it makes them visible from all around. Significant buildings such as cathedrals are similarly placed where topographically possible. A good example is the medieval Lincoln Cathedral which stands high on a rocky ridge running north-south through the middle of Lincolnshire and is the dominant building from east and west in the lower-lying areas. This is a striking image even today and in the medieval landscape, with Lincoln Castle close by, it was a powerful statement of church and crown visible for all to see.

Impacts of terrain and weather on both attack and defence

In terms of conflict such as wars, terrain and topography determined strategy for assailants and defenders alike. Landscapes that provide shelter and are difficult

British troops bogged down with their artillery, Flanders 1917.

British troops carrying supplies to the front at Flanders, 1917.

The problems of a flooded trench for sodden Allied troops, Western Front, First World War.

German trench and dugouts 1916.

French troops storming a German trench at the Battle of Aisne, 1914.

to traverse will always favour those seeking to avoid direct confrontation, who opt for guerrilla hit-and-run tactics. Open countryside such as the central European plains would find favour with invading cavalry such as the Huns of the Dark Ages, the Tartars and Mongols of medieval times, and the tank divisions of first Germany and then Russia during the Second World War. The development of new military technology has given advantage to the innovators throughout the history of warfare. However, terrain and topography can be great levellers and the outcomes of numerous conflicts bear testimony to this.

Finally, the impacts of seasons and seasonality combine to shape the

An Allied trench with German gas attack, Verdun.

effects and impacts of topography and terrain, especially when seasons bring extreme weather. Examples include northern high-latitude and alpine environments where snow and ice may make countryside or watercourses impassable. However, ice-bound rivers and lakes may be rendered crossable in winter but when spring meltwaters come, can be turned into impassable barriers. Frozen lakes in Scandinavia were used as seasonal landing strips for aeroplanes during twentieth-century conflicts. Similar patterns occur in regions subject to torrential rainy seasons such as many tropical areas, with drylands becoming sodden mud baths.

The Northern Crusades

An example of a battlefield catastrophe linked to seasonal extremes was during the Northern Crusades, authorized by Pope Innocent III to convert to Christianity the pagan communities of Latvia, Lithuania, and Prussia in the Eastern Baltic. In 1236, a force of Teutonic knights led the campaign which, because as Eastern Orthodox Christians they too were considered heretical, included attacks on Russian states. By 1240, the knights were taking the western Russian city of Novgorod and the nearby port of Pskov, but both were relieved by Russian Prince Alexander Nevsky. The crusaders began their assault again in 1242, but with good local knowledge of the terrain and the conditions the prince drew the knights, with their 2,500-strong army, onto the frozen Lake Peipus, located on the border of modern-day Russia and Estonia. The Russian infantry confronted the knights and held them in check. Then, as they tired, the cavalry joined the battle. Exhausted, and in a state of confusion, the knights withdrew from the conflict and moved further out into the icy lake. However, this meant they unwittingly manoeuvred into a zone where the ice was thinner and began to sink and break up under the weight of horses, men, and armour. As the ice gave way, the Teutonic army slipped into the frozen waters, and many were drowned. This proved too much for the eastern campaign of the Northern Crusade, from then on the knights focused their attacks on the western areas alone. The Narva River was accepted as the border between Russia and Estonia and remains so today. The Battle of Lake Peipus was an overwhelming victory for the Russian Prince Alexander and was brought about by superior knowledge of local terrain and clever military tactics.

The Bohemian Revolt

Another such example was the Battle of White Mountain during the Thirty Years War between the Holy Roman Empire and the Protestant Union. The conflict boiled over when in 1617, Catholic Ferdinand II was crowned the new King of Bohemia and began to jettison the religious freedoms previously enjoyed by his subjects, who were Protestants. An immediate response by the Protestants was for a mob to throw two Catholic lords and their scribes out of a high window in Prague – in an incident which became known as the Defenestration of Prague. This was in 1618, and by 1620 Ferdinand, as representative of the Pope and recognized as Holy Roman Emperor, set about the suppression of the Protestant uprisings against their Catholic overlords in what was known as the Bohemian Revolt.

The result of this situation was the meeting of the Imperial army of Johann Tserclae, Count von Tilly, and the Bohemian army under the command of Christian of Anhalt. The Bohemians were pushed back to the outskirts of Prague where they made a stand. Assembling on a high plateau called White Mountain the Bohemians, with 23,000 men, faced the Imperial army of around 25,000; both sides included many mercenaries. With bitterly cold wintry weather closing in, the conditions were atrocious, and the fight was over in under an hour.

The Bohemians were routed with around 4,000 killed or wounded to only 700 casualties in the Imperial army. Consequently, Prague fell to the emperor, the revolt collapsed, and Bohemia and the Czech region were reabsorbed into the Holy Roman Empire and its Catholicism. During the Thirty Years War, which ran on until 1648, around eight million lives were lost. The outcome of White Mountain was perhaps not determined by the extreme weather, but it probably tipped the balance of the conflict on the day on such an exposed battlefield.

How weather affected Clive of India

Similar importance of weather on the battlefield was demonstrated by the British in India. In the mid-eighteenth century the British were in the throes of their conquest of India. This involved conflict with local and regional rulers and with rival French interests. In 1756, a new nawab ruler, Siraj ud-Daulah, came to power in Bengal and revolted against the British East India Company, occupying their trading post in Calcutta. The British response was to send Colonel Robert Clive to suppress the rebellion, and ultimately to remove Siraj. These objectives were achieved through a mix of bribery, diplomacy, and military conflict. In June 1757, Colonel Clive advanced toward the Bengal capital of Murshidabad with a force of around 3,000, about three-quarters being Indian sepoys. At the Hooghli River he was opposed by an army of some 50,000 including artillery sent by the French. Despite the overwhelming odds, Clive gave battle, which was finely balanced until the weather intervened in the form of torrential rain.

The heavy downpour dampened the powder which meant muskets, pistols, and even cannon were inoperable. However, the better-trained British army kept their

Napoleon's retreat from Russia.

powder dry which the Bengalis did not. So, when the massed Bengali cavalry charged the British lines, they were cut down in droves by musket and cannon-fire. Around a third of the nawab's army stood to one side; their leader had been bribed by Clive. This overwhelming victory was a vital step toward British control of India. Siraj fled the battlefield on a camel and was later captured and executed by the newly incumbent nawab. A change in the weather was a key reason for the British success.

Napoleon Bonaparte in Russia

Seven years after Austerlitz, in June 1812, Napoleon chose to invade Russia at the head of an army of somewhere around 250,000 men. Learning from their earlier defeats and understanding Napoleon's way of fighting, the Russians managed to avoid major and decisive battles and Napoleon closed in on Moscow. However, by September and deep into foreign country, he had lost around half his army to a mix of disease, starvation, and desertion. Finally, the Russians decided to stand and fight with Marshal Mikhail Kutusov in command. So, at Borodino on the road from Smolensk to Moscow the Russian forces assembled along a line of hills fortified by additional earthworks. On 7 September, Napoleon launched a frontal attack.

Both sides suffered huge losses and the redoubts were taken and retaken with infantry and heavy cannon-fire. Eventually, late in the day, Napoleon's troops secured

Napoleon retrieving the eagle standard after the battle.

the high ground, but he hesitated to commit his final force and so the Russians were able to withdraw and regroup in good order. Due to the defensive and difficult terrain along the Kalatsha River the French had made negligible impact there. Both armies had lost around 35,000 men, and within the week Napoleon occupied Moscow.

However, this turned out to be a famously pyrrhic victory with much of the city razed due to fires almost certainly started deliberately by the retreating Russians. Without essential resources of fuel, food, and clothing, the French abandoned their goal of Moscow and set about a retreat from Russia. With bitterly cold weather, and what Russians described as their 'Generals January and February', the Grand Armée was starving and freezing and endured harassment from Russian partisans and the army. Fewer than 30,000 French soldiers survived the long march home.

Winston Churchill observed that 'Wars are not won by evacuations'. The catastrophic defeat at the gates of Moscow left Napoleon with three options in retreat. First, head north and west through poor countryside but areas unaffected by the war so far; second, go south and then west into much richer landscape in terms of available resources but having to face the Russian army in further engagements; or retreat along the same route they had come where they at least had some provisions deposited from the invasion. In the end, he fell back along the original route. Nevertheless, the provisions set aside within Russian territory were already under assault from Cossacks

French retreat from Moscow, 1812.

and local partisans. Then, as the Russians realized that Napoleon was abandoning Moscow and retreating, it was clear that the tables were turned, and they pursued.

Despite initially mild weather, the French army soon became stretched out over around sixty miles with loot, wounded, and civilian followers, the many who couldn't keep up simply fell behind and dropped out of formation. Soldiers, now half-starved, could not maintain orderly procession, and waggons of wounded were abandoned as the horses expired due to lack of forage. By late October 1812, the Grand Armée was once again at the battlefield of Borodino where 30,000 human corpses remained, half-eaten by wolves. For the army food was the major issue with men and animals starving. The countryside was littered with the bodies of 10,000 horse carcasses; some animals had been cut for flesh and blood while still alive. The landscape was littered with cannon, powder-waggons, and all kinds of military stores. Soldiers and followers described as 'naked wretches' were fleeing from mobs of angry peasants whose retribution was vicious in the extreme. Fifty French prisoners were burned alive while another fifty, still living, were buried in the earth. Other prisoners were lined up prone along a felled tree trunk while peasants, both male and female, bashed out their brains.

Things got worse as the weather turned bitterly cold, the north wind brought crippling low temperatures and heavy snow. Men running toward campfires in search of heat simply collapsed and passed out as the snowstorms hit them. On 9 November, when the French reached Smolensk which had been turned into a supply depot, starving stragglers ran amok and there was such chaos that the troops bringing up the rear guard got very little. The elite troops of the French army held off overwhelming forces of Russians for some time, but ultimately even the Imperial Guard and Napoleon's personal entourage had to join the flight as the Russians poured across the countryside taking thousands of frozen, starving French as prisoners.

Marshal Ney, at the rear of the French retreat, had refused to surrender at Smolensk and somehow broke through overwhelming Russian troops to follow a stream to the Dnieper River to a point where his soldiers could cross the frozen watercourse. Guns and waggons had to be abandoned, but with 900 men he was able to re-join the main body of the army.

However, the next river they came across was the Beresina which in the summer was no problem to cross, but now, only half-frozen, was impassable. Worse still, three main bodies of Russian forces were converging on the French at just the point where they met this barrier. The one bridge was held by Russians in the nearby town, but French reinforcements pushed them back. As the Russians abandoned the bridge, they destroyed it. The French column of 70,000 was by now actually only 30,000 soldiers with 40,000 stragglers and civilians, and waggons that the Russians believed held guns and ammunition but were mostly carriages for women. North of Borisov the French found a ford that at its deepest was about eight feet and was more than a hundred yards across. Using wood from the nearby village the French engineers began constructing a bridge out of sight of Russian eyes. The French successfully feinted to a southern crossing. With rafts and horses, the French army now began the crossing while the Russians guarded the wrong place. The makeshift bridges were lashed together across the ford and some 10,000 French troops managed to cross even though the bridges kept giving way, leading to panic. The Russians were now moving to the far bank of the crossing point, their Cossacks harassing those in the rear-guard left on the northern bank. The crowds of stragglers and civilians were pouring into the confined space of the pontoon bridges with 30,000 people, along with horses, pressed in by the Russians trying to cross the two narrow wooden structures. Survivors described struggling over dead and half-dead people, with the living desperately clinging onto the limbs of those walking over them. As the pontoon bridge swayed and sank people slipped and stumbled, grasping anyone nearby and taking them down with them. The crowd, now over a mile wide and about four hundred yards deep, jostled for position and even more panic ensued when the Russians began firing cannon into the seething mass at close quarters. People cried

Napoleon's retreat from Moscow through the Russian winter, 1812.

out to be shot or stabbed to death, and a mother was seen strangling her young child before allowing herself, already shot in the legs, to fall under the stamping hordes.

The Russian forces also suffered from cold and malnutrition, but they were on home turf and were in the ascendency, whereas the French were on the run in a foreign land. By the end of their march the French force was reduced to around 25,000 and about half a million men had been lost. The Russian army, under Kutusov, had begun with nearly 100,000 and ended with 40,000 men still available to fight; they had other armies too. The retreating French also had to endure constant harassment from Cossacks and local peasants and partisans, which of course the pursuing Russians did not.

Napoleonic battlefield sur le Nemen 1807, where the French army was victorious.

Flanders on the higher ground August 1917, showing the terrain above the wetland.

Passchendaele and the French in the First World War

Staying with French forces, but more than a century later, in the summer of 1916, the British and French looked to implement a joint offensive in the Somme region of the Western Front in northern France. By the end of this conflict, commanded for the Allies by Sir Douglas Haig, and with the November weather worsening, the casualties were around 400,000 British, 200,000 French, and 500,000 German troops dead. Indeed, the first day of the Somme was the worst military disaster in British history with 57,470 casualties of which 19,240 were dead. The objective was to shatter the German defences, but the exercise was an abject failure resulting from hopeless misreading of the situation: the landscape and the opposition defences. Haig abandoned the offensive in November 1916 having gained a maximum of seven-and-a-half miles (twelve kilometres) of ground. While he went on to modernize the British army, introducing new technology like tanks, and winning a series of important victories in the latter stages of the war, he demonstrated stubborn over optimism in the success of frontal offensives against the odds. To say the least, the problems posed by topography, terrain, and exposure to enemy fire on open ground made some of his tactics reckless and foolhardy. The costs in terms of men and suffering were incalculable. In part, this approach was heavily influenced by the earlier wars between

Dead Japanese sentries being replaced in their pits, Russo-Japanese War, 1905.

the Japanese and the Russians and their experiences of trench warfare. This interpretation of the Russo-Japanese conflict generated the mistaken belief that direct assault by infantry into the face of heavily defended trench positions could bring victory if the troops were sufficiently feisty and bold.

The operation was led by the British because the French were occupied with the defence of Verdun; Haig had assembled a force of half a million men plus about 1,500 guns. However, many of the soldiers were new to battle; having signed up following the famous Kitchener 'Wants you' campaign. Around 2.5 million volunteers had enlisted because of the Secretary for War's posters in 1914. With the need for at least basic military training for this mass citizen army of volunteers, many did not see active service until the autumn of 1915. Sadly, for many of these recruits, the Somme would not only be their first battle, but their last too. Haig assumed his mass bombardment of the enemy lines would shatter the German defences, whereas they were largely holed up safely in undamaged concrete bunkers.

So, on 1 July, when the British and French troops went 'over the top' they were faced by defences such as barbed wire, mostly intact, and exceedingly heavy machine-gun fire. The troops were instructed to advance in lines at walking pace on the ill-founded assumption that the artillery fire had removed most of the German defences. The French infantry attack made some progress but many of the British battalions never even reached the German lines before they were mown down. A particularly tragic event was that of the so-called 'Lost Regiment' of volunteers from Newfoundland, Britain's smallest overseas colony and forming the Royal Newfoundland Regiment. They were one of the groups ordered forward on the first day of the Somme but as a second wave assault on Beaumont Hamel. Not knowing that the first wave had failed to get to the enemy lines, they advanced unsupported across open ground toward the

Opening of the Battle of Verdun from a German perspective.

Taking a British field gun to the front near Ypres in horrendous conditions.

The Battle of Flanders illustrates the carnage; note also the extensive use of timber and brushwood in the Front.

German positions. Cut down by machine-gun fire from a total of 780 men, 684 were casualties.

Despite the atrocious losses Haig persisted with the tactic and some key points were for a while captured; Mouquet Farm was taken by the Australians but at a cost of 23,000 casualties. A major problem on the open shell-pitted battlefield was that of coordination and communication. With the lack of effective comms, it was impossible to effectively coordinate artillery and infantry.

Trench warfare was becoming more sophisticated; standard guidance saw them dug in zigzag lengths to prevent the enemy shooting directly down the line of a trench or an explosion ripping along its length. Between the opposing trenches were lengths of barbed wire strung across no-man's land as well as booby-trapped tunnels dug by both sides loaded with mines or other explosives. It was at the Somme that Haig first

This picture of the Battle of Flanders shows the appalling conditions.

introduced the tanks which, although having visual impact, were also vulnerable to artillery fire when on the open field of battle. As with other drawn-out conflicts disease and associated problems also took a huge toll. However, a major problem was the flat countryside and the awful conditions in the cratered and devastated landscape.

By the summer of 1917, General Haig was planning a major offensive action in northern France and Belgium across the great marshlands of the low countries of Flanders. The intention was to break the German lines and free Belgian ports which were used as bases for German U-boats that stalked the North Sea and the English Channel. The initial June assault was on the Messines Ridge and bore some success; the Battle of Passchendaele, also known as the Third Ypres, began in late July 1917. This assault used the creeping artillery barrage now favoured by both French and

Allied first aid post on the Somme battlefield.

British commanders behind which the infantry advanced over open ground. They broke the first German line with relative ease but then hit trouble as the German defences included concrete blockhouses and machine-gun nests. The British assault was then pushed back, and the territory gained was largely lost.

To understand Passchendaele the terrain must be fully appreciated as this area of the Flanders flatlands, was essentially an extensive marshy floodland. Some areas had been wrested from nature by agricultural

Fighting a gas attack. This *Chicago Daily News* postcard depicts First World War trench warfare.

Underground hand-to-hand fighting with sappers at Port Arthur, Russo-Japanese War 1904.

improvement over centuries, but this countryside was essentially wet. By August, heavy rains, combined with the effects of artillery shelling, turned a lot of the lower-lying battlefield into a vast quagmire. Men and supplies could only negotiate much of the area by means of duckboards. In every sense, the conflict was getting bogged down. In September the weather improved, and British advances were made to take the Broodseinde Ridge in October 1917. Despite no clear objective now, Haig continued the frontal assault with artillery and infantry to ultimately take the higher ground of the Passchendaele Ridge. This was achieved by 10 November but with little practical strategic benefit and the direct loss of life amounting to around 250,000 casualties from each side. The final assault on the Ridge from 26 October to 10 November was at a cost of 16,000 casualties from the British Canadian troops. The Ridge was subsequently abandoned without any fighting.

Collecting the wounded, Ypres 1917.

Chapter 5

The impacts of disease and infection

Combinations of terrain, topography, extreme weather, globalization, and catastrophic diseases can tip the balance of conflicts. Furthermore, lack information and understanding of any of these factors can prove disastrous. When battles and warfare become industrial in scale and static in terms of geographical location further problems ensue. The inability to provide for even basic sanitation, hygiene, potable water, and good food, is a recipe for truly awful mixes of noxious diseases and infections, compounded by the physicality of living and fighting in swamp conditions. Extreme weather simply makes all this even worse. The slightest injury or cut can result in life-threatening infection.

Disease, sanitation, and supplies on the Western Front

Often omitted from descriptions and analyses of the Battle of Passchendaele is

Western Front British gunners with a trench mortar, First World War.

the awful toll of disease and infection associated with fighting in constantly waterlogged conditions in rat-infected trenches, for months on end without effective sanitation. This is a distinctively unglamorous side to warfare. A later chapter considers the wider impacts and influences of disease in warfare and on the battlefield, but here we look in some detail at their impacts on the First World War because they are so significant in understanding the landscape of the conflict.

Seasonality influences things like food availability, vital supply chains, and in some situations the likelihood of debilitating diseases. Fevers, parasites, and infections were rife on the frontline of many conflicts. Combined with the

A cartoon illustrating the sheer misery of the communications trench in the First World War.

German trenches Vimy Ridge where the Germans benefitted from the higher, drier ground.

obvious stresses of major wars and their impacts on people, climate and terrain may trigger contagion such as typhus, malaria, cholera, typhoid, trench foot, and other similar ailments, especial dysentery. For aggressors and defenders, and both military and civilian populations, war may mean malnutrition, making people even more vulnerable to disease. Understanding and adapting to the changing conditions may be the key to success, but until modern times there was limited understanding of the nature and causation of infections. The spread of sickness was often attributed to toxic miasmas carried in the air from contaminated places such as bogs and marshes. This meant that effective action to combat the spread of illness was limited. Indeed, this situation was the case for societies where, even in peacetime, sanitation was at best rudimentary, and proper hygiene was unheard of or even actively shunned.

The outcomes of many conflicts have been determined by countryside and terrain on the one hand, but also by casualties from disease on the other. Throughout history conquering forces ultimately won because of diseases they carried for which they had immunity. This was the case for the Spanish Conquistadors in Central America, and later for other Europeans in North America. However, disease can be a double-edged sword in conflicts and lack of exposure, and thus immunity to indigenous diseases, can be debilitating for an invading force. In 1986, Alfred Crosby wrote a

Winter in the trenches, Western Front, March 1915.

Western Front burial trench, First World War.

Western Front dead German soldiers, First World War.

seminal book on the topic of ecological imperialism; he argued that the European colonial expansion from the medieval period through to the twentieth century was significantly influenced by the diseases that they transmitted.

The trauma of war and the toll of disease

The Great War was actually the first major conflict where the death rate from the trauma of war, largely inflicted by projectiles such as bullets and shells, was greater than that from disease. On the Western Front, this was a ratio of five to one. However, no soldier on the Western Front was entirely free from the threat of diseases born of the war, and the sheer number of casualties by far exceeded those of previous wars. This also omits the catastrophic impacts of Spanish Flu in the immediate post-war period. However, paradoxically, it is also probable that it was the first major war where the conditions created by the fighting reduced the amount of disease to less than that normally expected in a theatre of war. A particular example was the case of malaria, the plague of many wars even on continental Europe. In the battle zone, the extensive use of poison gases combined with the by-products of high explosives polluted the air and ground to such an extent that the disease vectors, Anopheline mosquitoes, were unable to live sufficiently long to transmit malaria. Fewer than 1,000 cases of malaria were recorded on the Western Front and deaths were only in the low teens.

Wounded German soldiers, First World War.

Of course, with the appallingly degraded living conditions in the trenches of the British Expeditionary Force (BEF) and imposed on the hapless trench dwellers of all sides, the result was a deplorable state of both personal and environmental hygiene. This meant that the incidence of most diseases soared to often chronic (constant) and epidemic (widespread) proportions, with significant implications for the health of the affected troops and their effectiveness on the battlefield.

Blinded for you – an image sold in aid of St Dunstan's Regent's Park.

Progressive industrialization during the First World War triggered numerous technological advances, including in medicine, embracing both diagnosis and treatment. An example was the widespread introduction of voluntary vaccination against some of the most

Collecting sphagnum moss for the war effort, First World War.

prevalent and deadly diseases such as smallpox, but because the uptake of these vaccinations in the British Army in 1914 was voluntary, its effect was significantly reduced. After 1915 the British Army made vaccinations compulsory. Antibiotics would transform the rate of cure of intractable bacterial diseases in the later stages of the Second World War but during its predecessor these were still undiscovered. In many cases the only available treatments were relatively ineffective medications such as *Sphagnum* moss dressings, potassium permanganate, boric acid, and the like. But even these, for example the *Sphagnum* moss dressings, were considered radical and new.

Well-established medical practices were often not utilized or effectively deployed by the British Army. Indeed, the treatment of malaria is a case in point. The Germans, in their East African Campaign, rigorously employed a malaria prophylaxis (prevention) campaign for non-immune European troops using the drug quinine, which they cultivated in East Africa. This enabled them to keep these key expatriate personnel in the field and effect tactical and operational military defeats on the British Army's European and Asian troops in East Africa who were less well protected.

An issue in Europe was that most troops arriving at the Western Front had led rather simple lifestyles until the outbreak of war. They were used to basic, but often quite effective, hygiene practices as part of daily life. These practices provided some basic protection against disease, and most had suffered the usual childhood infections.

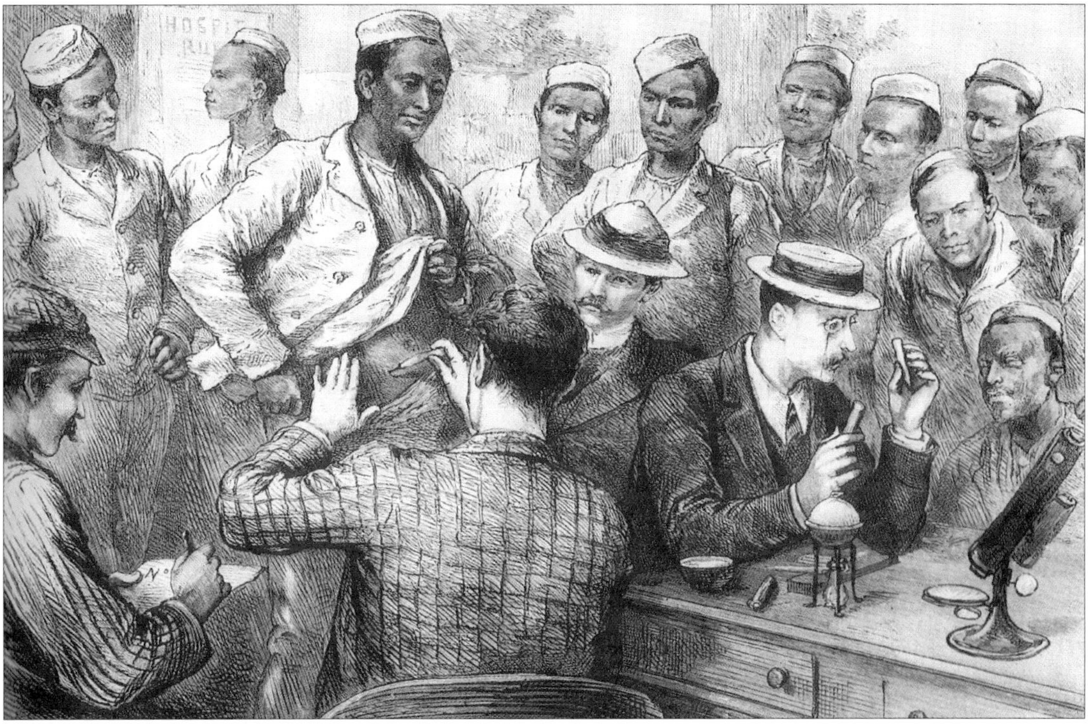

British Gurkhas are vaccinated against cholera, 1893.

This meant they had acquired specific antibodies to resist future infections from their expected lifespan diseases. However, when these soldiers arrived on the field of battle, they were placed abruptly into a new world of tightly packed soldiers from around the world carrying strains of diseases way beyond their previous exposure. Furthermore, they had close contact with large numbers of animals that had their own diseases and parasites. Along with all this was the hordes of infested vermin (rats) and most detested of all, infestations of human body parasites like lice and fleas.

Advances were made during the nineteenth century in terms of vaccination against otherwise debilitating diseases.

The disastrous experience of Gallipoli

One of the horrific catastrophes of the First World War occurred in March 1915 when British troops landed in Turkey at Cape Helles with the Australian and New Zealand (ANZAC) forces disembarking at Gaba Tepe. The naval support from French and British ships failed to dislodge the Turks and consequently the infantry was faced with overwhelming artillery barrages. They failed to make headway inland from the beaches; the ANZAC forces had landed in the wrong places and were

ANZACs in their dugout near Gaba Tepe Gallipoli, First World War.

pinned down by Turkish fire as they scrambled up rocky ravines and ridges above the shoreline. The Turkish resistance was led by General Mustafa Kemal with advice from German commander Liman von Sanders. For the Allies, the campaign was an unmitigated disaster and the British commander, Sir Ian Hamilton, was sacked. The decision was then taken to evacuate 140,000 troops leaving 44,000 dead on the battlefield. The conflict illustrates the difficulties inherent in frontal infantry assault against well-prepared defences.

However, one of the major factors that again reared its head on the Western Front was disease that killed and debilitated. The core problem was a combination of inherent disease in these conditions compounded by grossly unsanitary conditions and the abundance of corpses.

The Allied forces at Gallipoli were mostly the ANZACs. Many factors contributed to making the Gallipoli battlefield an almost unendurable place for all soldiers. The constant noise with cramped unsanitary conditions, diseases, the stench, the daily death of comrades, terrible food, and lack of rest and thirst all contributed to the most gruelling conditions. Incessant noise from shelling, bombing, artillery, machine-gun and rifle fire caused psychological and physiological problems for the soldiers. These

The Allied landing at ANZAC Cove Gallipoli, First World War.

Charge of Turkish soldiers at Gallipoli, First World War.

included shell shock, stress from unceasing exposure to loud mechanical noises, hearing impairment, and lack of sleep. The ANZACs were literally clinging onto the edge of a cliff with the sea at their backs and the Turks occupying the higher ground. They were forced to dig extensive trench and tunnel systems and to endure a semi-subterranean existence of cramped and filthy living conditions under constant shellfire. The cramped conditions and steep terrain left few safe places for men to rest on the frontline on Second Ridge above ANZAC Cove. Severe exhaustion from lack of sleep caused by the constant noise from frontline positions such as Silt Spur, Quinn's Post, and Tasmania Post meant that many men fell asleep at their posts.

Food was a major concern to ANZAC soldiers. Much has been written about the food rations provided for the ANZACs at Gallipoli, including the dark, humorous odes to bully beef and impenetrably hard army biscuits. There is no denying that the rations issued to the ANZACs provided very poor nutrition due to the unvarying diet of processed foods: canned meat – corned 'bully' beef, bacon, or Maconochie's beef stew – hard tack biscuits, and watery jam. The diet was sometimes varied with sugar, condensed milk, rice, and cocoa, but there was a distinct lack of fresh fruit or vegetables. These rations were intended to be lived on by British army divisions for only short periods of time, not for months as was the case at Gallipoli. Living on these rations caused major health problems for the soldiers. So prevalent on the ANZAC battlefields were the food cans in which these rations were issued that their remains can still be found around the sites of the trenches and dugouts. The Turkish forces were provided with a wider variety of food. This was centrally prepared by cooks and consisted of fresh local foods, although it was often lacking in meat. French and Indian divisions had much better rations than ANZACs, with more vegetables and bread. The poor nutritional content of the British rations contributed to the physical decline of the ANZAC and British troops at Gallipoli. The unappetizing and unvaried diet affected the soldiers' morale and psychological well-being. It also increased their susceptibility to disease, which spread rapidly during the summer months of the campaign.

Disease swept through both ANZAC and Turkish forces at Gallipoli. Dysentery, tetanus, and septic wounds plagued the soldiers and necessitated the evacuation of thousands of men from the battlefield. The latrines were open and rudimentary. There were no bathing facilities with few opportunities for body or clothes washing. Lack of sanitation in the ANZAC areas caused the rapid spread of dysentery, known as the Gallipoli Gallop. The unburied corpses in and around the frontline areas were the perfect breeding ground for flies. These were almost unbearable in the summer months; they were so thick that soldiers could not eat without their biscuits and

Lord Kitchener on the beach at Gallipoli.

jam being blackened with flies. Flies rapidly spread diseases through the troops living in cramped, over-crowded trenches and dugouts, unable to even wash their hands. Lice was also a major problem for soldiers during the summer months. With a huge proportion of soldiers suffering 'catastrophic dysentery' the only medical advice given was to tie string around the bottoms of their trousers!

The local water supply was very limited in the British- and ANZAC-held areas of the peninsula. At ANZAC Cove in particular the water supply was a serious problem that contributed to the soldiers' ill health and exacerbated the wretched sanitary conditions. Soldiers in frontline positions were issued only small amounts of water per day and the water quality was poor. Thirst and dehydration were common among the men. Often their only drink was extremely strong black tea.

Other factors that characterized the life of soldiers during the 1915 conflict were psychological. These included homesickness, fear and anxiety, the constant threat of death, and killing, and grief at the daily loss of mates, brothers, and comrades. Overall, these were appalling conditions, which indicate the wholly inadequate planning and response of the British and Allied military authorities to basic human needs and a failure in their duty of care for their soldiers. The ANZAC soldiers earned the respect of others largely because of the projected image of their laconic good humour in the face of the most terrible circumstances. However, some soldiers could not handle these conditions at all and understandably succumbed to mental, physical, and emotional injuries, which continue to be marginalized or completely unacknowledged in the ANZAC legend. The conditions took their toll on even the most stoic and fortunate of survivors, many of whom felt the effects of their time at Gallipoli decades after the conflict.

For Gallipoli, there was a massive lack of understanding of terrain and associated conditions. The Allies landed on open beaches and had to try and move upwards and inland but were faced by well-defended entrenched Turkish positions with heavy artillery. Pinned down and unable to make any significant headway the supply lines were non-functioning, so food and diet were dire, and the consequences were catastrophic disease and other problems. Furthermore, the misjudgement in terms of the almost total underestimation of the scale of the Turkish defences combined with a lack of appreciation of the problems of the terrain within which the Allies were operating, were inexcusable. Furthermore, the anticipated support for the land troops from shelling by the navy did not materialise. The term hellhole is often applied to battlespace scenes, but in this case if anything, the phrase was an understatement.

The Western Front

By late 1914, a complex line of trenches, stretching almost 500 miles (800km) from the North Sea to the Swiss Border, brought with it an extraordinary concentration of millions of men from many nations and cultures. These men were suddenly thrust together in an inconceivable existence of trench warfare, in a climate that over the year ranged from the balmy to the ferociously cold. Additionally, everywhere was well doused by frequent rainfall and affected by seasonal snowfall and frost. Northern France and Flanders could be particularly wet and inhospitable. Throughout history, even relatively small concentrations of military forces have suffered from outbreaks of disease, ranging from discomfort to catastrophic. These outbreaks were particularly associated with static warfare such as sieges or over-wintering in encampments. Epidemics of typhus, malaria, typhoid (the infamous enteric fever), diarrhoea, yellow-fever, pneumonia, and influenza were generously amplified by innumerable cases of venereal disease, scabies, and the like. These illnesses routinely wrought vastly more casualties on armies than those inflicted by the enemy's long bow or machine gun.

Trench diseases in wet landscapes

In general terms of diseases, the Western Front proved no different from what had gone before, but the situation was compounded by the terrain, weather, wetland, and general lack of sanitation. Perhaps the other overwhelming factor was the sheer number of people involved on both sides. One major consequence of the countryside and wetness in this battlescape was the prevalence of three particular diseases, the so-called Trench diseases. These became particularly important on the Western Front during the four years the war lasted and gained the permanent prefix 'trench'.

All three had previously been recorded in many campaigns, but never on the scale of the Western Front. At times, fears were expressed by the High Command that these diseases could actually affect the prosecution of the war. Moreover, to a significant extent, the public, then as now, were largely ignorant of the dreadful strain these diseases placed on the morale and fighting efficiency of the frontline troops. Partly because troops sought to spare those back home from such sordid details, but also because the Allied High Command wished to play down the crippling effect of these diseases from a strategic and morale point of view. As the war progressed many civilians became aware of these trench-prevalent diseases, but their knowledge about them went little beyond this.

Bringing troops to the front by motorbus 1914.

First World War fatalities

The First World War is estimated to have claimed twenty million lives and to have left twenty-one million wounded. The total number of military personnel deaths was just shy of ten million with a further ten million civilians, and of these deaths, more than half were Allied soldiers. Many died in combat, through accidents, or perished as prisoners of war. However, considerable loss of life was attributed to famine and disease with horrific conditions meaning that fevers, parasites, and infections were rife on the frontline and ripped through the troops in the trenches. Among the diseases and viruses that were most prevalent were influenza, typhoid, trench foot, and trench fever. Indeed, if the wartime and post-war fatalities to Spanish Flu are included, the death toll to war-associated disease vastly outnumbered the losses in combat, and much of this was associated with terrain, topography, and weather.

Infections and diseases

Infection posed one of the greatest medical risks. A simple cut to a finger from cleaning your rifle or digging a trench could quite quickly become infected and develop into pneumonia. In the trenches, the men were knee-deep in mud nine out of twelve months of the year, surrounded by bacteria from the bodies of men and animals in no-man's-land. Their own bodies were weaker from lack of sleep, wet, dirty clothes, and a restricted diet in which a piece of fruit or vegetable was a treat.

Field ambulance records show how the pattern of offensives and attacks correlated with the work of doctors and medical support staff. On a single day, up to 300 men could be admitted with gas poisoning. On days when there was no fighting, medics were able to treat non-urgent cases, such as tooth decay.

In the field and in barracks, epidemic typhus (causative bacterium *Rickettsia prowazekii*) was always the bane of armies. The disease was carried by lice and for soldiers there were two varieties, body lice (*Pediculus humanus* sub-spp. *corporis*) and head lice (*Pediculus humanus* sub-spp. *capitis*) that were the vectors of the disease. *Pediculus* was rife in the Western Front trenches and almost impossible to eradicate, causing huge discomfort to the troops. Some soldiers found that shaving the head and moustaches or beards generally controlled the head lice. However, body lice were able to hide away in the folds, creases, and pleats of heavy uniforms from where they emerged to feed, and so control was much more difficult. This was especially problematic in cold winter weather when warm clothing was essential. Topography, weather, and disease proved to be a toxic mix.

Surprisingly, given the prevalence of body lice in the Western Front trenches, outbreaks of epidemic typhus were quite limited. This contrasted with serious epidemics in 1915 among Serbian and Austrian troops on the Eastern Front. Nevertheless, body lice also caused an infection known as 'Trench Fever' caused by *Rickettsia quintana* and closely related to epidemic Typhus.

Lice are the long-feared vectors of epidemic typhus. This disease is caused by an organism, of the genus *Rickettsia*, which demonstrates characteristics of both bacteria and viruses, and like the latter, it only grows in living cells. The infection produces severe fevers, painful aching joints and body rashes. These often led to fatal gastrointestinal haemorrhage and serious failure of kidneys and other major organs.

The French Army on the Western Front suffered severely from epidemic typhus, with well over 100,000 cases recorded with a ten per cent fatality rate. However, the French Army was particularly notorious for its poor field hygiene. The British Expeditionary Force (BEF), on the other hand, only had around two hundred deaths from this infection despite the lack of vaccine. As both armies were essentially in the same terrain, it is assumed that the better field hygiene of the British Army was a key factor in this. Epidemic typhus was transmitted from lice to humans by biting and blood-sucking with infection mostly through feeding parasitic lice leaving their associated infected faeces on the skin of their host. Covered in louse bites the soldiers scratched the open wounds and in so doing rubbed the infective faeces into their own flesh. Plagues of biting body lice infested the unwashed clothing of all ranks of soldiers in the trenches, with the resultant intense itching causing severe discomfort and associated stress. This was even the case without infections and made life for many of the troops utterly miserable.

A similar bacterial infection produced a less severe but long-lasting, painful, debilitating disease commonly known as Trench Fever or Pyrexia of Unknown Origin (PUO). On the Western Front, the Allies recorded about 200,000 cases of this unspecified fever. Some sufferers experienced up to forty days of hospitalization which, spread among a military force, had serious implications for operations. Symptoms could remain at bay for maybe a week or a month, at which point a severe headache was combined with debilitating muscle pains. These pains were often on the shins and hence the alternative name of Shin-bone Fever. First reported from troops in Flanders in 1915, individuals suffered febrile illness in five-day relapsing cycles as the fever went into remission and reoccurred one or more times. When first experienced, the specific cause of the disease was unknown, but its debilitating nature affected between 380,000 and 520,000 soldiers in the British army. Many troops were rendered incapacitated, so research was undertaken in Britain and the United States to identify the causes and mechanisms of disease transmission. Because symptoms bore some resemblance to other fevers like malaria it was felt that lice or even mosquitoes were the vectors. However, effective treatments proved elusive, and prevention focused on the application of insecticides and de-lousing of clothing. When the causative agent of the infection was finally identified, it was grouped into *Rickettsia* genus and was called *Rickettsia quintana*, because of the five-day relapse, later changing to *Bartonella quintana*.

With no effective treatment for trench fever, other than bed rest, serious depression was common. Today the disease would be treated with antibiotics. Fatalities were very uncommon but around eighty per cent of soldiers infected were unfit for duty for about three months. Over the course of the First World War there were 800,000 British Army Trench Fever casualties. The other national armies suffered similarly from this problematic issue for all the forces involved in the conflict.

Dealing with non-fatal diseases

Non-fatal disease might prove very uncomfortable for infected frontline soldiers, but it could be a 'welcome' break from the intolerable conditions and dangers of life on the front. Due to the scale of infection and the lack of effective treatment, military authorities tried to limit lice infestations through things like hot baths, laundries, fumigation, and frequent changes of heat-sterilized clothes and bedding. These certainly helped and were the essential elements of realistic control. However,

Nineteenth-century German soldiers suffering from typhus.

for many soldiers mired in the frontline landscape, such luxuries and hygiene were unimaginable. Conditions and terrain on the frontline made achieving these basic aims incredibly hard. As the conflict developed it was only in the designated rest areas that such facilities were available. In the latter stages of the war there were primitive, partially effective insecticides (naphthalene, creosote, and iodoform). Despite the potential benefits of these treatments some of them had unpleasant side-effects on the soldiers and so the insecticides were not always welcomed.

Terrain, topography, and weather compounded poor diet and proximity to disease-ridden corpses. Particularly in the sodden trenches, where drying out was well-nigh impossible, fungal skin infections were rife and potentially very serious. In this respect, a common and serious problem was a disease called trench foot, prevalent particularly through the winter of 1914/15 with more than 20,000 Allied soldiers believed to have been affected. At the end of the war 74,000 Allied troops had suffered the ailment over the whole period. The cause of this debilitating condition was continual immersion in ice-cold water without any way to dry off. In fact, this was really a cold injury rather than an actual infection. Nevertheless, trench foot, left untreated, could

Bringing in the Allied wounded, First World War.

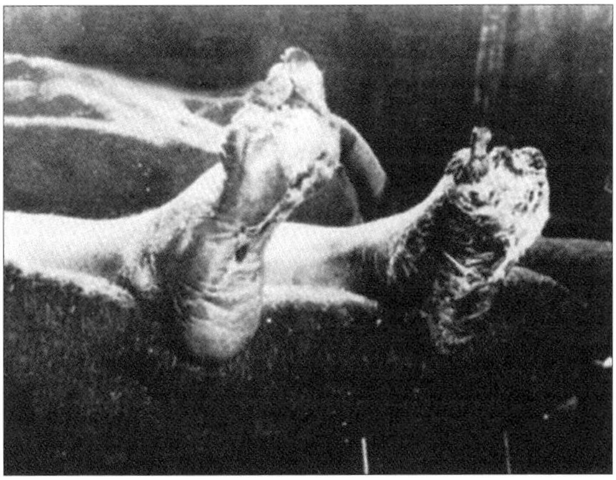

Effects of trench foot, First World War.

lead to serious secondary infections. For the American troops 1,800 cases were reported from 1917 to 1918 with five resultant deaths. Trench-foot troops had to be evacuated from the frontline to recover.

Once again, the landscape conditions were key factors in the discomfort and infection. As noted, this problem was especially significant in trenches dug on land at or near sea level, or in wetlands with the water-table close to the land surface. When digging the trenches, a couple of feet down, soldiers hit water which flooded the structures. In cold weather this was a doubly problematic situation of wet and chill. Then after long periods simply standing in soaking wet socks, and boots, trench foot began. Soldiers' feet swelled and went numb with the skin turning red or blue. As blood circulation became restricted the affected feet grew increasingly painful. With immersion and chill continuing the skin started to break down, the feet swelled, and with blisters forming they became

German soldiers and medical orderlies.

numb from nerve damage. Over time, the skin could become infected by fungus and as the problem progressed, untreated feet frequently showed signs of becoming gangrenous. The condition might then trigger tissue loss, and ultimately necessitate amputation. The guidance to reduce the possibility of developing trench foot was that soldiers were advised or ordered to change into dry socks as frequently as possible. This was easier said than done in the unimaginably awful conditions of the trenches. From 1916 onward, socks were being sold prepared with borax powder as an anti-fungal to help alleviate problems associated with wet feet.

With major trench-lines established in late 1914, the first winter of the war kicked in. It was soon apparent that these hastily dug trenches were likely to flood and become filthy, cold quagmires of mud and water. The situation was complicated further by the significant immobility of static soldiers in the trenches. This meant that in effect they spent long hours stationary and with their feet experiencing wet and cold. For the British Army the standard ammunition boot was made of leather and therefore not effectively waterproof. Furthermore, in the early periods of the First World War's trench warfare, drying out or changing into clean, dry socks was not feasible. After some hours, or days, of continuous exposure to the wet and cold, the skin of the soldier's feet became both waterlogged and chilled.

Following the early rash of Allied forces' trench foot casualties on the Western Front, frequent foot inspections were undertaken by regimental medical officers.

French soldiers in a flooded trench on the Western Front, First World War.

Additional pairs of dry socks were made available to troops so they could change several times daily and whale oil was provided so that it could be rubbed into the feet. This was a team project as soldiers applied it to each other. Application helped stimulate blood circulation and it was hoped that the whale oil might help prevent excessive waterlogging of the skin.

Terrain as a key to avoiding infection

Linked to the topography and terrain of the battlescape, the German forces had the relatively good fortune of occupying the higher and drier ground. The German trenches were better drained than those of the Allies. The other big difference in strategy was that the German forces tended to occupy semi-permanent fortifications. This meant the conditions could be better planned and executed in contrast to the British temporary structures. This approach was in part because the British intent was to press forward and occupy new ground. The conditions inherent in the British trenches were then necessarily more primitive and unsuited to long-term occupation. In the most wet and boggy situations the British had to impose drainage that was more efficient, and issue waterproof gumboots or waders to troops in areas more seriously affected. They also had to install elevated duckboards to keep the soldiers' feet dry.

Wooden inverted A-Frames were especially effective at supporting duckboards

Collecting the wounded at Ypres was not a simple task in a snowbound winter, 1917.

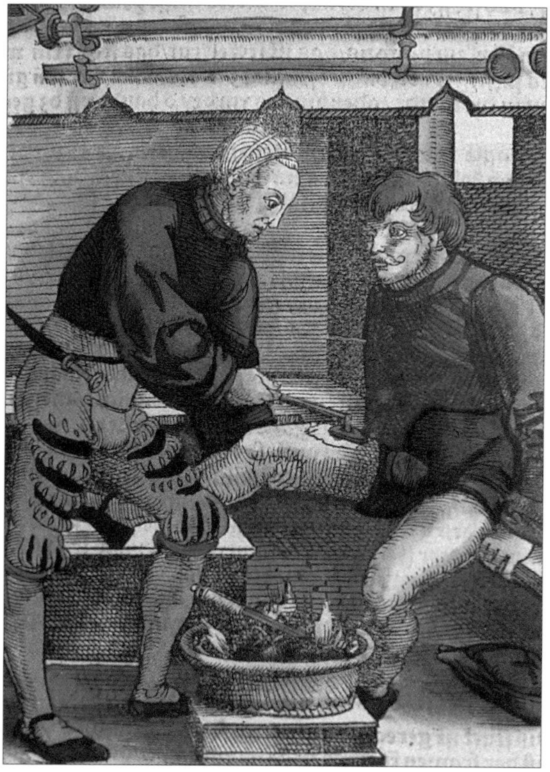

above water-level and were widely used throughout the trench systems of the British and Allied forces. Combined, these measures offered a degree of protection to troops in these appalling conditions. Indeed, as the war progressed, the occurrence of trench foot in British troops gradually declined perhaps associated with the adaptions to the conditions. Nevertheless, although the total British cases recorded was about 74,000, it is believed that many other cases simply went unrecorded or were misreported. The latter was the

Many aspects of the treatment of wounds were slow to evolve beyond medieval surgery such as cauterizing a wound. The development of antibiotics and of advanced reconstructive surgery during the First World War changed this.

case because in many units of the Force, to neglect the feet was a chargeable offence. Overall, trench foot was a particularly distressing and uncomfortable problem caused by conflicts in a wet landscape.

Not fatal but very unpleasant – Trench Mouth

The third of the generic trench diseases was trench mouth, and while this was rather more benign than the other two, it was no doubt both unpleasant and distressing. This was particularly the case when most of the frontline troops were in their teens and twenties. Despite the dangers they faced on the battlefield they would be aware of the importance of their attractiveness when they eventually returned home; a disfiguring infection was thus especially distressing.

Even the full name of the disease, Acute Necrotizing Ulcerative Gingivitis, was rather troubling. The condition was triggered by a malignant overgrowth of the normal mouth-dwelling bacteria (*Bacillis fusiformis*) and spirochaetes (*Borrelia vincentii*), which attacked and eroded the gums. The results were bleeding, ulceration, sloughing of gum membranes, and particularly bad breath. The gum pain made the basic processes of eating, swallowing, and even talking, very difficult. Infection was often accompanied by the painful swelling of the glands in the throat and neck. The underlying cause of this distressing condition was a combination of poor oral hygiene, both physical and emotional stress, poor diet, lack of rest, and heavy smoking. The latter was associated with the general issue of full-strength unfiltered cigarettes supposedly to help make the unbearable conditions slightly better, but a horrible infection was an associated consequence.

Indeed, all the causes noted above were realities of trench life on the Western Front during the First World War. The only effective treatment was palliative with removal of the source of stress, rest, good mouth hygiene, a reduction in smoking, and a balanced diet; all in short supply throughout the conflict. One consequence of this situation was a huge number of toothless ex-soldiers in the post-war years because of the damage wreaked by trench mouth on the unfortunates in and around the trenches of the Eastern and Western Fronts.

Globalization and crowded conditions in the spread of Spanish influenza

As topical today as it was catastrophic in the early twentieth century, a corona-type virus emerged on the global landscape. From 1915 onward, a new strain of influenza began to surface among the combatant armies on the Western Front. This was a result of the mixing globally of young men without wider immunity and then placement

A French soldier being tended by a nursing nun, late 1700.

into mixed and crowded conditions on the frontline. For American troops the problems began at the recruiting bases at home with youngsters drawn from a wide countryside of remote settlements houses together, and then shipped across the Atlantic in cramped troop carriers. Many arrived already ill or carrying diseases then passed on in the crowded wartime landscapes of the battlefields. Passenger. Spanish Flu was most likely a mutation of avian-type influenza (bird flu) in Asia that jumped species via domestic pigs to humans and emerged into the crowded military bases of both North America and Europe. Striking horror in the wartime authorities, the main casualties from this influenza were not the usual targets of the very young and very old vulnerable individuals. This disease struck down the very demographic of the war effort, namely eighteen- to thirty-year-olds. This was a young person's disease unlike the more prevalent flu and pneumonia which normally affect older people. To avoid panic the authorities kept it secret until the Spanish government acknowledged its existence. By late summer 1918, this especially virulent influenza was rife throughout the multi-national armies of the Western Front battlescape and associated base camps.

When the epidemic declined in the early 1920s, it had killed over fifty million people around the world. Indeed, the total may have been as high as a hundred million (six per cent of the global population at that time). With fatalities exceeding all the other First World War deaths combined, the frequent cause was pneumonia that followed viral flu infection. Death might occur within only a few hours.

A landscape infested by vermin

Many of the medical conditions and complaints experienced in the First World War were spread, caused by, or at the least exacerbated by vermin. The main culprits in this scenario of filth and disease were rats, fleas, lice, flies, and malarial mosquitoes.

Bringing huge numbers of men together in the awful conditions described, meant the trenches were soon home to millions of rats. These mammals might produce up to nine hundred offspring each year. This meant that actions attempting to kill and limit the rat populations were futile, and of course in the killing zones of the front, they had ample supplies of fresh flesh on which to feast.

Private Harold Saunders enlisted in the 14th London (London Scottish) Regiment in November 1915 and was despatched to France with the 2nd Battalion during June 1916. Suffering from a septic heel, when his mates left France for Salonika in Greece, he remained behind. He eventually transferred to the 1st Battalion and was discharged in April 1918. He wrote of his experiences in the 1930 anthology *Everyman at War* and described the rats in the trenches: 'One got used to many things, but I never overcame my horror of the rats. They abounded in some parts, great loathsome beasts gorged with flesh. I shall never forget a dug-out at the back of the line near Anzin. It was at the foot of rising ground, at the top of which was a French war cemetery. About the same time every night the dug-out was invaded by swarms of rats. They gnawed holes in our haversacks and devoured our iron rations. We hung haversacks and rations to the roof, but they went just the same. Once we drenched the place with creosote. It almost suffocated us but did not keep the rats away. They pattered down the steps at the usual time, paused a moment and sneezed, and then got to work on our belongings. A battalion of Jerrys would have terrified me less than the rats did sometimes.'

This short comment gives a clear summation of the problem and the impact on the lives of men in the war zone and battlescape.

One of the other consequences of life and death in the First World War battlescape were the ubiquitous and abundant flies. We gain some insight into the situation from the account of Harold Cronin, a lieutenant in the 5th Bedfordshire Regiment when he wrote of the disease-ridden state of the trenches in a letter home. 'In the trenches it was fairly bad, they are so narrow and smelly, and one is being potted at and shelled all the time.' His note continued, 'Although it is so gloriously sunny something is wrong with the place, and it really isn't as healthy as it looks. I think the flies have something to do with it as well as the heat and the still unburied dead bodies about'. He expands on the issue of flies, 'There are millions and millions of flies here and they are all over everything. Put a cup of tea down without a cover and it is immediately covered with dead ones, they are all round your mouth and directly you open it to speak or to eat, in they pop. It is a game. We have all got nets of course, we should have been worried, no medicine by now, if we hadn't'. This captures the essence of the problems with millions of flies, unburied corpses, disease rife, and limited medical support.

The Highlanders in the Crimean War at Gallipoli.

Like so many wartime accounts, the diary of Sergeant Horace Stanley was published many years following his death after his granddaughter found it hidden in the attic. He served in the 1st Cambridgeshire Regiment and was on the frontline at both Ypres and the Somme. He wrote of 'the same tragic story' repeated with 'Men march up singing and return wounded as fast as lorries can carry them. They return huddled together like carcasses of meat'. However, he paid tribute to the heroism and courage of frontline nurses. He wrote, 'There's another class of women whose heroism and courage is deserving of the highest praise but they too appear to be forgotten, the nurses in the front areas where romance and sentiment cease to exist, where life hangs but by a thread, where the work which they are called upon to do is even worse than the shells and aircraft bombs which number them among their victims. There is no holding patients' hands in flower bedecked rooms amid romantic surroundings where the gallant Dragoon staggers in with gold braid and a bloodstained bandage around his head'. He continued, 'No! The work is fast and furious, filthy and bloody, abdominal cases are bad at any time but when the casualty has been snatched from a muddy, gory swamp, hardly recognisable from the wind which is everywhere, as lousy as a cuckoo, and with no control over the lower organs, the smell and the groans, it is a miracle that these women don't lose their reason'.

The First World War was perhaps the first major conflict for which detailed accounts of at least some of the casualties, linked to specific diseases and particular injuries, are available. These are necessarily selective and overall impacts would be spread throughout the various combatant armies. However, specific figures such as given below do serve to highlight the broad spectre of disease and wounds throughout the battlescape. The overall mix of diseases and injuries is summarized from the British 51st Field Ambulance Brigade:

The Highlanders in the Crimean War over disputed territories in a strategic location characterized by difficult terrain.

Top twenty medical conditions treated by the 51st Field Ambulance:

Pyrexia of unknown origin (8.7%)
Inflammation of connective tissue (7.9%)
Trench foot (6.8%)
Influenza (6.6%)
Scabies (6.1%)
Shrapnel (4.9%)
Gunshot (4.7%)
Mustard and chlorine gas poisoning (3.98%)
Diarrhoea (3.0%)
Rheumatism (2.6%)
Shell shock (2.3%)
Gonorrhoea (2.2%)
Lung infection (2.1%)
Syphilis (2.0%)
Fractured femur (1.9%)
Urinary tract infection (1.8%)

Lice (1.8%)
Other STDs (1.6%)
Gangrene (1.3%)
Wasp stings (1%)

Industrialized warfare enters the battlescape

Following the American Civil War (620,000 deaths) and the Russo-Japanese War (165,000 dead or injured) the First World War was the third major conflict in the industrialized world. These other two wars preceded the First World War by fifty-three and ten years respectively. The casualties of the First World War reflect the emergence of industrialized warfare into the battlescape in both numbers and types. Of course, there had been other major conflicts on slightly lesser scales like the Boer Wars, the Crimean War, and the Franco-Prussian War. However, these first two examples of earlier industrial-scale wars highlight inflated casualty numbers, the likely result of industrialized munitions mass production. The civilian casualties associated with this manufacture also have to be added to the overall accounting.

Analysis of the American Civil War and the Russo-Japanese War also indicated that future conflicts were most likely to be relatively static and to involve protracted trench battles. This must have been a spectre obvious to those in power, but even so, the consequences and aftermath of the First World War proved to be totally shocking. Indeed, that entire battalions of infantrymen or at least large parts of them, might be obliterated almost instantly was inconceivable, but it happened and the battlescape concept was transformed in terms of both the scale of landscape over which a war was to occur, the numbers of troops engaged, and the expected levels of deaths and injuries to be incurred. With the First World War rather than Second the longstanding static battlescape where armies were quite literally bogged down in a swamp for years, emerged as a new phenomenon. This began with the American Civil War and the Russo-Japanese War, but it was in the First World War that the full impacts of long-term occupation of the same battlefield for months or years on end became apparent.

Endemic disease was now part of the battle zone, although as the First World War rolled on, the impacts of many were being addressed, at least in part. Treatments improved, diseases were more effectively contained, and death rates fell. The exception to this was clearly the later emergence of the influenza pandemic. For disease overall, about eighty per cent of the Allied forces treated were able to return to duty, though not all were sufficiently fit for redeployment to frontline service. The First World War was characterised by massed casualties caused by trauma and disease and the sheer

Transporting the wounded on wagons on a temporary rail track from the Vimy Ridge 1917.

misery associated with conflict, wet landscapes churned by shelling, climate, and weather. During the latter stages the Allied force was hugely expanded with men and equipment from both the Commonwealth and the United States. Furthermore, by the end of the conflict the armies were generally more experienced in industrialized warfare and more effectively equipped to treat the diseases and infections of this modern conflict.

Disease control improves

By the early twentieth century, improved understanding of both bacterial and viral infections brought about significant advances in public health to control infections. Health programmes included immunization through vaccination and actions taken to reduce common diseases such as smallpox, typhoid fever, and tetanus. Other strategic actions targeted diseases like malaria and yellow fever through their known insect vectors and associated habitats. So, in the years prior to the First World War there emerged the beginning of effective treatments and controls for many infections which undoubtedly saved millions of lives during the war. Nevertheless, antibiotics were yet to be discovered and many ordinary people knew very little about prevention. Fatality, associated with common infections such as tuberculosis and bacterial pneumonia, remained relatively commonplace by our modern-day benchmarks. One consequence of a combination of these factors was that the North American army suffered more deaths from disease than from enemy action during the First World War.

The problems began at the outset of the military recruitment process. Crowded military training camps became breeding grounds for those old childhood diseases like measles, mumps, and chickenpox. These infections spread quickly through the ranks of new recruits. On arrival, recruits were screened for obvious infectious diseases, which certainly helped. However, colds, influenza, and associated infections were ever-present issues and infections like meningitis and pneumonia were ongoing. Secondary pneumonia for example, brought significant risk of fatality, bacterial pneumonia proving forty to fifty per cent fatal. Meningococcal meningitis is a particularly deadly infection in young people, spreading through communities in crowded situations. The American army had 1,965 cases reported with 911 associated deaths.

Many American soldier recruits were from farming backgrounds, often in remote rural areas where they had not mixed very widely and had not been vaccinated. These young men were therefore especially vulnerable to infections when placed into a new environment where they came into contact with carriers. Then, shipped across the Atlantic in cramped troopship conditions to arrive in Europe, and into the frontline battlescape as described. The journey took a week to two weeks, and troops were packed in close quarters making influenza, for example, particularly difficult to control. Once soldiers reached their destination in France, the conditions were similarly poor with quickly constructed makeshift training camps and conditions almost as crowded as on the ships. These were wonderful breeding grounds for all sorts of diseases. Along with infections of the war zone terrain, they were exposed to mass childhood diseases. One of the most significant was mumps with 82,000 cases; there were one million days lost to illness, though only forty-three fatalities. Measles caused fewer (8,200) cases, but slightly more (eighty-six) deaths. Diphtheria was responsible for 4,700 infections and sixty-two fatalities.

The overall situation as discussed is a harsh reminder of the vulnerability of humans to new diseases spread globally and in world without modern antibiotics. Without effective antibiotics, once infected, there was little treatment other than basic supportive care and the body's immune system. The 1918 outbreak of Spanish flu has already been noted with a mortality rate of between two and three per cent and especially high among young people. So, if a thousand soldiers were infected then between fifty and a hundred developed pneumonia, of which twenty-five to fifty died.

The American medical records are difficult to interrogate because their statistics on infectious diseases concentrated on the American Expeditionary Force (AEF), in other words on their troops already in Europe. The bigger issue perhaps, was that many American troops arrived in Europe already sick from disease-ridden training camps and troopships crossing the Atlantic. Typhoid Fever was a big killer with 1,200 cases resulting in 155 deaths. This was considered a significant improvement on earlier wars like the Spanish-American war where there were 142 cases per thousand soldiers while infections in the First World War reduced to one case per thousand men. A key factor was that inoculation was available and made compulsory for troops serving overseas.

The threat of epidemic cholera from polluted water, late 1800s.

Smallpox is now globally eradicated but was once an appalling killer and a disfiguring disease for survivors. Despite almost universal vaccination, for the Americans, it caused thirty cases and five associated deaths. Malaria resulted in 850 cases with four deaths. One of the most unpleasant diseases for many troops was dysentery but the Americans managed to keep it relatively under control through better sanitation and because they were less involved in trench warfare. Nevertheless, there were 6,200 cases reported and thirty-one associated deaths, considered a big improvement on previous conflicts. Tuberculosis (TB) or 'consumption' was in decline but still endemic in many civilian communities and so recruits were screened, and sufferers discharged. Despite this, it was estimated that about ten thousand American soldiers had TB with 4,200 cases recorded and 433 fatalities.

Tetanus as a disease of muddy, wet, battlefields and war-wounds

In the conditions described already, the prevalence of tetanus infections might have been expected. Considering the appalling wet and muddy conditions in which much of this conflict was played out, one of the notable medical successes in the First World

Russians removing cholera victims in Manchuria, October 1902, Russo-Japanese War.

War was the dramatic reduction in tetanus through programmes of inoculation. Serum was taken from horses injected with modified tetanus toxin to produce an effective antiserum. For the Americans, from 500,000 wounds and injuries, there were only twenty-three recorded cases and no deaths. This was despite the mud and dirt of the trenches and wider battlefields being ideal places for tetanus (*Clostridium tetani* bacterium) in wounds to develop. Tetanus spores enter the body through deep wounds and the spores generate live bacteria which release toxins causing the clinical symptoms. Vaccination was combined with wound 'debridement' which is the removal all dead and damaged tissue, and the thorough surgical cleaning of wounds, mostly with minimal anaesthetic or painkiller. The cleansing was often by high-pressure jets of clean water. Painful though this was, even without the serum, this may have been sufficient to greatly reduce tetanus infections. The response to risk of tetanus in the wet, muddy, festering conditions of the frontline landscape did show that medical advances could help mitigate some of the horrors.

British troops dragging heavy guns through the swamp in Flanders.

Chapter 6
Water and wetlands

Water and wetlands in their various forms have had major influences on conflicts. This extends from the need for clean and potable water supplies for troops, to their impacts on landscape, countryside, and terrain. Troops soon die of thirst without drinking water and if water supplies are contaminated then they quickly succumb to disease. As battlescapes, waterbodies form topographic barriers, conduits, boundaries, and places of sanctuary; their roles and functions differ for indigenous and invading peoples.

Wetlands as battlescapes

Many individual battles have been influenced or determined by water and other natural resources. So, for example, at the battle of Marathon between the Greeks and the Persians in 490BCE the Greeks felled trees down each of their flanks to defend

German river crossing during the muddy season on the Eastern Front, 1941.

British tank on the Western Front, 1917.

Destroying a bridge in the Austrian crossing of the Piave, First World War.

their advance against their opponents. The result was that this, combined with the marshland and the shore, limited the manoeuvrability of the Persian force. When the Greek phalanx broke the Persian wing chaos ensued, and the Persians panicked and fell back toward their fleet moored offshore. With many men struggling in the marshes, the Greeks slaughtered numbers of the Persians including their general, Datis. Clever use of natural resources and the wet terrain won the day, and the Greek hoplites suffered a mere 192 casualties.

Wetlands, including rivers, have frequently been territorial markers and boundaries. Crossing major rivers may prove hazardous, and while lakes facilitate rapid transit by boat, other wetlands may be problematic. Furthermore, expansive wetlands are by their very nature flatlands, often without easily discernible features and markers. For incomers unfamiliar with such areas, they may prove a serious obstacle and lend themselves to ambush and similar strategies. To complicate matters further, some wetlands are seasonal or simply unpredictable and short-lived. The English Fenlands for example, might be relatively dry in summer but an inland sea of thousands of square miles of wetland in winter. The Russian rivers encountered by Napoleon in the eighteenth century were low and possible in the summer but in winter spate were wide, deep, and treacherous.

Examples of major conflicts where water and wetlands were influential and even decisive include the 1960s Vietnam War, the Western Front of the First World War,

Austrian gun detachment crossing a tributary of the Dunajec, First World War.

French troops going over the top and advancing behind their barrage, 1917.

the Seminole Wars in the US, the English Civil War – though this was one of numerous internal conflicts in England – and many others. Water plays many roles in conflict: supplying potable water is vital for troops, but contaminated water can bring horrendous outbreaks of transmissible diseases. Waterbodies provide a means of rapid transportation but also present difficulties in crossing them. They are also frequently

Moving heavy guns over waterlogged terrain.

sources of disease and parasites.

Particularly in the First World War, bogs, marshes, fens, mud, and peat, were immensely important. The Somme, Flanders, and other major battlefields were generally in flat or rolling landscapes dominated by bogs, rivers, marshes, and farmland, which quickly degenerated into fields of mud as the conflict developed. This is described in detail in the seminal volume by Johnson in 1921 and is a theme worth exploring further. The influence of wetlands on the Western Front and during the Second World War, in the case the Dutch Polders, are therefore discussed in a later chapter. Wetlands have provided battlescape settings throughout history and across the world.

German soldier at a waterlogged shell-hole, First World War.

Defining wetlands and separating them from other landscape types can be problematic, so this is essentially a broad-brush division: heaths, moors, and commons are considered separately but in practice many landscapes are in effect mosaics of different components. The relevance of micro-topography is imposed on that of macro-terrain.

The significance of rivers to the Romans

Furthermore, as noted earlier, the crossing of certain rivers was sometimes of significance beyond immediate military objectives. This is exemplified by many key events throughout history. So, when tribes on the borders of the Roman Empire raided into Roman territories and then retreated beyond the Danube, a river that at the time was not feasible to cross, the ability to strike back became an imperative. Rome's wider success was in part based on an image and widespread belief in its invincibility that could not be allowed to be compromised.

This was a key moment in the series of wars between Rome and the Dacians, firstly with Emperor Domitian and then with Trajan. Trajan undertook two major campaigns – the 1st and 2nd Dacian Wars – the key events were recorded on Trajan's Column in Rome. The Dacian Wars (AD101–102, and AD105–106) involved two military campaigns between the Roman Empire and Dacia during Trajan's reign as emperor.

These conflicts came about because of the ever-present threat from Dacia on the Roman Danubian province of Moesia, combined with the expanding resource requirements of the Imperial economy. Trajan focused his attention on Dacia, a region north of Macedon and Greece, east of the Danube. The area had been a problem for the Roman Empire even before the time of Julius Caesar, particularly when the Dacians defeated a Roman army at the Battle of Histria around 61–62BCE and again in AD85 when they crossed the Danube to pillage Moesi and defeated the Roman army sent by Emperor Domitian, at the Battle of Tapae. However, defeats for the Dacians three years later resulted in a truce and ultimately the Dacian king became a client ruler under Roman governance, at least for a time. Nevertheless, the Dacians remained hostile toward Rome, and as guardians of that border of the Empire may have used their enhanced access to Roman skills and warcraft to enhance their own military defences and technologies.

Following Domitian's assassination, and with the Empire suffering from economic and military challenges, the new emperor, Trajan, an experienced soldier, decided to strike decisively against the Dacian threat. Roman military ingenuity and engineering were demonstrated very effectively in this campaign with two legionary columns marching directly to the core of Dacia and burning towns and villages as they went.

Trajan defeated the Dacian army at the Second Battle of Tapae. In AD102, the Dacian king, Decebalus, negotiated peace terms with the Romans and received support to guard the empire against aggression from more northerly tribes. This truce only lasted a short while and soon the Dacians were once again inciting local tribes to revolt and were pillaging Roman colonies over the Danube River. Trajan assembled his armies again and prepared for another war which took place in AD105.

A key part of the campaign to end the troublesome threats from the Dacians was to construct a major crossing of the Danube River, behind which they would retreat, giving them security. The present-day river is around 2,600ft (800m) wide at this point and the bridge the Romans built was 3,724ft (1,135m) long, 49ft (15m) wide, and 62ft (19m) high. Each end of the structure had a Roman *castrum* built around an entrance which meant that crossing was only possible via the fortified camps. Built in AD105 under the direction of Emperor Trajan, it was designed by architect Apollodorus of Damascus (in Roman Syria). Some of the ruins of the bridge's piers are still visible. Trajan's Bridge over the Danube, also called the Bridge of Apollodorus, was a Roman segmental arch bridge and as the first crossing over the lower Danube; it ranks as one of the greatest achievements of Roman architecture. Only functional for 165 years, it was the longest arch bridge (total and span length) in the world for the next thousand years.

The construction utilized wooden arches spanning 125ft (38m) each, set on twenty masonry pillars made from bricks, mortar, and pozzolana cement (volcanic ash). The enterprise was remarkably speedy, taking around two years to complete in AD105. Work on each pier involved a watertight wooden box called a caisson from which water was pumped out to keep the working space dry. Apollodorus used a technique called river flow relocation, the principles of which were established by Thales of Miletus around 600BCE. During a period of low-water flow, the engineers dug a canal to redirect the water downstream of the construction area. Wooden pillars with a rectangular layout were then driven into the riverbed to provide foundations for the supporting piers. These were then coated with clay and the hollow piers filled with stones held together by mortar. The outer layers were then built over with Roman bricks. The piers were 145.9ft (44.46m) high, 58.3ft (17.78m) wide and 165.3ft (50.38m) apart. Most of the parts for the construction were probably assembled on land and subsequently installed onto the pillars. It is believed that the year of construction was very dry and the river levels therefore relatively low and almost completely drained when the foundations were laid. In total, there were twenty pillars with intervals of 160ft (50m) between them. The bridge itself was built of oak timber and was sufficiently high to allow ships to pass underneath.

The bridge served its primary purpose, it prepared the way for the Roman invasion of Dacia. The second Dacian War ended in AD106 with Roman victory. Furthermore, the impact of at last defeating the Dacians, and the not insignificant capture of their gold mines, was so important that celebratory Roman games were held for 123 days. These games involved 10,000 gladiators taking part in contests, and 11,000 wild animals being slaughtered. However, perhaps the greatest achievement was the statement that no matter where you were, no matter how powerful you were, there was no match for the might of Rome. One can only imagine the thoughts of the Dacian soldiers on the far bank, to the 1,000-foot-wide Danube River, the uncrossable barrier, as each day the pontoon bridge drew closer and closer. Throughout the rest of the known world, the Roman military machine must have appeared to be invincible.

How wetlands turned English history from Alfred the Great to William the Conqueror

In AD878, in England, the Saxon leader King Alfred the Great of Wessex was effectively standing alone against multiple invading forces of Vikings from northern Europe. They had initially arrived from around AD865. By the spring of AD878, following a surprise attack by Viking forces in January, Alfred spent months hiding in the Athelney marshes of Somerset. From his wetland hiding place the King of Wessex was able to wage guerrilla warfare against the invading armies. Backed into a corner, with the Viking forces massing and all the other Saxon kingdoms fallen to the invaders, Alfred began to summon a local army or *fyrd*; the call drew fighters to the cause from a wide area. Thousands of Saxon warriors assembled, and battle took place at Ethandun in Wiltshire (modern-day Edington) with a spear-wielding Saxon horde and shield-wall. Having emerged from their secret wetland base, the Saxons engaged the Vikings for a day-long battle after which the Scandinavians retreated to Chippenham; two weeks later they surrendered. The long-term result was that England was split into a north-eastern region under Viking control called the Danelaw, and a south-western zone ruled by Alfred and the Wessex Saxons. The Viking leader Guthrum also converted to Christianity.

Viking invasions

The post-Roman period in England witnessed waves of invaders and colonizers arriving from Europe and settling, each largely displacing the previous settlers. In a turbulent period during the middle of the eleventh century York was central to international power struggles in Britain and across the North Sea. Indeed, in England, York was a determining factor in the outcome of the Norman invasion of

1066. A century after the demise of the short-lived York-based king, Eric Bloodaxe, Viking invaders, with Northumbrian allies, were victorious at the Battle of Fulford. On 20 September 1066 King Harald III of Norway (Harald Hardrada) and the banished Saxon, Tostig Godwinson, King Harold's brother, defeated the northern earls Edwin and Morcar. However, the tables were turned at the Battle of Stamford Bridge five days later, when the English army under King Harold Godwinson routed the invaders. Nevertheless, considering the Battle of Hastings and the Norman conquest that followed, this was something of a pyrrhic victory. These events had major ramifications for York and its people.

The Battle of Fulford, Fulford Bridge, or Fulford Gate, fought on the outskirts of York, has been overshadowed by the great battles of Stamford Bridge and Hastings. The sequence of events flowing from the defeat of the northern earls at Fulford led, a few weeks later, to the Norman conquest of Britain. The Battle of Fulford was fought on the outskirts of the village of Fulford near York, when King Harald III of Norway, also known as Harald Hardrada (meaning 'hard ruler'), and his English ally, Tostig Godwinson, fought and defeated the Northern Saxon earls. Tostig was Harold Godwinson's banished brother and had allied with King Harald of Norway, and possibly with Duke William of Normandy, but otherwise there is no record of the reasoning behind his invasions. However, Fulford was a decisive victory for the Viking army. While the northern earls could have remained behind the protective walls of York, they met the Vikings across the river. All day the English tried desperately to break the Viking shield wall, to no avail. Tostig and Earl Morcar had a long-standing enmity, the latter having displaced the former as Earl of Northumbria; this meeting must have brought emotions to a bitter head.

The context to the contest for the English throne was that the Anglo-Saxon king, Edward the Confessor had died without an heir on 5 January 1066. This left Edgar, the young son of Edward Atheling, the only surviving member of the royal family. On 6 January, the day of Edward's funeral, Harold Godwinson, Earl of Wessex, and the head of the most powerful Saxon dynasty, made his way to London to be crowned king by Aldred, Archbishop of York in Westminster Abbey. Harold had been elected king by the Witenagemot whose members were already gathered to celebrate the feast of Epiphany. A complication was that two powerful earls, brothers Edwin of Mercia and Morcar of Northumbria, came forward to challenge Harold's authority. It seems that Harold went north to confront them and resolve the issue. This situation was resolved by him marrying their sister, Edith, the widow of Griffith of Wales, and thus securing the support of two very powerful allies. Furthermore, through the alliance with Edwin and Morcar, Harold strengthened his position in

Stamford Bridge and the site of the famous river crossing in 1066.

northern England and in the strategic centre and northern capital York.

However, while Harold was the senior Saxon claimant, his unpredictable and violent brother Tostig, felt that he too, was the legitimate heir to the crown. Exiled to Flanders because of his unruly behaviour in England in May 1066, Tostig invaded, gathering additional forces while sailing to the Humber to battle the forces of Edwin, Earl of Mercia. This foray ended in defeat for Tostig, and he retreated north to the protection of King Malcolm of Scotland and to make an alliance with another claimant to the English throne, Harald Hardrada, King of Norway. It may also be that Tostig travelled to Normandy to ask for support from William, Duke of Normandy but the latter was unwilling to offer this. Ultimately, Tostig and his supporters allied with Hardrada, and they fought side-by-side at the Battle of Fulford.

For Hardrada, Tostig was a useful ally not only being the brother of his main adversary, King Harold, but because he had a good knowledge of the country and the terrain. In August 1066 the Norwegians sailed for Orkney, arriving there in September. Here they collected supplies and met with Tostig, who brought additional soldiers and ships. Together they sailed around the coast and up the great Humber Estuary. They entered the mouth of the Humber on 18 September and from there

Hastings battlefield and Battle Abbey pictured in the 1970s.

the combined force made its way up the Ouse River toward their first objective, the strategically important city of York. Having disembarked from their ships, the armies moved speedily on toward York and on 20 September 1066, faced the forces of the earls, Edwin and Morcar.

Earl Edwin had brought soldiers to the east of the city in the expectation of an invasion by the Norwegian force; the conflict began with English troops moving wide to safeguard their flanks. For the Saxons had the Ouse River on their right and a swampy area called Fordland on the left. Strategically, the position taken up by the earls had disadvantages, one being that Hardrada held the higher ground and thus had a vantage point from which to oversee the battle. Furthermore, should one flank of the Saxon army falter, the other would also be in trouble. An additional problem was that while the marshes helped protect the Saxon position, they also meant that if the Vikings broke through, there was no easy retreat.

Hardrada and Tostig approached the field along three routes from the south and assembled opposite the Anglo-Saxons. Their force arrived piecemeal, and it would take time for all their troops to assemble. The least battle-hardened Vikings were sent to the right and the more experienced soldiers occupied the riverbank. The Saxon force attacked the Viking army to pre-empt its full deployment and Earl Morcar's soldiers forced the weaker Viking line back into the marshes. However, this early success was not enough to carry the day and reinforced, the Viking army was now supported by their better troops, the right flank attacking the centre and additional men moving along the riverbank. Despite a numerical advantage the Saxons were being made to concede territory, and Earl Edwin's men, defending the riverbank, were cut off from the rest of the army by the marsh. This was the topographic impact inherent in the weakness of their deployment.

The Northumbrian and Mercian Saxons now moved back to York for a final stand. On the beck the Saxon troops were hard-pressed and a further Viking incursion, with fresh men, meant a third battlefront. Now outnumbered and outmanoeuvred, the York army was beaten. The earls Edwin and Morcar survived the conflict and York surrendered to the Vikings. With Tostig presumably viewing York as his own future capital it was negotiated that there would be no forced entry or looting. Hostages were given and the Norwegian force fell back around seven miles eastward to Stamford Bridge.

Estimates suggest the Viking force at Fulford numbered about 10,000 with 6,000 used in the battle. The Saxons had around 5,000. Both sides suffered heavy casualties, estimated at perhaps fifteen per cent fatalities, total death toll of 1,650. There were many more injured. This was a consequence that was to prove significant in the later Norman invasion, in that much of the fighting power of the combined Mercian and Northumbrian armies was destroyed, or at least compromised, by these earlier battles.

With news of the defeat, the Saxon King Harold decided to force-march his own troops 190 miles from London to York. This strategic decision meant he arrived near York within a week of the Battle of Fulford, thus surprising the Viking army and defeating them at the Battle of Stamford Bridge. In the meantime, William, Duke of Normandy, landed his own army in Sussex on the now-undefended English south coast. In response, Harold marched back to the south of England where the two armies met near Hastings. Harold probably hoped that in catching William off guard he might repeat the success of Stamford Bridge. The twin battles at Fulford Gate and then at Stamford Bridge, fought within a single week of each other, must have significantly weakened Harold's available forces at Hastings, just three weeks later. Without the two battles near York, the outcome of Hastings might well have been very different. As it was, the strategic role of York as a gateway to Northumbria, on a major waterway amid extensive wetlands, probably changed English history forever.

The Battle of Stamford Bridge is one of the key conflicts in English history but is over-shadowed by the subsequent Battle of Hastings. It took place at the village of the same name in the East Riding of Yorkshire. On 25 September 1066, a Saxon army, under King Harold Godwinson, and the invading Viking force of King Harald Hardrada of Norway and Harold's brother Tostig, came to blows. Following a fierce battle, both Hardrada and Tostig were killed, along with many of their men. Harold carried the day only to be defeated shortly afterward by William of Normandy. Stamford Bridge has been viewed as symbolic of the end of Viking influence, or at least the Viking Age in northern England and in York itself. Nevertheless, there were significant Scandinavian campaigns in Britain and Ireland in the following decades as warring factions jostled for overall power; the Vikings clearly hoping to regain their lost kingdom. The Danish king, Sweyn Estrithson, made incursions from 1069 to 1070 and the Norwegian king, Magnus Barefoot, did likewise in 1098 and then again from 1102 to 1103. In truth, the Viking influence was never as powerful as it had once been.

The annihilation of the Vikings at the Battle of Stamford Bridge.

There is some dispute over the exact location of the Battle at Stamford Bridge, as indeed there is about the site of the Battle of Hastings. However, it is almost certain that there was a bridge over the Derwent River close to the present-day village, and that at least part of the battle centred on or about this point. The suggestion is also that there was a fording point close to the modern bridge site. So, while local tradition puts the battlefield east of the Derwent River and just southeast of the modern town, in a location called Battle Flats, the precise position is unknown. It is believed that the Viking force, at the start of the battle was split into two groups: on the west and east banks of the Derwent, with the majority sited latterly. They may even have been on the move, heading back from Stamford Bridge toward York along the old Roman road.

It may be that there was a two-pronged attack by Harold's forces via the ford and possibly an older Roman bridge about one mile to the south of Stamford Bridge itself. This tactic would have utilized the two roads to the battle site from York. On the east bank of the Derwent River from the crossing, the topography rises quickly up to about a hundred feet (thirty metres) at High Catton. This is the only higher ground in this low-lying, predominantly flat landscape, and therefore a strong defensive position for the Viking army. However, it seems Hardrada and Tostig were caught unawares by the sudden appearance of Harold's army as he came around the Gate Helmsley ridge and his Saxon forces swept downhill toward their troops.

Clearly, the unexpected arrival of the Saxon army took the Vikings by surprise; their response to an imminent assault was to deploy rapidly into a defensive circle, presumably with a traditional Viking shield wall. Topographic details become important here; if they were on Battle Flats, this deployment by the Viking troops would make little sense. However, located east of the Derwent the defensive circle would be a logical move. It seems that when the main English army arrived, many of Hardrada's men on the west bank were already killed or retreating across the bridge or ford. The Saxon advance was held up by the river-crossing pinch-point. A local legend, recounted in the *Anglo-Saxon Chronicle*, tells of a giant Norseman armed with a Dane-axe blocking the crossing to single-handedly hold back the whole Saxon army, supposedly felling around forty Saxon warriors. The Norseman was finally defeated by a Saxon soldier floating under the bridge in a half-barrel. He reputedly thrust his spear through gaps between the planks of the bridge to skewer the unfortunate Viking. Of course, this story requires a bridge rather than just a ford.

The time taken to cross the river allowed most of the Viking force to form a shield wall in anticipation of the Saxon assault. Harold Godwinson's soldiers now crossed the river and formed a line somewhat short of the Viking 'wall'; they locked shields and charged at the invaders. The action spread way beyond the river crossing, the battle raging for hours. The need for haste meant the Vikings had not had time to put on full armour, and that was now a big disadvantage. After several hours, the Viking army began to break up and the Saxons were able to press through the shield wall. Now outflanked and their leaders killed, Hardrada with an arrow through the windpipe and Tostig slain too, the Viking force fell apart and was effectively annihilated.

As the battle progressed, the Vikings were joined by fresh soldiers who had been left with the ships at Riccall. These new troops were led by Hardrada's prospective son-in-law, Eystein Orre. In their haste to get to the battlefield, it is suggested that some of the men collapsed and died of exhaustion. Those remaining were fully armed for battle and their brutal counterattack, known from Viking sagas as 'Orre's Storm', checked the Saxon advance. However, now heavily outnumbered, the Vikings were soon overwhelmed, with Orre himself killed, and the Viking army routed. Finally, chased by Saxon troops, many fleeing Norsemen drowned attempting to cross the local rivers. It was said that so many died in such a small area the field was still whitened with bleached bones more than fifty years following the slaughter.

Typical Anglo-Saxon soldier, c. 1066.

Eventually, King Harold Godwinson and the few surviving Vikings agreed to a truce. These included Harald's son Olaf and the Earl of Orkney, Paul Thorfinnsson who were allowed to leave after pledging to never attack England again. The losses endured by the Vikings were colossal, and from the fleet of over three hundred ships which had arrived, twenty-four were enough to carry the survivors away. These few headed back to Orkney for the winter, and the following spring, Hardrada's son Olaf, returned home to Norway where the kingdom was divided between him and his brother Magnus who had been left to govern the homeland during the invasion of England.

The arrival of the Normans

The final throw of the dice in this epic time in English history was when only three days after Stamford Bridge, on 28 September 1066, William, Duke of Normandy, landed in Pevensey Bay, Sussex, on the southern English coast. Exhausted from the battle with the Vikings and having suffered major casualties in two huge conflicts, King Harold and the Saxons now had to force-march south to meet the Norman army. Less than three weeks following victory at the Battle of Stamford Bridge, on 14 October 1066, the Saxon army was heavily defeated by the Normans. King Harold

Hastings battlefield from Battle Abbey taken in the 1920s.

II fell in action at the Battle of Hastings, and the Norman conquest of England was underway. The outcome and longer-term strategy were made so much easier by heavy losses to the Saxon military commanders from these three battles, all within a month.

To fully understand the locations and the associated battle tactics, including the advance to the sites by both armies, it is necessary to reimagine the landscapes as they might have been before modern-day farming. Agricultural drainage has altered these landscapes beyond recognition. This is particularly so for the enigmatic location of the Battle of Hastings. Re-wetting the countryside impacts on the field of battle itself but also on the routes taken by the two forces advancing to the conflict, and the attempted escape routes of the English Saxons after their defeat. Harold's forces occupied the ridge of high ground and thus the topographic advantage where they assembled their characteristic shield-wall (a tactic by now used by both Vikings and the trained Saxon troops) and in this case of housecarls with battle-axes. Even with the Saxon forces depleted and tired, the Normans found this tactic, and the position, extremely difficult to break through. Attempts to charge up the hill were hindered by the marshy ground, and they were cut down by spears launched from the high ground above. After a day's pitched battle between 8,000 Normans and 7,000 Saxons, around 6,000 men had died. Harold and his brothers were killed, and the Saxons withdrew in tatters as the Norman

Saxon housecarls at Hastings 1066.

cavalry rode them down. The battle was probably decided when the Breton soldiers retreated downhill and were pursued by the relatively ill-disciplined Saxon fyrd troops rather than by the professional housecarls. This was enough to break the shield wall and leave the Saxon warriors open to the Norman cavalry. What followed is history; England and the world were changed forever. However, water and topography had played a major role in this and the preceding battles.

The wet fens of England

Water, reedbeds and wetlands were at the core of the English Fenlands and the fenlanders. Even in medieval times the image of the people of the south Lincolnshire and Cambridgeshire Fens harked back to their history. They were steeped in the vast wetlands, and this was reflected in their stubborn resistance to external influences and change. In 1536, the commoners of Lincolnshire made a complaint to King Henry VIII about the selection of his ministers and advisors and by association the suppression of the monasteries, abbeys, and other religious houses. Henry replied in his 'Answer to the Petition of the Rebels and traitors of Lincolnshire'. In this response he described them as 'the rude commons of one shire' and Lincolnshire itself as 'one of the most brute and beastly of the whole realm'. This gives some insight into how the Fenland region was viewed, both from within and from the outside.

The vast areas of farming commons and often-extensive wetlands retained independence and even a stubbornness and resistance to change or innovation. In terms of context, it is an amazing transformation, which in a little over five hundred years, has turned the Northern Fens of South and East Yorkshire and north Lincolnshire, and the Southern Fens of Lincolnshire, Cambridgeshire, and East Anglia, into one of the world's most productive farming landscapes. For a region so resistant to change, it is surprising perhaps that these earlier landscapes and cultures have been erased almost entirely from the regions, and even from the cultural memory. Much of this loss took place over just two or three centuries.

Early writers put this stubbornness down to a deep retention of their Anglo-Saxon roots. It was around Ely for example, that Hereward the Wake, the last great Saxon warlord, held out against the Norman invasion until he was betrayed by the church. Hereward's life is shrouded in mystery, but it seems that in 1070, anticipating the likely conquest of England by Danish king Sweyn II, he and his followers came to Ely, in what is now Cambridgeshire, with a group of Danish sailors. Together this force sacked Peterborough Abbey motivated in part by a wish to stop the church's treasures passing to Turold, the new Norman abbot. However, Sweyn negotiated a peace with King William and consequently the Danish force returned home.

In the meantime, Hereward set up a base on the Isle of Ely, which in 1071 became a refuge and gathering place for Anglo-Saxon fugitives, most notably Morcar, Earl of Northumbria. At the time there were Saxon uprisings breaking out sporadically across the country; each resulted in violent suppression by the Norman overlords. Hereward and his troops held out in the Isle of Ely in the heart of the vast swamps of the Fens, effectively an inland sea. Eventually the clerics on the Isle, threatened with seizure of their wider estates by the Normans, gave away the secret of the safe routes through the reedbeds and the Isle was conquered. Consequently, William's forces captured the Isle after a prolonged assault, but Hereward managed to escape. Quite where he came from originally, why he was there in 1066, and what happened

Stirling Castle in the 1970s.

to him after the fall of Ely, are all part of the mystery. It is believed that he was pardoned by William and lived out his days at the Norman court. Whatever the truth, the Hereward saga, like Alfred in Athelney, demonstrates the importance of sanctuary in vast wetlands, and the significance of local knowledge of terrain. Water presents territorial barriers and boundaries, along with cultural identity. Identity and landscape breed resistance and set the scene for major battlescapes.

From the Norman conquest of Anglo-Saxon England, we move to conflicts in medieval Europe where, once again, rivers bound territories and wetlands prove significant.

Wet battlescapes in medieval Europe

In the Baltic countryside of medieval northern Europe, war broke out between the Polish-Lithuanian Union and the Teutonic Knights when King Wladyslaw II, Jagiello of Poland, sided with a revolt in Lithuanian Samogita, which was held by the Teutonic Knights. In combination with his cousin, Grand Duke Vytautas of Lithuania, he led an army of around 39,000 across the Vistula River and headed for the Teutonic Order's headquarters in northern Poland at Malbork. In 1409, close to the two villages of Tannenberg and Grunwald, their force was met in battle by the Grand Teutonic Master Ulrich von Jungingen. The Teutonic Knights forcibly repelled an early charge by the combined force and followed this by a rather ill-disciplined pursuit as the Polish-Lithuanian cavalry retreated. However, the Teutonic Knights soon became bogged down in the wet forest and marshland and so were unable to drive home their advantage. Indeed, as they floundered, potential victory was turned to defeat when they failed to break the Polish right wing. Now regrouped, the Lithuanian forces were able to surround the knights, and the Grand Master was killed in the ensuing struggle. Retreating to camp, the elite knights of the Teutonic Order fought to the death. The forces of the Polish-Lithuanian alliance were unable to take the Teutonic castle at Malbork, but the Order's influence was vastly reduced and never fully recovered from the setback. Terrain and conditions, combined with poor tactical decisions, tipped the conflict from victory to a cataclysmic defeat.

The Anglo-Scottish wars

From European conflicts in wetlands, it is worthwhile considering the long-running sagas of the Anglo-Scottish wars. The borderlands between northern England and Scotland have been contested landscapes throughout their long histories, and much of the conflict has occurred in wetland or been influenced by water. So, once again, topography, rivers, marshes, and bogs were frequently factors on which a conflict was decided. The geographic location of Stirling with its precipitous, rocky position overlooking the River Forth (and one of the few safe crossings) and the massive, impenetrable peat bog of Flanders Moss, gave it huge strategic significance. It was said that he who controlled Stirling controlled Scotland as this was the spatial pinch point between the lowlands and the gateway to the Highlands. The mix of strategic position, topographic significance, and terrain meant Stirling was the battlescape for some of the most famous Anglo-Scottish conflicts.

The Battle of Stirling Bridge

The first Anglo-Scottish battle to consider is the Battle of Stirling Bridge during the First War of Scottish Independence. On 11 September 1297, the forces of Andrew Moray and William Wallace defeated the combined English army led by John de Warenne, 6th Earl of Surrey, and Hugh de Cressingham. It took place near Stirling on the River Forth.

English kings during the medieval period repeatedly tried to extend their rule and influence north of the border into Scotland. At the same time, the Scots habitually raided southward into northern England. So, in 1290, the death of Margaret, the

Stirling Castle overlooking the River Forth in Scotland, early 1900s.

Scottish queen, gave King Edward I of England the opportunity to effectively take over the country. However, his aspirations were famously dashed by the resistance led by Sir William Wallace. With the throne of Scotland vacant, the Scottish lords asked Edward I to choose the new king, he picked John Balliol. Balliol was a distant descendant of the great Scottish king, David I, but was regarded as weak, potentially subservient, and someone who would do Edward's bidding. Nevertheless, Edward's plans soon fell away as Balliol refused to join his campaign in France and, worse still, in 1295, signed an alliance with England's traditional enemy, the French. Furious, Edward marched his army north to invade Scotland where he massacred the Berwick garrison and defeated King Balliol at Dunbar the following year. The latter was deposed, and Edward ruled Scotland directly.

Prior to this, however, in 1257, the Scots had risen in revolt, led by William Wallace. The two armies met at Stirling Bridge where an English force, commanded by the Earl of Surrey, attempted to cross the River Forth over a narrow bridge in front of the Scottish lines. This was the key crossing point to Stirling and its castle with the great morass of Flanders Moss and the marshlands of the meandering River Forth to either side. Together these formed a formidable natural barrier. The smaller Scottish army, with Wallace and Andrew de Moray leading, assembled in an advantageous

Stirling Castle with a view over the strategically important wet landscape.

position on the slope above. From their vantage point they hurled spears and other missiles into the advancing English knights below.

According to accounts, Wallace and Moray waited until as many of the English cavalry had crossed the bridge as they felt they might overcome. They then breached the previously sabotaged wooden bridge so that no more could cross. It seems that around 2,000 English troops had come over when Wallace gave the signal to collapse the bridge and the Scottish spearmen stormed down from the high ground to repulse a charge by the English heavy cavalry and counterattack against the English infantry.

Having achieved control of the eastern side of the now-collapsed bridge, preventing English reinforcements from crossing, the Scots caught the cavalry on the low, marshy ground in the river meander; there was no hope of relief or retreat. The heavily armoured knights soon floundered in the marshy terrain and many thousands were killed. Indeed, it seems that most of the outnumbered English were killed, though a few hundred perhaps escaped by swimming across the river and some, such as Marmaduke Thweng, fought their way back over the remains of the bridge. Those English soldiers stranded on the far side of the river ceded victory to Wallace and the Scots and then fled the scene. This was an ignominious defeat for the English with losses of around 5,000 from their force of 12,000. The Scottish losses are unknown.

The Battle of Bannockburn

By 1314, the English, now under the weak and militarily naive King Edward II, had been largely driven from Scotland by King Robert the Bruce. The English gains of the now-late Edward I, had been mostly reversed. Stirling Castle, a Scottish royal fortress was the last English stronghold and under siege by the emboldened Scottish army. Edward II led 2,500 cavalry and up to 25,000 infantrymen to relieve the castle, the largest English force ever to cross into Scotland. They were met by 8,000 Scots, mostly infantry. Battle commenced in the New Park situated south of the town.

Most medieval battles were short-lived affairs and often over in just a few hours, whereas unusually, Bannockburn was fought over two days, 23 and 24 June 1314 during the First War of Scottish Independence. The decisive victory for Robert Bruce became a major turning point in the wider conflict although the war continued for another fourteen years. Ultimately Scottish independence was restored under the Treaty of Edinburgh–Northampton. Edward II's foray into Scotland was triggered by Bruce, in 1313, demanding that all supporters of the deposed Scots king John Balliol acknowledge Bruce as the true monarch or else forfeit their lands.

The Scottish army was divided into four divisions of schiltrons commanded by King Robert Bruce, his brother Edward Bruce, his nephew Thomas Randolph, Earl of Moray, and one under shared command of Sir James Douglas and Walter the Steward. Angus Og Macdonald, Lord of the Isles, was accompanied to Bannockburn by thousands of Islesmen, and they took a place of honour in the king's personal schiltron with his men from Carrick and Argyll.

In the build-up to the battle, Bruce chose a flat field flanked by woodland known as the New Park to set up camp and prepare for the fight. The woodland provided advantage for the Scots foot soldiers who would face the English cavalry, and whose four divisions assembled in a diamond formation. Bruce covered the south with Douglas to the east, Randolph to the north (towards Stirling), and five hundred horsemen to the west under Keith and as a reserve. On 23 June 1314, two English cavalry formations advanced towards the Scots positions with one led by the Earl of Gloucester and the Earl of Hereford. They were behind a smaller group of around three hundred soldiers marching closer to the River Forth commanded by Sir Robert Clifford and Sir Henry de Beaumont. The two detachments proceeded ahead of the main army with the objective of breaking the siege of Stirling. The Hereford-Gloucester force was first to cross the Bannockburn stream and proceeded towards the woodlands in which the Scots were hiding.

At this point however, Bruce himself had moved away from the main troop, and, not fully armed for combat but instead on a small horse for reconnaissance with only light armour. His only weapon was an axe to defend himself and in this apparently vulnerable situation the nephew of the Earl of Hereford, Henry de Bohun, saw an opportunity. In full combat armour, de Bohun charged forward with his lance and the two faced off single combat. As the two combatants passed, Bruce nimbly slipped to one side and broke Bohun's head with a single blow from his axe. This incident swung the course of the first day as the Scots rushed at the English forces under the joint command of Gloucester and Hereford. Now in full retreat the English troops struggled to get back across the stream; with many lost in the chaos, they withdrew for the day. Overnight a defector to the Scottish camp confirmed the low morale of the English army. This information perhaps tipped Bruce's decision to launch a full-scale attack on the following day with his trained schiltrons as offensive units, a strategy totally different from that of one of his predecessors, William Wallace.

Over two days, the English cavalry failed to break the Scottish line and its dense, defensive formations of spearmen. With a narrow crossing of the stream and wet, marshy ground to either side of the grassland on the other side, the English could not bring their numerical superiority to bear. The topography and terrain meant the fight was on a narrow front with no opportunity to outflank, and Edward's troops, especially the heavy cavalry, were increasingly frustrated. Then, under full assault from the Scots, the English fell back and were lured into pits and trenches previously set into the marshy ground by the Scots and which caused major injuries to horses and riders. Many of the pits were lined with short, sharpened stakes, and in the ensuing chaos resulted in thirty-four English barons and thousands of soldiers being slaughtered. Stirling Castle was lost and in 1328, Scottish independence was formally recognized. Topography, tactics, and clever use of the terrain gave the numerically outnumbered Scots a significant victory.

Solway Moss

In November 1542, the two armies were at loggerheads again. The Battle of Solway Moss was a short-lived affair, described as being over almost as it began. With hugely superior numbers the Scottish army should, in theory, quickly have annihilated the English force, but this was not the case. Lack of cohesion and clear leadership by the Scots, together with effective military deployment by the English, taking advantage of terrain and topography, triggered a humiliating defeat. This engagement took place on the English side of the Anglo-Scottish border on Solway Moss near the River Esk.

Despite being urged by his uncle, King Henry VIII of England, the Scottish king, James V, refused to break from the Roman Catholic Church. In retaliation, Henry launched a major punitive raid into southwest Scotland. On 24 November, Scotland sent an army of around 15,000 to 18,000 soldiers across the Solway Firth and into

England, but the Scottish army was poorly led and badly organized. The force was in effect commanded by Lord Maxwell, but there were internal disputes among the Scottish hierarchy as to who was the designated leader.

However, the Scottish army's advance into England was checked by English commander Lord Wharton with around 3,000 men close to Solway Moss. The start of the battle had a major influence on the outcome. As a small cavalry vanguard of perhaps 500 English stormed the Scottish encampment at night, the Scots, thinking the entire English force had arrived, panicked and in the darkness wandered into the peat bog, lost their way, became bogged down, or drowned. The battle was described as uncoordinated and soon became a rout as the rest of the English force arrived on the scene.

Sir Thomas Wharton noted the battle as between the Esk and Lyne rivers. After the initial interaction with the English cavalry vanguard at Akeshawsill (now Oakshawhill), the Scottish force moved away but became trapped on the south bank of the Esk River. This was on English territory located alongside the river and the nearby peat bog. Following a period of bitter fighting the Scots surrendered. From the English force of around 3,000 men there were few reported losses; for the 18,000-strong Scots army it was estimated only twenty died on the battlefield, but several hundred drowned in the marshes, bogs, and rivers. About 1,200 Scots were captured, many of whom were later ransomed. The battlescape terrain and the effective deployment of a well-coordinated force won the day with an overwhelming victory achieved against very unfavourable odds.

Flodden Field

On 22 August 1513, a Scottish army of many thousands, and estimated at this early stage to include between 7,500 and 10,000 accompanying people (men, women, and children), crossed the border into England along an eight-mile front from Wark Castle in the west to Norham Castle in the east. The strategic aim of the manoeuvre was to force Henry VIII to withdraw his army from France and return to English soil. The Battle of Flodden, Flodden Field, or occasionally Branxton or Brainston Moor, was fought on 9 September 1513, during the War of the League of Cambrai between England and Scotland. The result was a resounding English victory. The conflict was fought near Branxton in Northumberland, northern England, between an invading Scots army under King James IV and the English army, commanded by the Earl of Surrey. In terms of troop numbers, it was the largest of many battles fought between the two countries. Declining a challenge to fight in an open field, James camped his invading army on a commanding hilltop position at Flodden where he could overlook

Flodden battlefield pictured in the early 1900s.

the battlescape and await the advance of the English force. The Scots had superior large cannon facing the expected line of the English attack. However, in view of the superior military power of the Scots, Surrey's army undertook a circuitous march under the cover of darkness to bypass the Scottish troops and position themselves to the rear of their camp. With dawn revealing the changed positions the Scots countered the English ploy by abandoning their camp and moving to occupy nearby Branxton Hill. Their cannon were here, although initially placed facing the wrong way. These were large guns, some of the biggest in Europe, but cumbersome and hard to turn.

At about 16.00 hours on Friday, in wet and windy weather, James started the battle with an artillery duel, but his big guns performed rather badly. Although the Scots faced the difficulty of shooting downhill, the guns were poorly sited; instead of the careful placement normally applied to these heavy weapons, they were hastily located on the hilltop, further slowing their already ponderous firing. The marked silence of the Scottish artillery, with just occasional massive cannonballs, allowed the lighter English cannon to target relatively rapid firepower onto the massed Scots infantry to apparently devastating effect.

The battle began with an artillery duel but again the English came out the better of the two forces because, while the big Scottish cannon were fearsome weapons, they overheated and had to cool for long periods before re-loading. The smaller English cannon fired faster and sent lop-sided cannonballs spinning into massed infantry causing havoc. The exchange of cannon-fire was followed by a downhill advance of Scottish infantry armed with long pikes and marching in uniform disciplined ranks. However, unknown to the Scots, an area of marshy land lay in their path halfway down the slope. By chance, the first troops passed through on drier ground, but those to the sides began to sink in and soon the boggy area became a quagmire. The soldiers to the rear, unaware that the leading ranks were stuck, carried on marching forward until the whole area was a mass of struggling infantrymen sinking into the marsh. With the Scots' formations broken and the troops mired down, the English were able to engage in close-quarter fighting for which they were better equipped. The battlescape became the scene of a rout and King James IV was killed in the conflict. He became the last British monarch to die leading his troops in battle. His death, and the loss of a large part of the Scottish nobility, created a political crisis in Scotland. Indeed, British historians often cite the Battle of Flodden as marking the end of the British Middle Ages, though another candidate is the 1485 Battle of Bosworth Field.

Considering the importance of this single battle, it is worthwhile examining how it played out in a little more detail. James' army had been reduced from its initial strength of about 42,000 because of sickness and desertion. Even so, he still commanded around 34,000 men in the field and outnumbered the English army by about 8,000. This Scottish army was organized into four divisions, or battles, with that on the left flank commanded by the Earls of Home and Huntley with combined Borderers and Highlanders. Adjacent, the battle was commanded by the Earls of Erroll, Crawford, and Montrose with soldiers from northeast Scotland. Third in the line was the force commanded by James himself along with his son Alexander, and the Earls of Cassillis, Rothes, and Caithness. Finally, on the right flank were the Earls of Argyll and Lennox commanding a battle from the Highlands and Islands. There may have been a fifth reserve battle under the command of the Earl of Bothwell.

The Scottish infantry was equipped with eighteen-foot-long (5.5m) pikes. This was a new weapon, supplied by their French allies, and one that had proved devastating in conflicts in continental Europe. However, it did require training, discipline, and suitable terrain for effective deployment. The Scots troops were not as expert at handling the pikes as the Swiss mercenary soldiers that had honed the original weapon. Nevertheless, they were sufficiently practiced advancing down Branxton Hill onto the English army 'silently and in good order'. This could be devastatingly effective as demonstrated by the left flank (western side of the battlefield) which was where the Scots unit under Lords Hume and Huntley was first to advance. By sheer good fortune they went over a gap in the bog where the water-table was lower and the ground relatively firm and dry. At the foot of the hill, they advanced on the English right, commanded by the Earl of Surrey's youngest son Edmund Howard with 'pikes charged' (lowered for combat). This sort of battlescape situation suited the long pikes and powered by the momentum of descent, the impact on the English infantry was clearly devastating. This effect is confirmed by burial pits found in the late nineteenth century marking this area of the battleline on the field. These Scottish troops either pushed the English infantry back to their original position or perhaps were able to cross the open ground quickly enough to engage them before they had advanced. This Scots attack was effective, and Edmund's troops were overwhelmed.

However, this was as far as the Scottish success went. Indeed, the formation and tactics of the Scottish pikemen has been questioned. It has been suggested that it was the organization of the Scottish divisions, or schiltrons (a compact body of troops forming a battle array, shield wall, or phalanx), which were in squares or columns eighty- to 100-men wide and eighty- to 100-men deep (8,000–10,000 men). These were closely packed together, marching in serried ranks; the tramping broke the surface tension of the saturated ground. The troops went forward in what was described as 'German fashion' which may have caused the wet surface to become a mire that could, and indeed did, cripple an army. The consequences would be horrible. As each line of marching men stalled in the bog, all forward movement halted. The pressure of their countrymen pushing forward from behind meant that the front rows probably died from suffocation. Furthermore, being eighteen feet in length, the pikes were essentially over-long spears and were only effective if delivered in an ordered mass and with forward momentum. Mired down in the boggy ground the pikes lost their effectiveness. A result was that the English soldiers were able to close in and join battle with an enemy unable to move, confused, and incapable of defence or attack.

So it seems that a key factor in the conflict was the interaction between the English infantry and the Scots pikemen. The determinant of the outcome of the fighting was a mix of tactics, formations and terrain. The Scottish style of battle could be highly effective but not on boggy or marshy ground. The other main influence on the outcome of Flodden was the artillery firepower, and the serious misjudgement of the deployment of the advanced Scots' technology in respect of this topographical context of this battlescape. The Scottish artillery was very advanced for the time but had some inherent problems associated with size and calibre; these were essentially heavy siege guns. The fearsome weapons consisted of five great curtals, two great culverins, together called 'the Seven Sisters', along with four sakers and six great serpentines. These impressive modern weapons fired iron cannonballs weighing around sixty-six pounds (thirty kilograms) with a range of about 2,000 yards (1,800m). This is where the problems began; the sheer size and preferred deployment as weapons of siege warfare yielded them ineffective on the open battlefield. The heaviest of the Scots' cannon needed a team of thirty-six oxen to move it. Moreover, they could only fire one round every twenty minutes or so because of overheating. Finally, for some bizarre reason the artillery was commanded by the king's secretary, diplomat Patrick Paniter, a man with no previous artillery experience. This really was a recipe for disaster and so it turned out. The English cannon were smaller, more mobile, and fired cannonballs which spun through their target infantry troops due to lop-sided weighting, with devastating impact. This was a catastrophic battle resulting from misunderstanding the topographic conditions and terrain, and appalling military misjudgement.

Wetlands and medieval Japanese warfare

Strategic benefits and territorial markers have influenced conflicts around the world. Looking further afield now, to medieval Japan, military technology and innovation may prove decisive, but terrain and topography cannot be ignored.

The 1575 conflict, as part of the Sengoku (Warring States) Period, was an attempt to unify control across the country. To achieve this ambition, Takeda Katsuyori, in the eastern provinces, needed to claim the capital of Kyoto, controlled by Odo Nobunaga. However, to do this Takeda had to cross through territory supportive of Odo, and held by Tokugawa Ieyasu, and lay siege to the fortress of Nagashino. In opposition to this attack, a combined force of around 38,000 troops came to the aid of the defenders, outnumbering Takeda. Nevertheless, despite the numbers, Takeda's cavalry were renowned as fearsome warriors, and Odo, a clever tactician, had his men construct a wooden palisade with his frontline behind a stream to make cavalry assault more difficult. This was innovative use of the terrain in terms of setting the battlescape for the conflict.

Furthermore, he had a technological innovation in his favour which was the use of matchlock muskets set in three ranks to enable constant firing and re-loading. The result of this combination of terrain and technology was that Takeda's invading army was slaughtered and Odo went on to become the most powerful warlord in Japan. This use of concentrated volleys of gunfire was around a quarter of a century before it was used in Europe. Tokugawa Ieyasu followed Odo into power and unified the entire country under the Tokugawa Shogunate.

Ottomans, Habsburgs and wet battlescapes

Conflicts in Eastern Europe between the Ottoman and Habsburg empires seemed to oscillate during the late 1600s. In 1697 the Ottoman Sultan Mustafa II arrived with his army at Belgrade. The commander-in-chief of the Habsburg army was Prince Eugene of Savoy; his forced engaged the Ottomans in battle while they crossed the strategic Tisa River close to Zenta. While the Ottoman force was thus exposed, using cannon-fire to good effect put them in disarray and they retreated toward the bridge under pressure from a cavalry attack. At the bridge over the river, the Habsburg infantry cut off the Ottoman retreat. Thousands were killed, and the Habsburgs captured a significant amount of treasure too. The battle, which ended Ottoman influence in Europe, hinged on an important river-crossing. A battlescape of wetlands and waterways proved critical in the decisive moments.

Wetlands in European warfare of the eighteenth century

In the early 1700s, Britain, Austria, and the Dutch Republic had formed a Grand Alliance to curb the expansionist ideas of King Louis XIV of France. By 1704, the British leader, Duke of Marlborough, was worried about a possible French attack on Vienna; he led a joint force into Bavaria with Austrians under Prince Eugene of Savoy. Here they faced a combined army of French and Bavarian troops led by the Duc de Tallard. The Franco-Bavarian force was camped at the Danube River and, being superior in number to their adversaries, did not expect an assault.

Indeed, the French and their allies were in a strong defensive position behind extensive marshy ground along the Nebel River, with their right flank secured by the massive Danube. They had around 60,000 soldiers compared with around 52,000 under Marlborough. However, on 13 August Tallard was shocked to see the Grand Alliance army advancing toward him across the great plain and then crossing the Nebel River. Despite fierce resistance, the French centre weakened, fell back, and were ultimately routed. With the French faltering, the battle was clearly lost, and the Bavarians fled the field. It is estimated that around 30,000 troops from the Franco-Bavarian force were killed, many of these drowned in the river while attempting to flee. Flatlands can make ideal battlegrounds on the one hand, but their often-associated rivers, streams, bogs, and marshes, are hazardous during and after a conflict. In this example, the terrain and superior numbers probably imbued the French force with misplaced complacency, and the Duke of Marlborough's army played the topographic factors to their advantage and ultimate victory.

Sedgemoor and the Monmouth Rebellion in England

The final battle of the Monmouth Rebellion, the Battle of Sedgemoor, was the last and decisive engagement between the English crown under King James II, and rebels following Charles II's illegitimate son James Scott, 1st Duke of Monmouth.

The conflict was known as the Monmouth Rebellion, and the battle took place on 6 July 1685 at Westonzoyland, near Bridgwater in Somerset. The outcome was an overwhelming victory for the forces of the monarchy. The major battle followed various smaller skirmishes in and around southwest England between Monmouth's rebel forces and the Royal army loyal to James II. Many were slaughtered during the fighting and around five hundred rebel prisoners were taken. Monmouth escaped the field of battle but was later captured and taken to London where he was executed as a traitor. A good number of Monmouth's supporters were also tried during the so-called Bloody Assizes.

The context to this battle lies in the Duke of Monmouth being a popular and charismatic alternative to the Catholic-leaning James II, a king who was both disliked and mistrusted as a monarch in Protestant England. This situation encouraged the ambitions of a pretender to the throne. Monmouth was residing in Holland, however, with encouragement from supporters in England, he landed at Lyme Regis in Dorset having sailed from the Dutch Republic in the expectation of a popular uprising to his cause. There followed a series of marches and skirmishes across Dorset and Somerset. Finally, Monmouth's rather motley and poorly equipped force was driven back to the great fenland of the Somerset Levels, and by 3 July was contained around Bridgwater. Here the troops were directed to fortify the town. The Monmouth army comprised about 3,500 mixed religious nonconformists, farm workers, and other artisans armed largely with farm tools such as pitchforks.

The force that came against them was royalist, many of them professional soldiers, commanded by Louis de Duras, 2nd Earl of Feversham, and Colonel John Churchill. The infantry included five hundred of the 1st Regiment of Foot (the Royal Scots, known as Dumbarton's Regiment) commanded by Lieutenant Colonel Douglas; two battalions of the 1st (King's Royal Regiment of Guards or Grenadier Guards) under Henry FitzRoy, 1st Duke of Grafton and Major Eaton; six hundred of the Second Regiment of Guards (which would become the Coldstream Guards) with Lieutenant-Colonel Sackville; five companies of the Queen Dowager's (Tangier Regiment and later 2nd Foot); and five companies of the Queen Consort's Regiment (King's Own Royal Regiment) commanded by Lieutenant Colonel Charles Churchill. Then there was the Horse and Foot, the Royal Train of Artillery camped by the main road to Bridgwater. Also present were the Royal Cavalry – seven troops of four-hundred-and-twenty men of the Earl of Oxford's, the King's Regiment of Horse (Blues and Royals), with Colonel Sir Francis Compton commanding; the King's Own Royal Dragoons; and finally, three troops of the King's Horse Guards (Lifeguards). This made up the royalist army that camped by the Bussex Rhine, a West County rhyne or major drain through the wetland, at Westonzoyland on the day of the battle. These numbers and identities are given to provide some insight into the overwhelming odds stacked against the ramshackle gathering of mostly farm labourers.

Eventually, at about 22.00 hours, Monmouth led his makeshift army from Bridgwater, with the intention of attacking the King's army under cover of darkness. Guided along the old Bristol Road toward Bawdrip by Richard Godfrey, the servant of a local farmer, their few cavalrymen made up the vanguard. The troops turned south along Bradney and Marsh lanes until they came to the open wet moor criss-crossed with deep and potentially dangerous rhynes. There was a short delay as the main rhyne was crossed and immediately the first soldiers to reach the other side met a royalist patrol. This led to a shot being fired raising the alarm; a royalist horseman from the patrol hastened back to report to Lord Feversham at the main camp. With surprise now compromised, Lord Grey of Warke led the rebel cavalry forward to engage the King's Regiment of Horse which alerted the other royalist forces. In the chaos of the darkness and the treacherous wet moor, the professional soldiers of the regular army outflanked and routed the rebel army.

The Battle of Sedgemoor is frequently described as the last pitched battle to take place on English soil, although this depends on the subjective definition of a 'battle'. There are other claimants to the title like the Battle of Preston in Lancashire (14 November 1715) during the First Jacobite Rebellion, and the Clifton Moor Skirmish, near Penrith in Cumberland (18 December 1745) during the Second Jacobite Rebellion. However, the last pitched battle on British soil, in this subjective view, was the Battle of Culloden on Drumossie Moor near Inverness on 16 April 1746.

Sedgemoor gained notoriety for other reasons, especially the aftermath of the resounding victory. King James despatched Lord Chief Justice Jeffreys to round up the defeated Duke's supporters across southwest England where they were tried in the Bloody Assizes. The courts were at Taunton Castle and elsewhere cross the region. Around 1,300 individuals were found guilty, resulting in many transported abroad, and others executed by drawing and quartering. Some people were fined, these included the writer and diarist Daniel Defoe, later the author of the novel *Robinson Crusoe*, who took part in the uprising and the battle; aside from a heavy fine he lost much of his land and money. Brothers Benjamin Hewling (commander of a troop of horse), and William Hewling (lieutenant of foot), were both condemned to death, though Benjamin was hanged rather than drawn and quartered after his sister paid £1,000 to the court. Harsh times indeed.

Three years later, the Glorious Revolution led to the unpopular King James II being overthrown in a coup; William of Orange, a Protestant, returned to the throne.

Sedgemoor was always tipped in favour of the government army and away from the rebels. However, it once again illustrates the power of a wetland as a place of sanctuary or in this case, a fruitless last stand for an army under immense pressure. The battlescape of the expansive wet moors, deep rhynes (drains), and major rivers, was a terrible place to engage the enemy, especially at night. No doubt some of Monmouth's rebels did seek sanctuary in the fenland, and while most were rounded up, perhaps some evaded their pursuers.

America's First Vietnam War

The Florida Everglades and the Seminole Wars provide an example of the deep complexities of conflicts and warfare over territorial disputes and between indigenous, migrating, and invading peoples. Furthermore, they provide insight into some of the issues of conducting warfare in hostile wet terrain on the one hand, and against overwhelming military odds on the other. We consider these three disputes in some detail because they give considerable evidence for some of the wider aspects of topography and terrain as determinant factors in battlescapes.

In 2006, Michael Grunwald wrote a classic account of peatlands and human conflict in his book *The Swamp: The Everglades, Florida and the Politics of Paradise*. This details not only the battle with wetlands by American capitalist aspirations, and business, but the warfare with native American Seminoles during the early 1800s. Seminoles were citizens of a Native American nation formed in the region in the early 1700s. Knowing the landscape and being able to subsist deep in the swamps, for many years the natives outwitted and outfought the American military. The thankless task of eradicating the native people from what was once over four-thousand square miles of waterlogged South Florida forest was described as America's 'first Vietnam War'. The Native Americans held out in the Florida Everglades until a final assault from the European North Americans during the later 1800s.

The Seminole Wars (also known as the Florida Wars) were three related military conflicts in Florida between the United States and the Seminole people. Hostilities commenced in about 1816 and continued through to 1858, with two periods of uneasy truce between active conflicts. The Seminole Wars were the longest, and most expensive in human and financial cost to the United States, of the American Indian Wars.

From the early 1500s, the native people of Florida had declined following the arrival of European explorers. The impact of European diseases for which they had little immunity was probably the main cause. Under Spanish rule, until the early 1600s, native revolts were violently suppressed, further reducing the native population of northern Florida. As relations gradually improved the population stabilized. However, from the late 1600s, raids into Florida by English settlers and their Indian allies from Carolina triggered a further sharp fall in the indigenous population. Indeed, by the early 1700s, Carolinian settlers and their Yamasee Indian allies had killed, carried off, or driven away most remaining indigenous people from the Florida peninsula. The result of persistent raiding was the virtual depopulation of the region with, according to the governor of La Florida, ten thousand or more Native Americans taken as slaves. It was into this vacuum that, during the mid-eighteenth century, small groups of various southeastern United States Native American tribes started to migrate into the vacant lands of Florida. In 1715 the Yamasee Indians moved into Florida, after conflicts with colonists from the Province of Carolina. Then the Creek people, at first the Lower Creek but later also the Upper Creek, arrived from Georgia and the Mikasuki (Hitchiti-speakers) occupying Lake Miccosukee near Tallahassee. The influx of various tribes of Native Americans continued as they were pushed out of their homelands by White settlers. The name Seminole may have originated from the Spanish word *cimarrones* meaning 'wild ones' or 'runaways'.

African-American slaves, escaping from the southern United States, who reached this Spanish-controlled territory were offered freedom and land by Spanish authorities in Florida. Former slaves were actively recruited as militiamen to help defend Spanish Pensacola and Fort Mose, a free black settlement; others joined Seminole bands. Many escaped slaves, now at Fort Mose, left for Cuba with the Spanish when they abandoned Florida in 1763. Others continued living with, or near, the Seminole tribes and were joined by other escapees from Carolina and Georgia. The black slaves who joined the Seminoles were integrated into the native American tribes, learned their languages, adopted their dress, and often inter-married. Indeed, the former slaves had knowledge of farming and could have value as interpreters between Seminole tribes and the white American settlers; some became influential tribal leaders.

There is some disagreement about when this conflict began and ended with some US military sources giving 1814–1819, others have the conflict starting two years later, while some cite 1817–1818 or just 1818. It was preceded by the Creek War (1813–1814) from which Colonel Andrew Jackson emerged a US national hero because of his victory against the Creek Red Sticks at the Battle of Horseshoe Bend. Jackson enforced the Treaty of Fort Jackson on the Creek Nation, taking much Creek territory in southern Georgia, and both central and south Alabama. This triggered mass movements of Creek Indians to Spanish West Florida where the refugees coalesced with the Florida Seminoles.

The First Seminole War (c. 1817–1818)

It is likely that this conflict ran from 1817–1818, though its beginnings were somewhat earlier. From the 1730s, the Spanish in the region had provided refuge for runaway slaves from the American Carolinas. However, in the 1770s these escapees began to congregate around 'Negro Fort on the Apalachicola River'. The Americans considered the Negroes among the Seminoles a threat to slavery north of the then Spanish border in the south of the area. Plantation owners, mostly from Mississippi and Georgia, accused the Indians of stealing their Negroes. Indeed, the Seminole Indians did keep black slaves that white Americans attempted to steal with raiding parties.

On 26 December 1817, the US War Department ordered General Jackson to take personal command of the situation and to bring the Seminoles 'under control'. However, the areas of Florida where the main Seminole 'problems' were experienced were under Spanish control, and they objected strongly to these punitive expeditions. Nevertheless, the Spanish rule was teetering in the face of local uprisings, and they would shortly cede Florida to the United States (Adams-Onís Treaty, 1819) with official transfer taking place in 1821. Following these changes, under the Treaty of Moultrie Creek (1823) between the United States and Seminole Nation, the Seminoles were to move from northern Florida to a designated reservation on the central Florida peninsula. To ensure the treaty was honoured, the American government-built forts and trading posts down the Gulf and Atlantic coasts.

The terms of the treaty meant the US government had to protect the Seminole tribes, as long as they abided by US law. The authorities were committed to distributing farm implements, cattle, and hogs to the Seminoles, and to compensate them for the travel and losses incurred in relocating to the reservation. They would provide rations for one year to give time for the Seminoles to plant and harvest their own crops. The tribe would also be paid US$5,000 annually for twenty years and for the same period would support an interpreter, school, and blacksmith. The Seminole Nation would then allow the construction of roads across the reservation and were committed to capturing and returning any fugitives, such as former slaves from the US territories.

The Second Seminole War (1835–1842)

The US reneged on the Treaty of Moultrie Creek starting the second war (1835–1842). The American government now insisted that the entire Seminole Nation move from the agreed reservation to a new location, imaginatively called Indian Territory, in what is today Oklahoma and is detailed in the Indian Removal Act 1830. Following threats and ultimatums some Seminole clans moved (Treaty of Payne's Landing,

1832). However, with many Seminoles refusing to move, the war began in December 1835; the first confrontation was the Dade Battle. The conflict carried on for several years and saw violent engagements across the Florida peninsula, as far as the Florida Keys. Numerically disadvantaged, the Seminole warriors were able to fight a guerrilla war to good effect, and to use tactics and terrain to outwit and outmanoeuvre the US Cavalry.

US officials in Florida realized the Seminoles would object to being forcibly removed to the new reservation and prepared for outright war. In mid-December 1835, with White settlers fleeing to safety as Seminole warriors attacked, first plantations and then a militia waggon-train, two companies of US cavalry, with 110 men, were sent from Fort Brooke under Major Francis L. Dade to reinforce Fort King. On 28 December the force was ambushed by Seminole warriors and wiped out. The only survivors were two badly wounded soldiers who made it back to Fort Brooke. Similar attacks occurred over the next few months as increasing numbers of US soldiers were engaged in fruitless pursuits of the elusive Seminoles through the expansive wet forest. They were lured into what were effectively killing grounds; the Seminoles lay in wait, ambushed, and then melted away into the dense forest. The Seminoles struck throughout the state, attacking isolated farms, settlements, plantations, and army forts. The US troops experienced serious problems of illness and lack of supplies with several American forts consequently being abandoned.

In late December 1835, Major Benjamin A. Putnam led a troop of soldiers to occupy and fortify the Bulow Plantation. Surrounded by cotton bales and a stockade, local planters and their slaves sought sanctuary. However, the soldiers fled the area on 23 January 1836, and the Seminoles burned Bulow Plantation. By February 1836, the Seminoles and their allies, former slaves, had attacked and destroyed twenty-one plantations throughout the area.

In February, the remains of the massacred Dade party were found by Major Ethan Allen Hitchcock and others. He wrote in his journal that the US government was in the wrong which is why the Indians persevered. In his view, they had defended their country nobly against an attempt to inflict a fraudulent treaty and had used all possible means to avoid war; they were forced into it through the tyranny of the American government.

The conflict grew and on 21 November 1836, at the Battle of Wahoo Swamp, an American government force of around 2,500 men came up against the Seminole tribes who successfully drove them back. The American dead included Major David Moniac who was the first Native American graduate of West Point military academy. This battle reinforced Seminole confidence in their ability to take on the established armies of the American government. However, the United States military forces committed to the affair increased, until there were over 30,000 regular soldiers, militiamen, and volunteers. In 1836, the US sent General Thomas Sidney Jesup to take command of the failing campaign; with over 9,000 men, his initiative was to change tactic completely. So, rather than chasing parties of Seminole fighters through dense, wet, Everglades Forest, as his predecessors had done, Jesup sought, captured, and destroyed Seminole homes, livestock, farms, and supplies. The new aim was to starve them out and wear down their resistance. This strategy was later used by General W.T. Sherman during the American Civil War and is said to have shortened that conflict.

By January 1837, the US Army was having more success in capturing or killing Seminoles. In late January a group of Seminole chiefs contacted Jesup to arrange a truce; in March a capitulation agreement was signed. In this document it was agreed that the Seminoles and their allies, 'their negroes, and their bona fide property', would be protected as they moved west to the reservation. The Seminole uprising was collapsing, and by late May, most of the chiefs had surrendered. Nevertheless, two significant chiefs, Osceola and Sam Jones held out and remained opposed to the forced relocation. Then, on 2 June, along with around 200 warriors, they attacked the holding camp at Fort Brooke. This was poorly guarded, and they succeeded in releasing the 700 Seminoles that had previously surrendered.

This indicated to Jesup that the Second Seminole War was still very much alive; he would never again trust the word of an Indian. Jesup arranged for so-called conferences to be established by Brigadier-General Joseph Marion Hernández under a white flag of truce. In fact, this was a cover to draw out the Indian chiefs and capture them, including Osceola and Micanopy. Some of these leaders later managed to escape from Fort Marion, but Osceola did not accompany them and died in prison, probably of malaria. Jesup's authorized abductions under a flag of truce was regarded as very controversial. He spent the next twenty-one years trying to defend himself against accusations of treachery.

General Jesup's troops were sent with multiple columns to sweep down the peninsula and push the Seminoles southward. On Christmas Day 1837, Colonel Zachary Taylor's column of 800 men came up against a force of approximately 400 warriors, holding the northern shore of Lake Okeechobee. The Seminoles were led by Sam Jones, Alligator, and the recently escaped chief Coacoochee. They had chosen the location well. The Indians were carefully positioned in a hammock surrounded by tall sawgrass and fronted by about half a mile of swamp. Away from the hammock was Lake Okeechobee where the sawgrass was around five-feet high. With mud and water three-feet deep, the cavalry's horses would be useless. The Seminole warriors had selected their battlescape with good knowledge of the terrain. Furthermore, they had prepared the ground and cut the grass to provide an open field of fire with notched trees to hold and steady their rifles. With scouts in the tall treetops, they were able to track every move of the US troops coming their way. When Taylor's troop arriving at this point, he gave the order to attack and, just past noon, with quiet all around, the sun directly overhead, and the air still, he moved his troops into the centre of the swamp. The plan was not to move around and entrap the Seminoles but rather to attack directly. Taylor's soldiers were on foot and when the frontline, led by Missouri volunteers, were within range, the Seminoles opened fire. Under this opening volley the volunteers broke ranks and scattered. With their commander, Colonel Gentry, fatally wounded, they retreated in confusion across the swamp. Conflict in the dense sawgrass was catastrophic for five companies of the Sixth Infantry; all officers bar one, and most non-commissioned ranks were killed or wounded. The units pulled back to re-form but only four men of the leading companies were unharmed. As the battle raged on the Americans forced the Seminoles from their defensive lair, but they then made off over the lake. Taylor's troops' casualties were twenty-six dead and 112 wounded; the Seminoles lost eleven with fourteen wounded. Nevertheless, the American army heralded the Battle of Lake Okeechobee as a major victory.

In late January 1838, the US force found a number of Seminoles east of Lake Okeechobee, again holding their ground in a hammock within the swamp. The Seminoles were pushed back over a wide watercourse by volleys of cannon and rocket fire. They then made a further stand before once more slipping away with fewer casualties than the Americans, ending the Battle of Loxahatchee. Then in February 1838, Seminole chiefs Tuskegee and Halleck Hadjo proposed to Jesup that if they were allowed to stay south of Lake Okeechobee, instead of being sent west, they would cease fighting. Jesup was in favour of this solution. The Seminoles camped close to the US Army while waiting for approval from the government in Washington. However, the Secretary of War rejected the suggestion and General Jesup captured the five hundred Seminoles in the camp and deported them to the Indian Territory anyway.

In May 1838, General Jesup requested that he be relieved of the Florida command; his request was accepted with Zachary Taylor taking control. With fewer men at his disposal Taylor worked to keep the Seminoles away from northern Florida. This strategy was achieved by constructing numerous small military posts at twenty-mile (30-km) intervals with a connecting network of roadways across the peninsula. By the winter, things across the region were quiet and national support for the conflict

Billy Bowlegs, leader of the Seminoles.

Osceola (Billy Powell) 1804 to 30 January 1838, leader of the Seminoles.

was dwindling. Indeed, many Americans were starting to think the Seminole Nation had earned its right to remain in Florida, and the Everglades. Far from being over, the war had also become very costly. With all this in mind, US President Martin Van Buren despatched Alexander Macomb, commanding General of the army, to oversee peace negotiations with the Seminole leaders. On 19 May 1839, General Macomb reached an agreement whereby, in exchange for a reservation in southern Florida, the Seminoles would cease hostilities, or so it seemed. Taylor, who had served longest of the Florida war commanders asked for a transfer, which was granted; he was replaced by Brigadier General Walker Keith Armistead.

The summer arrived and the truce seemed to hold but on 23 July around 150 Seminoles attacked a Caloosahatchee River trading post guarded by twenty-three soldiers under Colonel William S. Harney. The Colonel made off via the river, but most of the garrison and some civilians were slaughtered. There is some dispute as to who was responsible for the attack and whether it was Seminoles or so-called 'Spanish Indians'. Local Seminole leaders promised to find and turn those involved over to the authorities; before this could happen, two troopers visiting the Seminole camp were killed. Using bloodhounds, the army tracked the Indians, but with limited success.

Army patrols and blockhouses in northern Florida helped contain the situation, but the Seminoles kept on the move. Armistead now went on the offensive searching out hidden Seminole camps. The army burned 500 acres (two square kilometres) of Seminole crops, and drove off livestock such as horses, cattle, and pigs.

The US Navy was also involved now and sent sailors and marines up streams, rivers, and into the Everglades. By late 1839, navy Lieutenant John T. McLaughlin led a joint army-navy amphibious force operating in the Florida Everglades with its base at Tea Table Key in the upper Florida Keys. Significant advances occurred in December 1840 and into mid-January 1841, when McLaughlin's troops, in dugout canoes, managed to cross the Everglades east to west. They were the first White Americans to do so, and the Seminoles kept away.

Armistead had now received US$55,000 to bribe Seminole chiefs to surrender; some did, others did not. Senior chiefs received up to US$5,000, lesser ones around US$200; each Seminole warrior was given US$30 and a rifle. By spring Armistead had despatched 450 Seminoles west to the reservation with a further 236 awaiting departure at Fort Brooke. It was estimated that 120 warriors had gone, leaving fewer than 300 in Florida. In May 1841, Colonel William Jenkins Worth replaced Armistead as commander of the Florida forces; he had orders to reduce expenditure on this increasingly unpopular war; around 1,000 civilian employees were axed, and his command structure was rationalized. Over the summer, Worth now ordered his remaining troops to undertake 'search and destroy' tactics to drive remaining Seminoles out of northern Florida. The final action of the second war was when General William Bailey and planter Jack Bellamy led fifty-two men on a three-day chase after a small group of Seminoles that had attacked settlers. Having come across their encampment in the Florida swamp, they killed all twenty-four Indians. At sixteen years old, the youngest member of the posse was William Wesley Hankins, it was claimed he fired the final shot of the Second Seminole War.

Colonel Worth now advocated for the remaining Seminoles be left in peace. He then received authorization to allow the Seminoles that remained to stay on an informal reservation in southwest Florida. On 14 August 1842, he declared that the war was over. Also in August, the US Congress passed the Armed Occupation Act to provide free land to settlers that improved the farmland and were willing to defend themselves from Indians. In late 1842, any remaining Indians outside the reservation in southwest Florida were sent west. This meant that by April 1843, the armed force in Florida could be cut to just one regiment. In November, Worth announced that there were only ninety-five Seminole men and around two hundred women and children left on the Florida reservation, and they were no longer considered a threat.

By the early 1840s, numerous Seminoles had died at the hands of the American force and others had surrendered due to starvation and were removed to Indian Territory. Despite all this, there was no formal peace treaty and several hundred Seminoles stayed in southwest Florida even as the conflict faded; but this was still not the end. The Seminoles remaining in Florida at the end of the Second Seminole War in 1842 were on an informal reservation.

It is estimated that the Second Seminole War cost up to forty million dollars with over 40,000 regular US soldiers, militiamen, and volunteers involved in the war. Around 1,500 soldiers died from disease and accidents, and over 300 regular army, navy, and marine corps troops were killed in action together with a further fifty-five volunteer officers and men. There is no accurate record of how many Seminoles died but the numbers are obviously considerable. Many were lost to disease or starvation in Florida itself, and on the journey west, others died once they arrived in Indian Territory. There were also unknown numbers of American civilians killed by Seminole attacks.

Time passed, and by late 1855, there were around 700 US soldiers stationed in Florida when a Seminole gathering took place, near Taylor Creek on northeast Lake Okeechobee, in the fall. It was decided that they needed to strike back against the rising pressure being placed on them by increasing numbers of white settlers. They would attack when the opportunity presented itself, although while some chiefs argued for war others opposed it.

Then, on 7 December 1855, First Lieutenant George Hartsuff left Fort Myers with ten men and two waggons to undertake a routine patrol of the reservation. They passed cornfields and three deserted villages, including that of Chief Billy Bowlegs, but saw no Seminoles. As evening fell on 19 December, Hartsuff announced that they were to return to Fort Myers the following day. In the morning the troops were busy loading up waggons and saddling horses when forty Seminoles, led by Billy Bowlegs, attacked their camp; several soldiers were shot. The casualties included Lieutenant Hartsuff though he was able to hide while the Seminoles killed and scalped four of his men. They killed the waggon mules, looted, and burned the waggons, and took several horses. Seven men, four wounded, were able to get back to Fort Myers. The Third Seminole War was underway.

The Third Seminole War (1855 to 1858)

With more and more American settlers moving into southwest Florida, tensions with Seminoles living in the region increased. This growing stress between indigenous Seminoles and the White settlers triggered the third conflict from 1855 to 1858.

As stress levels rose, in December 1855, the US Army found and destroyed a large Seminole plantation located west of the Everglades. It is suggested that this was a tactic designed to trigger a violent response from the Indians to then allow for punitive action which would remove the last of the Seminole Nation from the Everglades. The response from the Seminoles was swift as Holata Micco, known to the Americans as Billy Bowlegs, led a raid near Fort Myers. This triggered a series of retaliatory reprisals and minor skirmishes, without major conflict. Again, the American military strategy targeted Seminole civilians through the destruction of food and ultimately starvation.

When the news of the Bowlegs' attack reached Tampa, the citizens elected militia officers and set about organising volunteer companies. The militia force marched to Peace River Valley and on the way collected more recruits. Some of the abandoned forts along the river were now manned and Governor James Broome began organizing volunteer companies. With limited state funds he persuaded the army to take volunteers; they accepted two infantry companies and three mounted companies. This totalled about 260 men. A further 400 men were mobilized under state control. Private donations supported the arming and supply of state troops including those in the US Army and others under state administration. Governor Broome made General Jesse Carter commander of the state troops as 'special agent without military rank'. Carter set half of the state troops to growing crops, and so only 200 of his men were available for patrols. It was noted that mounted patrols preferred open country (easier for the horses), but there was a downside in that the Seminoles could spot them more easily.

The situation continued to deteriorate and on 6 January 1856, two men were killed south of the Miami River and local settlers fled to Fort Dallas and Key Biscayne. Outside Fort Denaud twenty Seminoles attacked a wood-cutting patrol, and five of the six men were killed. Even with militia units placed to defend the area, the Seminole braves raided south, down the coast beyond Tampa Bay. One man was killed, and a house was burned, and on 31 March 1856, they attacked 'Braden Castle', the plantation home of Dr Joseph Braden. They were beaten back but took seven slaves and three mules. Carrying their loot, and with slaves in tow, the Seminoles slowed as they stopped to eat, and the militia found them. Two Seminoles were killed and scalped; these trophies were displayed in Tampa and in Manatee.

In April there were patrols by both regular army and militia around the region and into the reservation, but there was little contact with the Seminoles. However, a six-hour battle occurred near Bowlegs Town when four regulars were killed and three wounded before the Seminoles pulled back. Small Seminole raids continued across

Florida including on 14 May 1856, when fifteen attacked the farmhouse of Captain Robert Bradley north of Tampa. Two of Bradley's young children were killed along with one Seminole. This may have been a revenge attack for Bradley killing a chief's brother in the Second Seminole War. Seminoles attacked a waggon train in central Florida and three men were killed; mail and stagecoach services from Tampa were suspended until military protection could be given.

Seminoles attacked the farm of Willoughby Tillis two miles (3.2km) from Fort Meade on 14 June 1856, but the household withdrew into the farmhouse and held off the attackers. The gunfire was heard at Fort Meade and seven mounted militiamen responded but three were killed and two wounded. Along Peace River some of the Seminoles were killed on 16 June when twenty Fort Fraser militiamen surprised a Seminole band. The militiamen lost two men killed and three wounded and they withdrew. It was claimed they killed around twenty Seminoles, but the Indians suggested four dead and two wounded. Nevertheless, the significance was that one of the fatalities was an important chief who was actively leading the attacks against settlers.

However, Florida settlers were increasingly unhappy with the militia. There were complaints of idleness, drunkenness, and thievery. Most significantly, the initiative had not been effective in stopping the raids on settlements. So, in September 1856, Brigadier General William S. Harney returned as commander of the federal troops in Florida. With his experience from the Second Seminole War, he established a series of forts across the state and patrolled deep into Seminole territory. His strategy was to confine Seminole activities to the Big Cypress Swamp and the Everglades. He believed that come the wet season they would not be able to survive there. His plan was to capture the Indians as they left the wetlands for drier ground to grow essential corn. He would use boats to reach islands and other dry areas in the extensive swamps and so flush the Seminoles out. He did attempt to negotiate but was unable to make contact. Therefore, in early January 1857, he sent his troops to actively pursue the Seminoles throughout their territory; this bore little fruit and he and his men were transferred elsewhere.

General Harney was replaced as commander by Colonel Gustavus Loomis. However, the withdrawal of the Fifth Infantry now left him with just ten Fourth Artillery companies. These were soon further reduced to just four companies. Loomis had volunteers grouped as boat companies, with metal 'alligator boats' previously built specifically to use in the Big Cypress Swamp and Everglades. These boats were thirty feet (9.1m) long, pointed at both ends, and drawing two to three feet (0.91m) of water. The boats were able to take up to sixteen men and penetrate deep into the swamps. The boat companies captured many of the Seminole women and children. The regular soldiers did less well, and it was observed that this was because most of the enlisted men were recent immigrants to the region who had no skills in woodcraft. The Seminoles were easily able to avoid the patrols.

By 1857, there were ten companies of Florida militia in federal service with around 800 men. In November of that year, they captured eighteen women and children from Billy Bowlegs' group. The militia also found and destroyed several camps and associated crops and, starting on New Year's Day 1858, began to move into the Big Cypress Swamp. They again destroyed any settlements and crops they found.

A delegation from the Indian Territory arrived in Florida in January to contact Bowlegs and the US troops stood down during this period. In 1857, the Seminoles had finally been granted their own reservation in Indian Territory separate from their old enemies the Creeks. Furthermore, cash payments of US$500 were promised to each warrior (more to the chiefs), and US$100 to each woman. On 15 March, Bowlegs and other bands took the offer and agreed to go west. And so, on 4 May, 163 Seminoles were shipped to New Orleans and four days later Colonel Loomis declared the Third Seminole War over.

However, small family bands of Seminoles, totalling around 200–500 people still refused to move. Instead, they retreated into the heart of the Everglades and the Big Cypress Swamp where they lived on land unsuitable for the American settlers; they continued living there until into the twentieth century.

Taming the wet landscape - unsuccessfully

Beginning in the late 1800s, flood control and drainage projects opened more land for development. These schemes significantly altered the natural environment causing inundation of some lands and the drying of former swamps for arable fields. Such projects, combined with new roads bisecting the Everglades in 1928, effectively ended the old ways of life. New opportunities developed and more white settlers, developers, and then tourists came to the region. In this changed situation some of the Seminoles began working on local farms, ranches, and even tourist souvenir stands. By 1940s, the Florida Seminoles were mostly moving to reservations with official tribal governments forming links to the Bureau of Indian Affairs. By 1957, most Seminoles had formal connections with the US government through the Seminole Tribe of Florida, with headquarters in Hollywood, Florida. They now control the Big Cypress Indian, Brighton, Fort Pierce, Hollywood, Immokalee, and Tampa reservations. The Miccosukee Seminoles still have a more traditional lifestyle in the Everglades region, mixing privacy with tourism as they wrestle alligators, sell crafts, and offer eco-tourism experiences of the area. Finally, in 1962, they were granted federal recognition as a separate nation and received their own reservation lands.

The removal of the Native Americans was only one part of the bigger attempt to wrest the Everglades from nature and bring them into good, capitalist production. The longer story is that the attempts largely failed, and the eventual outcome was the establishment of the Everglades National Park and the celebration of the landscape as one of America's true wilderness areas. Most remaining Native Americans were finally displaced to allow the region to become a 'natural' wilderness area within the National Park. Further north, in Virginia, there are extensive peatland nature reserves including the National Wildlife Refuge site evocatively named 'The Great Dismal Swamp'. The name alone gives an insight into how European settlers viewed this peat landscape when they settled the eastern seaboard of the US. Florida and the Great Dismal Swamp were each regarded as derelict, disease-ridden wetlands that needed to be converted and reclaimed to good, productive, capitalist landscapes. This was at odds with the indigenous viewpoint and ultimately was largely a failure. For Florida and the Everglades, America's 'first Vietnam war' should perhaps have provided a salutary lesson.

The Chinese Yellow River Flooding by Chiang Kai-shek

We now move around the world to consider one of the biggest manmade environmental disasters of all time, the military flooding of the Chinese Yellow River valley.

The 1938 Yellow River flood, (the Huayuankou Embankment Breach Incident), was triggered in central China by the nationalist government during the early stages of the Second Sino-Japanese War (1937–1945). This human-created disaster was an attempt to halt the rapid advance of Japanese forces. The sabotage has been described as the 'largest act of environmental warfare in history' and is taken as an example of scorched-earth military strategy. The year 1937 was very much the end of the beginning of the Second Sino-Japanese War and saw the rapid incursion by the Imperial Japanese Army into the Chinese heartlands. By June 1938, the Japanese controlled all northern China and on 6 June captured the ancient regional capital of Henan Kaifeng. It seemed that they would soon take the significant railway junction serving the Pinghan and Longhai Railways at Zhengzhou, endangering the major regional city of Wuhan.

The Chinese nationalist government was desperate to halt further Japanese inroads into western and southern China. With only limited strategic options, and at the suggestion of politician Chen Guofu, General Chiang Kai-shek decided to open the dikes (or levees) on the great Yellow River near Zhengzhou. The initial idea was to

Seminole Indians in the Everglades c. 1919.

Japanese artillery bogged down, Second Sino-Japanese War, 1930s.

break the Zhaokou dike, but they experienced difficulties there and so turned their attention to the Huayuankou dike on the Yellow River's southern bank. This was breached by tunnelling on 6 and 7 June 1938. The result was that water flooded into Henan, Anhui, and Jiangsu covering and destroying thousands of square kilometres of farmland. The effective course of the Yellow River was shifted hundreds of kilometres southward to flow into the Jialu River through Zhongmu County. This modified watercourse took the Yellow River into the Huai River via the Shaying River in Zhoujiakou. However, these were relatively small channels and they burst their banks causing widespread destruction in the floodplain. It was suggested by a post-war review that floods covered thirty-two per cent of the land and forty-five per cent of the settlements across twenty counties. With thousands of villages flooded, several million inhabitants had to flee their homes and became refugees. It is not known how many Japanese soldiers were killed by the flood, but the post-war commission estimated overall casualties may have been up to 800,000 fatalities including hundreds of thousands of Japanese.

The precise numbers of casualties from the inundation have been disputed with estimates revised by the Chinese government and other researchers in the post-war decades. Any assessment is problematic because many people, including government officials, fled. This meant there was nobody left to count the casualties. In the shifting battlescape of uncontrolled banditry, and ongoing warfare between nationalists, communists, and the Japanese, a headcount of casualties was not a concern. The nationalist government implied that the disaster was caused by Japanese bombing but then suggested the massive casualties suffered reflected the depth of sacrifice needed from the Chinese people in their war against Japan. They stated that twelve million people had been affected by the flood with the official Chinese history of the war estimating 900,000 dead and around ten million refugees. More research has reduced the estimates, but they are still horrific, with about 500,000 dead, three million refugees, and perhaps five million people affected with 500,000 left homeless.

Besides the massive death toll, the flooded areas were affected for years to come. The inundated countryside was virtually abandoned, and all crops destroyed. As the waters receded, most land was left uncultivable with a covering of silt. Many public buildings and other structures were destroyed along with housing, and survivors were left destitute. To compound the impacts on farmland, the agricultural irrigation channels were damaged. The widespread damage was also hard for the Chinese community to come to terms with; people were unsure whether the blame lay with the Chinese government or the Japanese invaders. Perhaps most people felt both sides were responsible. In the belief that the rural communities would support them, the Chinese communists used the flooded regions as recruitment grounds against what were seen as common enemies. By the 1940s, the region was an important guerrilla base called the Yuwansu Base Area.

As in other European examples, such as Holland in the Second World War, water can be a powerful weapon. However, its impacts can be indiscriminate and uncontrollable. Furthermore, the longer-term damaging effects of triggering a catastrophic flood may outweigh the immediate 'benefits'.

Wetlands as sanctuaries

The use of water as a weapon is just one aspect of the wetland battlescape. Another is that they have often been places of sanctuary that foster independence and non-conformism. Governments are not favourably inclined toward independent thinking and may seek to suppress it.

From China and the wars with Japan, and the subsequent conflicts between nationalists and communists, our attention turns to another very ancient seat of civilization: Iraq.

The Iraqi Marsh Arabs

The Marsh Arabs have lived in the Iraqi wetlands for millennia, on the fringes of mainstream society. Estimates in the 1950s suggested there were around 400,000, but numbers were higher when hundreds of thousands fled Saddam Hussein's repressive regime, becoming economic migrants. The original Mesopotamian marshes covered around 7,700 square miles (20,000 square kilometres) and their drainage took place from the 1950s into the 1990s in Iraq, less so in Iran. This was mostly to clear large areas of the Tigris-Euphrates River complex for farmland. Boats, called *mashoof* and *tarada*, were traditionally used for transport through the marshes and their associated channels, formed mostly by herding water buffaloes. The constantly wet environment meant that diseases like schistosomiasis and malaria were endemic.

The Marsh Arabs come by various names: Arabs of the Marshlands, the *Ma'dān* (dwellers in the plains), or *Shroog* (those from the east). Some of the terms are derogatory for people on the fringes and outside of society. These people inhabit the Mesopotamian marshlands in southern Iraq along with the Hawizeh marshes across the Iraq-Iran border. Consisting of different tribes and tribal groups their unique culture centres on the natural resources of these extensive wetlands. However, this lifestyle was severely compromised with the drainage, especially following the 1991 Iraq conflict. The draining of the remaining marshlands badly affected the natural landscape and resources it provided, though since Saddam Hussein's overthrow water

The Iraqi Marshes Kut El Amara, early 1900s.

The Marsh Arabs pictured in the early 1900s.

has been let back in and there has been a degree of recovery. The Marsh Arabs had two main occupations: one group bred and raised water buffalo and the other grew crops like rice, barley, wheat, and pearl millet. Sheep and cattle were also reared. Some Marsh Arabs were nomadic pastoralists with temporary shelters for living as, guided by the seasons, they herded their buffalo through the wetland. Living in a vast and productive wetland fishing with spears and poison was popular, but using nets was frowned on. This nomadic or semi-nomadic lifestyle led to the distrust of the Marsh Arabs by wider Iraqi society, compounded by long-standing rivalries between Sunni and Shia Muslims in Iraq. The marshes had long been a refuge for those persecuted for their religion by governments, and in the past, such as during the Zanj Rebellion (AD869–883 around Basra), they were a haven for escaped slaves and serfs.

In the 1970s, the expansion of irrigation projects in adjacent agricultural areas disrupted waterflow to the marshlands. By the mid-1980s, there was low-level insurgency in response to drainage and resettlement projects. Opposition was led by Sheik Abdul Kerim Mahud al-Muhammadawi of the Al bu Muhammad, known as Abu Hatim. Following the First Gulf War (1991) the Iraqi government expanded its programme to divert the Tigris and Euphrates rivers from the marshes as retaliation for an attempted Shia Muslim revolt. The objective was to remove the food supplies of the Marsh Arabs and discourage militiamen from taking refuge there. The wetlands were systematically converted to arid desert with marsh villages attacked and burned, and the water poisoned.

In this context of suspicion and a demand for retribution, Saddam Hussein accused the Marsh Arabs of treachery during the 1980–1988 war with Iran. Understanding the importance of the marshlands and the difficulty fighting, or even pursuing, a foe familiar with a vast wet battlescape, he decided to destroy their habitat instead. In the 1990s, the marshes were dammed and drained to drive out the potential insurgents finding sanctuary in the extensive reedbeds. The 1990s drainage was mostly for political ends and to drive the Marsh Arabs out of their waterscape. It was achieved by water-diversion tactics and was punishment for supporting the 1991 uprising against Saddam Hussein's regime. Nevertheless, the stated objective was reclamation for agriculture and the removal of malarial mosquitoes breeding grounds. However, the real reason for the actions was to displace over 200,000 Marsh Arabs and to inflict state-sponsored violence on them which led the international community to declare an act of ecocide and ethnic cleansing. The result was a tragic human and environmental catastrophe. Eyewitness accounts of Iraqi army tactics during the draining included the bombing of marsh villages and spreading of landmines in the

A munitions wagon, with shells for the front, plunging through a muddy swamp of a road October 1917, Western Front.

Second German crossing of the Marne, 1918.

Americans defending the bridge at Chateau-Thierry, 1918.

London Territorials at Pozieres, the Somme.

water prior to departing.

Observers stated that this was one of the worst environmental disasters of the twentieth century with several thousand Marsh Arabs killed. Of those remaining, most were driven out of the marshes, abandoning traditional lifestyles to assume more conventional agriculture or migrating to towns and camps elsewhere in Iraq. Between 80,000–120,000 escaped to Iranian refugee camps. Following Saddam Hussein's overthrow in 2003, local communities broke many of the dams to allow the land to re-wet. In the 1970s, these wetlands had extended over around 3,500 square miles (9,000 square kilometres), but by 2005 this

Hand-to-had trench fighting near Bordeaux, 1916, Western Front.

Adapting to the wetland environment with a French First World War hydroplane.

had been reduced to a mere 293 square miles (760 square kilometres). In 2002, the region had recovered around forty per cent of the pre-drainage area with the intention of increasing this to about seventy per cent. Some of the Marsh Arabs have returned to their old lifestyle but with current political and social disruption and uncertainty, the remote and expansive wetland has been used for illegal activities connected to drugs and arms smuggling, receiving stolen goods, and taking hostages for ransom. Furthermore, full recovery of the marshlands is unlikely because of ongoing agricultural abstraction and irrigation. The tribal leaders present outwardly submissive personae and

A French trench with loopholes for firing 1915.

appear to collaborate with the coalition and Iraqi government officials. At the same time, they actively engage in smuggling and other illicit activities. These challenges are exacerbated by poverty, political instability in the region and local feuds in the marshlands.

Canadian soldiers collecting cartridge cases and trench-mortar bombs, October 1917.

Wetlands, territories, and communities

Wetlands do not merely influence conflicts, as noted earlier they also shape and determine communities and attitudes. Waterbodies are often territorial boundaries and as such may be the focus of aggression and claims, along with providing barriers to movement between areas of land as well as routes for inland-bound waterborne transport. Communities living and evolving in these waterscapes, especially when they are large like the Iraqi marshlands, often develop distinctive characteristics and significant degrees of independence, and can be viewed as separate from mainstream society.

Throughout history, peat bogs and fens have provided sanctuary for people in times of conflict or oppression, and for non-conformists and those seeking to distance themselves from the law or the church. Rich in natural resources for those who know and understand their ways, but difficult to enter or transverse if you do not. These have been ideal hideaways from the time of Alfred the Great to Hereward the Wake, and from the nineteenth-century French forces in the Franco-German war, to the Marsh Arabs of Iraq seeking protection from Saddam Hussein. One consequence of the sanctuary wetlands provide from those in authority, is that central powers sought to remove them from the landscape and control both environment and people. Wetlands have been controlled by draining, dredging, and in every sense, converting them into conformity. Indeed, this has been the fate of many wetlands large and small over the last thousand years especially. Effective removal of major wetlands

Japanese artillery crossing a river under fire, early 1900s, Russo-Japanese War.

however does require political control, economic and other resources, and sometimes appropriate technology. Some large wetlands, marshes, bogs, and fens survived late into modern times due to the lack of one or more of these prerequisites for removal.

American soldiers cutting through the barbed wire, Western Front, First World War.

Chapter 7
Heaths, moors, and commons

The military significance and use of moors, heaths, fens, and bogs, extends back a long way. Across the countryside of many areas around the world, 'unimproved' wood-pasture (i.e., grazed, open landscapes with scattered trees) where a major part of the landscape and its economic systems. In Britian and much of Europe such lands were managed as various forms of commons which provided local resources and especially grazing for livestock. Many of these areas were relatively flat or else merely rolling hills, and were often dry, sandy heaths, or else if wet, were lowland moors, bogs, or fens, and in the uplands wet moors of blanket bogs. In upland zones the tops of hills provided important panoramic views across the wider countryside, and the flatlands generally, were suitable landscapes for organised conflicts. Certainly, once formal military warfare ensued, then heaths, commons, and drier flatlands were often the chosen battlescapes.

The moors and bogs of the English uplands

The moors and bogs such as around the western edge of Sheffield in England, with their Iron Age hillforts can trace a military presence across millennia. Terrain and topography were key factors in determining early settlement patterns with relatively limited early use of the wetter low-lying areas and zones of dense forests with large trees. Prehistoric sites tended to be on the higher uplands of northern England for example, where smaller trees were easy to remove, lighter soils were easy to till with primitive ploughs, and high elevation meant good distant viewing. This might enable easier communication with friendly neighbours but significantly helped identify the approach of potentially hostile tribes. Nomadic Mesolithic and Neolithic people hunted across these hilly landscapes, and then Bronze Age and Iron Age tribes formed villages, and farmed the land as settled communities. Some early cultures were transhumance, living with their domestic animals in summer shielings on the high ground but retreating downhill in winter. Certainly, by the Iron Age, the major settlements were on hilltops and tors where topography and terrain provided a defensive advantage and a visual significance in the landscape. In modern times, these lands of the Peak District were not only used as military training grounds, but as decoy areas to protect the vital steel industry to the east of Sheffield during the Second World War.

The flatlands of lowland England

Moors and heaths also provided the sites for airfields for the Battle of Britain and the strikes against Nazi Germany. Indeed, many these so-called wilderness landscapes have histories of conflict going back thousands of years. However, wetlands, especially peat bogs, fens and moors were of huge significance to military campaigns. In the landscape, these treacherous areas of neither firm ground nor navigable water, were a fundamental problem for soldiers or warriors, most of whom could not swim anyway. Furthermore, slip into a fen or bog when wearing armour and you sink slowly to a very unpleasant death. The Saxon troops of Hereward the Wake, holding out on the Isle of Ely in Cambridgeshire, drove the Norman invaders off the fragile causeways by firing the dry reeds. The Normans, in their chainmail, sank deep into the quagmire. Stamford Bridge had earlier been settled in a vast wetland landscape in which the one river crossing was a vital strategic key. This aspect of wetlands, moors, and bogs in the landscape was used to great effect by the Scots against the English at the battles of Stirling Bridge and Bannockburn. Battles such as Solway Moss, Culloden, and Flodden were all decided on the impact of a bog or wet moor.

Flanders Moss and the River Forth were of huge strategic significance in Scotland

Scottish Highlanders and English Redcoats around 1715.

and it is said that he who controlled Stirling Castle, the gateway to the Highlands, controlled Scotland. In England, many of the battles of the civil wars, such as the Wars of the Roses, and the English Civil War, were acted out on heath, moor, and bog. The Battle of Sedgemoor itself was a tragedy played out in a foggy, dank marshland; earlier, Alfred the Great had sought refuge in the nearby wetlands of Athelney.

Peat bogs and fens

The significance of these landscapes carried on throughout history and around the globe. In the European arena of the two World Wars, peat bogs and fens played major strategic roles, with the Dutch flooding the former peat cuttings to halt the German advance as they retreated. The Somme, and other catastrophic campaigns, were fought in vast wetlands and peat bogs. Transport or transit through fens and bogs was problematic and since early times, channels or canals were constructed to facilitate effective movement. With the coming of the Romans for instance, the English fenlands and bogs were brought under varying degrees of control through ambitious drainage schemes. However, the primary function of what were waterways rather than drains, was probably military. The canals were used to move men, animals, and supplies speedily and efficiently through otherwise difficult, dangerous, and slow terrain.

Definition becomes complicated here because, as the reader will already have noticed, there is a huge and often blurred overlap between habitats like heaths, moors, bogs, and fens. Furthermore, historical ecology indicates how in regions like Great Britain, dry moorlands today were much wetter until perhaps three or four centuries ago, and many fenlands included extensive heaths and bogs because of their patchy, underlying geology with sands and gravels deposited by glacial action.

Battlescapes by choice

Historically, moors, heaths, and commons in Great Britain and other similar countryside, were chosen as places for battles and skirmishes as well as for military training. Often this was because they were frequently flat, but particularly because they were open. Here, face-to-face military confrontation could take place. This face-off type of warfare is and was the complete antithesis to guerrilla warfare or hit-and-run skirmishing. However, the conditions of particular sites, and their landscapes, were very variable and many lowland moors were wet fens and potentially difficult terrain to traverse without good local knowledge. As noted, upland moors were generally much wetter than they are today, and indeed many would have been extensive boglands. Since the 1700s, there have been increasingly successful efforts to drain many of these lands.

It is worthwhile considering some better-known battles of moors and heaths.

A Scottish moorland – the battle of Culloden

The Battle of Culloden, fought on a bleak, wind-swept moor above Inverness in Scotland, marked both the end of the British Jacobite cause and in many ways the final death-throes of the old Highland clan system. With the French at war with Britain in 1745, they backed Charles Edward Stuart (Bonnie Prince Charlie or the Young Pretender) to gain the British throne at the expense of the Protestant Hanoverians, and hence re-establish Catholicism in the country. Having landed in the Outer Hebrides, Charles had marched south into England with some considerable success. However, lacking a popular rising of support from the English Catholics, Charles and his Jacobite supporters, having penetrated deep into England, waivered and then retreated to Scotland. By now they were hotly pursued by a Protestant loyalist army led by the Duke of Cumberland. So, on 16 April 1746, the two armies met on Culloden Moor. This was the sort of terrain familiar to the Highlanders and suited to the Highland Charge (see below), followed by hand-to-hand skirmishing, a fearsome tactic that might have been quickly deployed to great effect. This was indeed the advice of Charles's senior and more experienced generals. However, being in personal command, the prince hesitated to act and, while dithering, his Highland clansmen were mowed down by heavy gunfire from the highly trained British troops. The ill-disciplined clansmen were slaughtered, and the battle was over within an hour. Charles fled to France with his hopes of monarchy dashed and the Highland Clearances swept through the countryside. Scotland was changed forever.

The battle tactic of the Highlanders was in fact well suited to this sort of terrain. Before the seventeenth century, they fought in close formation fronted by heavily armed warrior elites bearing heavy battle-axes or claymores (two-handed swords or great swords). This approach was very effective until the introduction of muskets and cannon which rendered these formations very vulnerable. In response, the clansmen developed lighter, one-handed broadswords that were basket-hilted to protect the hand. This new weapon was mostly used in combination with a shield or 'targe' strapped to the weaker arm, and with a dirk or long knife clasped in that other hand. The tactic was called the Highland Charge and its use resembled older Celtic fighting styles of battle when one side rushed at the other to break the line of battle and disrupt their formation.

In practice, the charge was terrifying to face and a tactic which demanded a high level of commitment to implement. Clearly, the men rushing headlong into musket range would suffer serious casualties from at least one volley before they had reached their target. Since speed was vital, the Highlanders preferred to use this tactic downhill and preferably over firm ground. They removed clothing from their lower body to enable them to run faster. The charge worked by running forward in groups of a dozen at a time, frequently blood relatives, these groups forming part of a larger wedge-shaped formation to spearhead the attack. When the first groups came within musket range (about sixty yards) the clansmen with firearms would shoot. The resulting gun-smoke from the mass discharge would help obscure their enemies' own aim. To get some protection from the expected return volley discharged by the opposing force, the Highlanders crouched low to the ground immediately after their own volley had gone off. They then dropped their firearms, drew their sharp-edged weapons, and with a Gaelic battle-cry, made the final rush onto the enemy line. Once in striking distance, the Highlander attempted to catch his opponent's sword, bayonet point, or pike on his shield while at the same time striking low with the delivery of an upward thrust of his sword into the enemy's lower abdomen.

Culloden Cumberland Stone marks where the Highlanders made their last stand, April 1746.

The Highland charge was a potentially devastating tactic ideally suited to warfare on rough, dry, open moorland. However, against highly trained infantrymen armed with muskets, and on open ground, surprise is essential if this is to be effective. So, on Culloden Moor with its open topography, leaving the Highlanders exposed as Charles did, was a catastrophically bad decision, or perhaps indecision. If the moorland was wet and boggy as it may well have been, then that too would slow the advanced when the charge came. Overall, the Highlanders' battle-plan might have worked if executed immediately and with full force. Once the element of surprise was gone and their numbers depleted, the outcome on the open moor was a foregone conclusion. The British army of around 8,800 lost about sixty men on the day and a further 200 died later of their wounds. The Jacobites, with 6,000 men, suffered around 1,500 killed or died of their wounds. There followed widespread persecution and slaughter across much of the Highlands. Overall, Culloden was an example of tactics, technology and terrain combining, but compounded by catastrophic errors of judgment in taking forward the battle plan.

Military training grounds

Open heaths, moors, and commons were often used to stage mock military training battles from the medieval period up to the present day. In medieval England, such landscapes were locations for practice warfare, battles, and major jousting events. Furthermore, for royalty and aristocracy, the arts of riding and hunting were used to develop necessary skills for the battlefield. In times of peace, this was an essential way of keeping knights and others in top condition for when inevitable conflicts arose.

Around Sherwood in Nottinghamshire, England, the famous heaths of old Sherwood Forest became military training grounds, and in the Second World War, Clumber Park was a transit and camouflaged storage site for tanks and other military vehicles. Dartmoor, Cannock Chase and other heath and bog sites were used for military manoeuvres probably as far back as the Crimean War and had extensive permanent camps too.

Furthermore, these flatland sites of peatlands, heaths, moors, and commons were also brought into action as military bases during conflicts. An example of this was the wartime use of countryside areas in Britain for military aerodromes during the First, and especially the Second World Wars.

In the English counties of Yorkshire, Nottinghamshire, Lincolnshire, Suffolk, and Norfolk especially, commons, heaths, and fens were converted to use as airfields, some still surviving today. Some sites were acquired at short notice during the First World War to launch defensive fighter strikes against German Zeppelin raids into England. Later, in the Second World War, moors and heaths provided the sites for airfields for fighters in the Battle of Britain (July–October 1940), and then increasingly for the RAF Bomber Command raids into Nazi Germany. Additionally, some sites were made up as mock airfields and other military bases to lure incoming bombers to waste their payloads destroying airfields that did not actually exist.

War graves and passive roles

Bogs and moors especially, had further unplanned passive roles in warfare as the last resting places for stricken or lost bombers during the Second World War, the landscapes becoming the war graves of aircraft and their crews. Many of these crashed on Kinder Scout and Bleaklow in the uplands of Derbyshire's Peak District in England, and others on the extensive lowland bog of Thorne Moors in South Yorkshire and Lincolnshire. This is a tragic history, which should not be forgotten.

Other examples of the passive roles of peat bogs include places for troops to take shelter near frontline shelling in the First World War as described by a descendant of an Italian soldier. Shells dropping into deep, wet peat may fail to explode or if they do, then the impact is significantly absorbed by the peat. Similarly, during Allied

Mud bath. German shell landing harmlessly in the soft mud of the Western Front, 1914. Peat and mud were good at absorbing the impact of explosions.

bombing raids into Second-World War Germany, the returning bombers dropped any excess or unused payload on their route home. This served two main purposes including reduction of weight and hence reduced risk of running short on fuel, and a less hazardous landing on the return to Base camp. Again, according to a descendant, the German residents took to the nearby peat bogs as the safest places to hide and shelter from the impacts.

Contributions to the war effort

Peatlands, especially bogs and fens, provided materials of immense value to wartime efforts. For the First Word War these landscapes generated supplies of horse-litter for warhorses, sphagnum moss for surgery, alder buckthorn to make fine charcoal for explosives, and peat fuel. Similar usage also occurred during the Second World War but are now almost forgotten.

One of the main uses of peat in the late 1800s and early 1900s, was litter for animal bedding. Extraction from the moors of peat fuel had gone on since at least Roman times but was now on the wane. However, with vast numbers of animals powering farms, towns, and cities, there was a big demand for material to keep stables clean, and peat was ideal. Once soiled, its nutritive qualities were enhanced, and it went back on the land as fertilizer. Although raw peat was widely used as litter by farmers and peasants, this wider usage took off in the early 1900s. Processed and packaged as a commercial product, with its absorbent and fibrous nature combined with antiseptic properties, it was used extensively as horse bedding for the military animals during the First World War. For instance, at Thorne Moors in South Yorkshire, the English Moss Litter company extracted peat moss up to the 1960s, and from 1923–1962, the Midland Litter Company took moss from Fenn's Moss near Wrexham. Mixed with green fodder and perhaps molasses, peat was even used as animal feed, either coarse or as a powder mixed into a cattle cake or peat cake. Again, its antibacterial

Flat-bottomed peat barge on the Thorne Moors canals carrying peat for horse litter, 1900.

Dutch crew and a flat-bottomed peat barge, Thorne Moors, 1900.

German peat barge with turf on the north–south canal near Essen camp, 1941.

properties may have had a therapeutic effect. Peat dust was used for packing fruit.

To give some indication of the emerging demands for peat moss litter in the early twentieth century, nationally there was an increase in numbers of working horses to around 98,000 between 1901–1906. These were employed by railways, tramways, omnibus companies, various local authority undertakings, and of course many other businesses. Peat moss litter (dried peat) made an ideal bedding material for these working animals. Consequently, by the late 1890s, at Thorne Moors, the British Moss Litter Company was formed and took over various peat-works across the region, establishing themselves between the Don and Trent rivers. Alongside the system of canals and boats, there developed a network of narrow-gauge railways and connections to the wide rail network. A new pressing mill still known as the paraffin mill or the paraffin works was built in 1895, to produce gas for fuel, ammonia water, paraffin, creosote, methyl alcohol, tar, and even alcohol for motor cars. There is relevance of this history to a discussion of miliary landscapes. Established as a major centre for moss litter production, and employing, at its peak, around 350 men, Thorne Moors in South Yorkshire produced vast quantities of peat litter for the many warhorses sent to the First World War frontline. These had to be catered for and this included copious amounts of bedding. Furthermore, peat distillation along with that of cut bracken, was considered for production of vital petrochemical substitutes to power vehicles. These business diversifications at Thorne did not last long, and the mill closed post-War in 1922 as the use of horses for industry and transport declined and the moss litter business collapsed.

Conflict in peacetime

Nevertheless, another use emerged in the 1930s and 1940s, that of peat processed for horticulture and gardening. Horticultural peat was an afterthought in the exploitation process that brought catastrophe to the region's peat moors and bogs. This intensive and highly destructive use triggered conservation 'battles' into the 1990s by the so-called Bunting's Beavers and others. These were campaigns to save the remnants of the once-vast South Yorkshire moors that grew and spread nationally and ultimately internationally, in a battle for the planet's ecology called the 'Peat Campaign'. This is increasingly relevant today in terms of the use of landscapes to capture atmospheric carbon and to battle climate change. As described, the English moors and bogs supported and influenced many aspects of warfare over the centuries. Perhaps some of the least known of these uses was the harvesting of sphagnum moss for wartime medical uses, and the use of peat as horse-litter.

Fuel for fire ships

Another instance of the role of bogs and fens in warfare was the use of dried reeds from fenlands to fuel fire ships in maritime conflicts, a naval tactic used throughout the ages. For example, it was recorded that during the Late Han Civil War in China, around AD208, two rival armies numbering about 50,000 soldiers on the one hand and 220,000 on the other, came head-to-head in a naval conflict. The rebel admiral, under the pretext of seeking peace, sailed fire ships laden with dried reeds and inflammable wax into the opponent's vessels. These ships had previously been lashed together to provide greater stability but now proved immovable under this sudden, unexpected attack. Panicking under the surprise assault and consequent conflagration, the Han soldiers retreated ashore. However, thousands died as they went overland through unknown and unplanned terrain, because the road they followed led into a swamp where many of the soldiers drowned. This example combines the clever use of resources from the wetland with the impact of a forced passage over land that turns out to be a swamp.

A return to the Anglo-Scottish wars

The Anglo-Scottish conflicts ranged over many centuries and varied from localized border raids to full-blown wars and invasions by one side or the other. The countryside in which these bitter conflicts often raged was dominated by heath, moor, bog, and common. Having already suffered major problems in Scottish campaigns, relief for the English King Edward II did not last overlong. He was soon defeated again by the Scots, this time at the Battle of Old Byland, Byland Moor, or Byland Abbey in England. The battle was a significant conflict in October 1322, between English and Scottish troops as part of the on-going Wars of Scottish Independence. With victory for Edward over his English baronial opponents at Boroughbridge, supposedly heralding a new start for the king, and his internal opposition temporarily quashed, this battle was a military high point in his reign. Probably emboldened by his rare victory he now set out on a final invasion of Scotland. However, this was to end in disaster for the English crown.

When Edward began his military advance during early August, King Robert Bruce of Scotland was ready and prepared. The usual tactics were brought into play. As the Scots slipped away northward, the crops were destroyed, livestock removed, and the Scottish army withdrawn beyond the River Forth. Here they simply played a waiting game. Consequently, when the English arrived, they found no food and no opposition. It is said that in the whole of Lothian the English found only one lame cow, sparking a remark from the Earl of Surrey that, 'This is the dearest beef I ever saw. It surely has cost a thousand pounds and more!' As Edward marched on Edinburgh, the troops at Leith were forced to retreat for want of food, suffering sickness and famine. Additionally, Edward's light horse troop was defeated by James de Douglas and because of harassment from the Scots, few soldiers dared leave the main ranks of the English army to forage for food. By the time the English army arrived back in Newcastle, rampant disease and starvation meant the army had to disband.

In a gesture of anger and defiance, as they retreated southward across the border, English troops destroyed both Holyrood Abbey in Edinburgh and the borders abbeys of Melrose and Dryburgh. The invasion of Scotland achieved absolutely nothing but distress and acute embarrassment with worse to follow. The impact on English national morale of this ignominious retreat by their starving army was up there with the loss to the Scots at Bannockburn. But the English retreat was not the end of this sorry saga since it heralded further Scottish attacks and incursions. Already, based on good knowledge of local conditions and terrain, plus avoidance of a single, major, face-to-face conflict, the tactics and strategy had paid dividends.

Now, however, King Robert Bruce and his army crossed the Solway in the west and then turned southeast toward Yorkshire and York. He brought with him many soldiers from Argyll and the Scottish Isles. The speed and boldness of this incursion south, known as 'The Great Raid of 1322', was a stark reminder to Edward of the dangers lying in wait deep into his own kingdom. After his retreat from Scotland, the English monarch resided with Queen Isabella at Rievaulx Abbey in North Yorkshire, but the attack by Bruce, sudden and unexpected, meant that by mid-October there was little between the Scots and a decisive royal prize. The only significant barrier was a large English force commanded by John of Brittany, the Earl of Richmond.

The battle of Byland

Earl John took a position on Scawton Moor, between Rievaulx and Byland Abbey; to ease him from this strong station on the high ground, the Scots employed tactics that had brought victory at the earlier Battle of the Pass of Brander. Lords Moray and Douglas attacked up-slope toward the English while a troop of Highlanders climbed the cliffs to the side of the English flank to mount a Highland charge downslope and into Richmond's rear-guard. English resistance soon crumbled under this double assault and Old Byland became a rout. Numerous nobles, including Henry de Sully, Grand Butler of France, Sir Ralph Cobham ('the best knight in England'), Sir Thomas Ughtred, and Richmond himself were captured, with others killed on the battlefield or in flight.

As events unfolded, Edward, regarded as 'ever chicken hearted and luckless in war', had made a rapid and undignified exit from Rievaulx. This was so hasty that he left his personal belongings behind. Following Byland, it was said the Scots became so fierce, and their chiefs so daring, that the English before them were cowed, like a hare before the greyhounds. This battle in Yorkshire, within striking distance of York itself, was a major victory for the Scots, and though far smaller in scale, was the most significant since Bannockburn.

Site of the Battle of Tewksbury on the River Severn, 4 May 1471.

The role of York in the northern battlescape

During this period of the Anglo-Scottish Wars and the weak-willed reign of Edward II, some of the most significant, yet today little-known, battles were fought in and around Yorkshire. Indeed, for much of a forty-year period York itself was the functional working capital of the English kingdom, and an important forward-base for major military operations. York is strategically placed, between rivers and wetlands with good, navigable access, in northern England. The royal court was at York and key functions of government, such as the exchequer or treasury, were based there. York was at this time the lynchpin for national politics and warfare and therefore any threat so close to the strategic city was a direct assault on the English seat of government. This situation continued until in the 1330s when Scotland and England reached a degree of relative peace; the city lost its significance as the war capital, and the English Government returned home to London. However, wars within England were ongoing as factions vied for political control, and battles in the war zone of the Yorkshire rivers, heaths and moors continued over the centuries.

The Wars of the Roses

Originally known as the Cousins' War or simply The Civil War, of all the English civil wars, the Wars of the Roses were perhaps the bloodiest. They were fought in

England between the Houses of York and Lancaster for over three decades during the fifteenth century. The 'royal' houses were both branches of the same royal family.

Civil war tends to be bloody and bitter, and this especially nasty conflict continued with the son of Richard Duke of York, having crushed the Lancastrians in battle, claiming the throne as King Edward IV. Although briefly deposed in 1470, he regained the throne soon afterward and enjoyed a long and successful reign. While the conflict was spread over more than thirty years, the Wars of the Roses included relatively few months of actual combat and fewer than twenty significant battles. some of them particularly gruesome.

Ferrybridge

The most dreadful battle of them all, perhaps one of the worst ever fought on English soil, was Towton. The preliminary engagement was the Battle of Ferrybridge, also in Yorkshire west of York, fought on 28 March 1461. Following his father's bloody death, Edward proclaimed himself King of England and marched north to the Lancastrian stronghold beyond the Yorkshire River Aire as King Edward IV, gathering a substantial army on the way. On 27 March, in charge of the York vanguard, the Earl of Warwick crossed the river at Ferrybridge. The bridge had been broken by Lancastrian soldiers and so the Yorkists repaired the gaps with planks. During the hazardous crossing, Warwick and many men were subjected to a combination of ice-cold river water and a hail of Lancastrian arrows from the northern riverbank. However, once the river was crossed the Lancastrians were driven back, the bridge repaired, and Warwick and his force well established on the north bank.

The following morning, the York vanguard was ambushed by a large Lancastrian troop under Lord Clifford and John, Lord Neville, Warwick's cousin. Surprised and confused by this, the small Yorkist force suffered serious casualties including second-in-command Lord FitzWalter. He was mortally wounded while rallying the troops and died a week later. Warwick's half-brother, with the unfortunate title of The Bastard of Salisbury, was also killed. While retreating, Warwick was himself struck in the leg by an arrow. Overall, it seems around 3,000 men died at Ferrybridge. Topography, a key river crossing, and extreme cold weather were all significant factors in the outcome. These were compounded by the element of surprise in the counterattack and a big difference in numbers between the two sides.

After Ferrybridge, Edward arrived close to the scene and with his main force. Now combined with Warwick, they returned to the Aire River bridge which was again broken by the Lancastrians. Warwick sent his uncle, Lord Fauconberg, upstream with the York cavalry to cross via the Castleford ford. From there they set off in

View of Clifford's Tower, York, in the 1970s.

The siege of York in 1644.

pursuit of the Lancastrian force. Within sight of the main army, Fauconberg caught Lord Clifford and his troop, beating him in a furious struggle. Clifford was killed by an arrow to the throat after he inexplicably removed his protective armour. The preliminaries were now over.

The battle of Towton

Ferrybridge was the precursor to the Battle of Towton fought on 29 March 1461. This second bloody conflict involved the Yorkist forces of Edward IV against the Lancastrians of Margaret of Anjou and took place near the village of Towton located southeast of York, south of Tadcaster. This horribly violent battle confirmed Edward, Duke of York, as King Edward IV (1461–1483) in place of the troubled Lancastrian, King Henry VI (1422–1461). The head of the Lancastrian claim to the throne, together with the principal Lancastrian supporters, was driven from England. The battle was described as the largest and bloodiest ever fought on English soil, though Boudicca's defeat to the Romans at the Battle of Watling Street runs it close. It is believed that around 50,000 troops took part, with some estimates as high as 80,000. Fighting for hours in a snowstorm on that bleak Palm Sunday, close to 28,000 men died on the battlefield. This was a battlescape where weather, water, and topography took their toll.

The engagement began with Edward considerably outnumbered because his ally, the Duke of Norfolk, was late arriving at the field. The battle started with an exchange of arrow volleys followed by the armies closing for fierce hand-to-hand fighting. While the Lancastrians had a strong topographical position on high ground, the appalling weather became a key factor. With snow blowing into their eyes in this exposed and open countryside, the Lancastrian archers could not see their targets, and importantly for archers, the wind was also against them. For the York archers, the strong wind behind them, their arrows were carried high and far. They were also able to reuse the fallen arrows from the Lancastrian bowmen that had fallen short. After ten hours of unrelenting fighting the nearby river in this wet landscape ran red with blood. Finally, as the Duke of Norfolk arrived with fresh troops, the battle turned in York's favour and defeat for the Lancastrians. Edward IV was confirmed as the incumbent king, and aside from a brief period in 1470, he ruled a relatively stable country until his death in 1483.

The English Civil War of King versus Parliament

As indicated previously, much of England's long history has involved civil wars of one sort or another. The conflict known as The English Civil War was especially

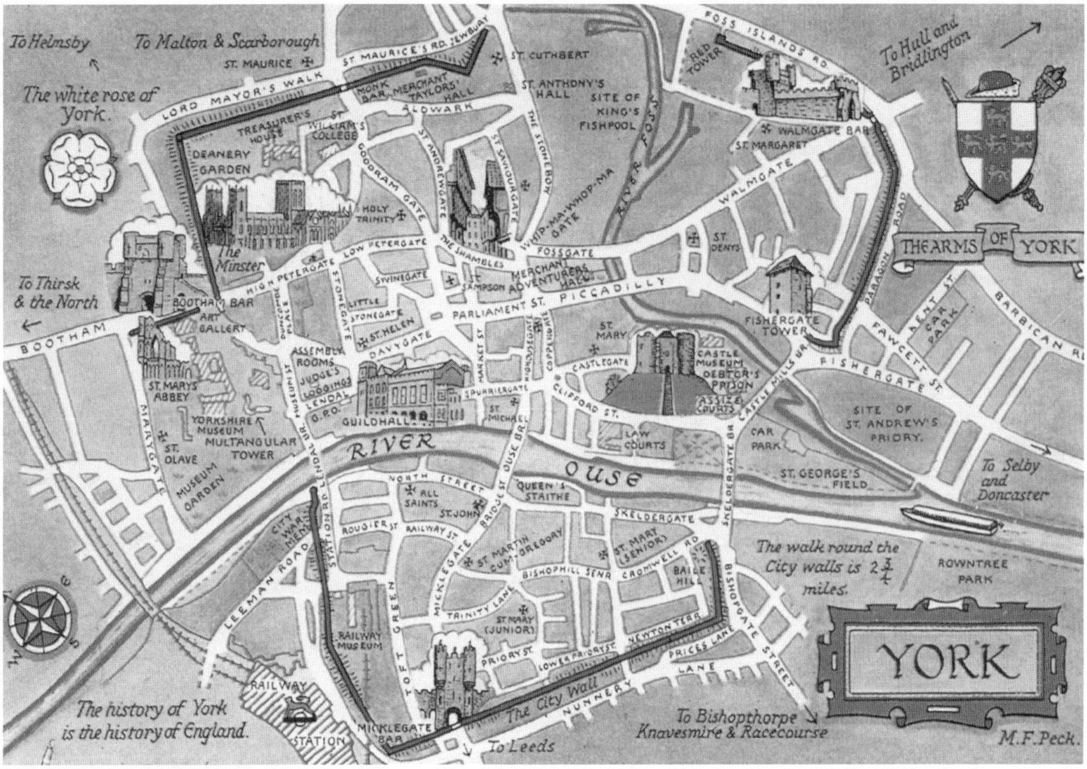

York City shows the strategic position of the castle between the two rivers and the extensive marshland with the massive city walls build between Roman and medieval times.

unpleasant and in very many ways changed the course of history. Many of the individual battles took place on the open flatlands of heaths, moors, and commons. Conflict began around 1629 when King Charles I dismissed Parliament and arrested MPs and finished in 1649 when he was tried and executed.

Throughout its long military history, England has endured or experienced many conflicts that amounted to civil war. However, the term is generally reserved for the bitter conflicts of the mid-seventeenth century between the royalists and the parliamentarians. Within this rather drawn-out endeavour, the Siege of York (a city whose battlescape significance has already been discussed), and associated Battle of Marston Moor on yet another wet, lowland flatland site, were a turning point in the overall conflict. In both the wider strategic context, and the closer detail of the final battle, topography and terrain played major roles. Medieval York was situated on largely dry ground in a site established in Roman times and occupying land between two rivers, the Ouse and the Foss, with the Derwent close by. Extensive marshes, carrs, and peat bogs dominated much of the landscape. The city was at a high point up the navigable River

View of the York city walls in the 1970s.

Ouse with effective access downstream to the great Humber Estuary and the North Sea. Moreover, from Roman times, throughout the post-Roman times and into the medieval period, York was strategically well-placed to control or at least influence much of northern England.

Adwalton Moor and Newcastle

In 1643, the royalists won the Battle of Adwalton Moor near Bradford and so established control over much of Yorkshire. However, parliamentary forces under the command of Sir Thomas Fairfax, moved north to counter this and, during the summer of 1643, laid siege to York, a royalist

A typical soldier of the Stuart period.

stronghold defended by the Marquess of Newcastle. Earlier in the year, during March and into early April in 1643, the Marquess acted to delay or prevent the Scottish Covenanters – sympathetic to the parliamentarian Puritan cause – from crossing the Tyne River. This was to stop them surrounding Newcastle-upon-Tyne and securing, and then controlling, the river crossing which was of major strategic importance. However, a parliamentarian cavalry force under Sir Thomas Fairfax had crossed the Pennines and entered west Yorkshire from Lancashire. To prevent Sir Thomas joining his father, Lord Fairfax, in Kingston-upon-Hull, the royalist troops south of York occupied Selby. However, Sir Thomas's Roundhead army with infantry reinforcements under Sir John Meldrum, took Selby, capturing the royalist leaders.

York's Monk Bar pictured by H. Earp about 1820.

For the Marquess of Newcastle, this confirmed York as under immediate threat, and as the principal centre of royalist power in northern England, its loss would be a catastrophic blow to the King's cause. The Marquess left Newcastle to counter any possible attack by the combined Fairfax force on York itself. The Scots Covenanters' leader, Lord Leven, now took the Newcastle garrison which he left under the Earl of Callendar and also went south toward York with his main army. By 2 April the parliamentarians and Scottish Covenanters joined up at Wetherby, perhaps fourteen miles west of York. From here they proceeded east to lay siege to the city.

York under siege and the impacts of royal commands

The siege of York began as a relatively loose blockade by the parliamentarian allies as they attempted to take the smaller royalist garrisons around the city. It was these smaller forces that were particularly important as they potentially controlled or severed communications with parliamentarian forces at Hull. However, by 3 June, the parliamentarian force had been reinforced by the Army of the Eastern

Association under the Earl of Manchester, and York was encircled. The siege now began in earnest with Lord Leven commander-in-chief of the combined armies, described as the Army of Both Kingdoms. This was an astute move to bolster the Scottish Covenanters in the north where the Royalists were traditionally stronger than the parliamentarians. Furthermore, Lord Leven was a veteran of the European Thirty Years' War and therefore an experienced, highly respected, battle-hardened soldier. York was now under serious and direct threat of being seized for parliament.

Prince Rupert of the Rhine, King Charles' cousin, was the primary military commander of the Royalist armies. Indeed, he was one of the outstanding military leaders of the English Civil War. So as news of the York siege reached Oxford, King Charles' wartime capital, from 24 April to 5 May, there was a council of war with his advisors including Prince Rupert. It was decided that Charles would play for time in Oxford, while Rupert took an army to relieve York. Rupert gathered his troops and marched through northwest England capturing Liverpool en route. As he went, his army gathered reinforcements along the way. From Lancashire he cut across the Pennine hills and down to the plain of York. With the intention of relieving the city. Rupert arrived at the head of an army of about fifteen thousand and the parliamentarian siege was broken.

Aware that Prince Rupert's force was near, the parliamentarian allies hoped that expected reinforcements with Sir John Meldrum and the Earl of Denbigh might arrive from the English Midlands. However, when it was realized that these forces would be too late, their vulnerability was clear: although their troops encircled York they were separated by the city's rivers and wetlands. This meant they might be exposed to attack one-by-one, and on 30 June the siege was abandoned. The allied armies moved close to Hessay village before assembling on Marston Moor to block Rupert's expected path to York, the old Roman road of Ermine Street (today's A59). Now placed in a strategically advantageous position, the parliamentarian force could also move south to stop Rupert's army cutting through the alternative route via Wetherby, if that proved to be the case. When Rupert arrived at York he was unsure how best to proceed, and news from Oxford compounded his doubts. Charles had sent a rather ambiguous message:

'But now I must give the true state of my affairs, which, if their condition be such as enforces me to give you more peremptory commands than I would willingly do, you must not take it ill. If York be lost, I shall esteem my crown little less; unless supported by your sudden march to me; and a miraculous conquest in the South, before the effects of the Northern power can be found here. But if York be relieved, and you beat the rebels' army of both kingdoms, which are before it, then (but otherwise not) I

A city of massive medieval defences – York's Walmgate Bar pictured in the early 1900s.

may possibly make a shift upon the defensive to spin out time until you come to assist me. Wherefore I command and conjure you, by the duty and affection that I know you bear me, that all new enterprises laid aside, you immediately march according to your first intention, with all your force to the relief of York. But if that be either lost, or have freed themselves from the besiegers, or that for want of powder, you cannot undertake that work, that you immediately march with your whole strength, directly to Worcester to assist me and my army; without which, or you having relieved York by beating the Scots, all the successes you can afterwards have must infallibly be useless onto me.'

Rupert took it as a command to relieve York, defeat the allied army, and *then* go south to support the King at Oxford. When he departed Liverpool to travel to Preston, his army was around fourteen thousand. On arrival the parliamentary forces surrendered without resistance. He had gone to Clitheroe to cross the Pennines at Skipton, stopping there for three days from 26–28 June, to take stock and undergo necessary maintenance. Reinforcements had also arrived from Cumberland and Westmoreland. From here, on 30 June, Rupert and his army reached Knaresborough Castle where the garrison was another royalist stronghold. Now just fourteen miles northwest of York the next move was on to the city itself. Then, with the allies having abandoned the siege, some of Rupert's cavalry were able to reach the city to contact the garrison.

The Battle of Marston Moor

With York relieved, the Marquess of Newcastle, who was overseer of the city's defence, sent Rupert a message of welcome and congratulations. Rupert responded with a command for the defending army to march from the city walls and to meet with his troops on the field of battle. The intention was to face the parliamentarian army on Marston Moor, but the troops occupying York were reluctant to leave the city. Some were unwilling to fight until being paid money already owed to them. Because of these problems, Rupert's force was depleted even before the battle commenced. This was to prove critical to the outcome.

Eventually Rupert was joined on Marston Moor by the Marquess of Newcastle and a mounted troop of 'gentleman volunteers'. The prince greeted them with, 'My Lord, I wish you had come sooner with your forces, but I hope we shall yet have a glorious day'. Erring on the side of caution, Newcastle wanted to await the arrival of an expected force of 3,000 troops under Colonel Clavering and another 2,000 from garrisons gathered en route before joining battle. However, Rupert was persuaded by his message from King Charles that he should engage and defeat the enemy immediately. Surprising the enemy might help the cause by catching them unawares, thus countering their numerical inferiority.

Nevertheless, deprived of Newcastle's infantry and his own men exhausted from their long march and allowed a short rest, the numbers tipped even more in Parliament's favour, especially as additional Scottish and parliamentarian infantry and artillery arrived on the scene. Early on 1 July, the royalist cavalry, having advanced from Knaresborough Castle, assembled on the moor and the two forces prepared for battle. Rupert had taken his main force on a twenty-two-mile northeastern flanking movement, crossing the Ure River at Boroughbridge and the Swale at Thornton Bridge. These two rivers merge to become the Ouse River that flows to York. Using the natural wetland topography of the York district Rupert placed his troops behind this defensive terrain. Significant also was the defeat of the Earl of Manchester's dragoons by Cavalier forces at a bridge over the Ouse at Poppleton north of York, the only river crossing available to the allies above the city. With the other crossing, constructed from boats, at Acaster Malbis five miles south, its loss prevented attempts by allied troops to cross the river and restricted their engagement with the royalist army.

As these skirmishes began, the two armies of Rupert for the king and Fairfax for Parliament, locked horns on and around Marston Moor. This was to become one of the biggest Civil War battles and one of the largest battles ever fought in England. The Battle of Marston Moor took place on 2 July 1644 and involved a combined allied force of English parliamentarians under Lord Fairfax and the Earl of Manchester, and Scottish Covenanters under the Earl of Leven. They faced the royalists under Prince Rupert and the Marquess of Newcastle. The allies gathered on a ridge of higher ground overlooking the moor, with the royalists on the moor itself with Wilstrop Wood behind them. Marston Moor has long since been obliterated by modern farming, but at the time it was a 'wet moor', very flat and marshy or boggy. Often such flat sites like commons, heaths, or moors were chosen for battle locations because troops could be assembled there and cavalry could readily be deployed. However, in such terrain, there are inherent problems of exposure to cannon fire and open vulnerability to enemy assaults. Furthermore, there is nowhere to hide.

The casualties at Marston Moor were exceedingly high but, as is often the case, difficult to assess accurately. The main engagement began around 19.00 hours and two hours later, with a gathering thunderstorm, it was almost fully dark but with a rising full moon. With orders from Lord Leven, Oliver Cromwell and his Roundhead cavalry launched a surprise attack under cover of darkness. This assault smashed into the royalist cavalry's right flank to devastating effect, though the left flank withstood a second cavalry charge. The royalists then attacked the parliamentary infantry; the final phase was as Cromwell turned and successfully attacked the cavalry at the rear of the royalist stand. As the battle ran its course, the countryside around York lay littered with the dead; confused fugitives from both sides wandered aimlessly in the riverine wetlands and marshes. The two armies probably numbered about 18,000 royalists and 28,000 allies. Something like 4,000 royalist troops were killed, many were Newcastle's 'whitecoats', slaughtered in a final brave stand. Furthermore, with something like 1,500 royalist soldiers captured, their army lost all its guns and hundreds of other weapons.

Prince Rupert's right wing and reserve were routed by a combination of Cromwell's cavalry and the covenanters' infantrymen. He only avoided capture by hiding in a nearby beanfield; this whole episode was a disaster from which he never fully recovered. For Rupert especially, defeat was a bitter blow with Marston Moor being the first time in the Civil War that he suffered loss. Deeply affected by this he kept the king's letter close to him for the rest of his life. During the battle, his faithful dog Boye, a constant companion throughout his campaigns, was killed; something that was celebrated in parliamentarian propaganda after the conflict.

The outcome was a crushing defeat for the heavily outnumbered royalists, whose leaders actively distrusted and disliked each other. Many of their troops had refused to fight. The parliamentarian allied army claimed only 300 soldiers killed but given the scale and ferocity of the conflict, this seems rather optimistic. Regardless, the parliamentarians suffered significant individual losses. One mortally wounded officer was Sir Thomas Fairfax's brother, Charles, another was Oliver Cromwell's nephew, Valentine Walton. The latter was struck by a cannonball early in the battle.

Late into the night, royalist generals and the stragglers from their army made the short journey back to the sanctuary of York. The city's defenders were worried that parliamentarian cavalry might enter York with, or close behind, the fugitive royalists, so Sir Thomas Glemham, the Governor of York, only allowed those who were part of the garrison in, just those few officers who had volunteered to take part in the action. However, the streets leading to Micklegate Bar, the western gate into York were already crammed with wounded and fugitive soldiers.

With his forces broken, defeated, and slaughtered, the Marquess of Newcastle had spent his fortune supporting the royalist cause. He decided to leave, to avoid the 'laughter of the court', and departed for Scarborough the day following the battle, 3 July. With many of his senior officers, he sailed to exile in Hamburg. Two days after the defeat, Rupert gathered about 5,000 cavalry and a few hundred infantrymen mounted on spare horses, and left York via Monk Bar. He went northeast to detour around Richmond and avoid interception, going back over the Pennines into Lancashire and then south to join up with King Charles at Oxford. Following Marston Moor, the siege of York began once again with the city surrendering on 15 July 1644. Pillaging and looting followed, with considerable damage to many important buildings though some were saved by the personal intervention of Lord Fairfax, a native Yorkshireman who sought to limit damage to York's churches, and especially the Minster.

Marston Moor, the siege of York, and its associated skirmishes, demonstrate the important roles of terrain and topography as critical determinants in conflicts. The rivers and wetlands were especially significant in influencing the choice of the battlefield and in limiting movement around and within the battlescape. The deployment of troops in the countryside was strongly affected by topography of hills and dales, and then by the rivers, marshes, and other wetlands. These factors were utilized by both sides in terms of their tactics and strategies, ultimately in the retreat from the field. Overall, the result of the conflict was achieved through sheer force of numerical advantage, in part due to a refusal of many of the incumbent force to fight, which turned the battle into a rout by the allied force. York and Marston Moor demonstrate the complex interactions between topography and terrain, together with leadership and politics in determining a battlescape outcome.

The loss of royalist influence in northern England

With the exile of Newcastle and the escape of Prince Rupert, and apart from a few isolated garrisons, the royalists lost their significant influence in northern England.

One by one, remaining loyal forces were gradually overcome, though a northern counties royalist cavalry detachment called the 'Northern Horse' continued to fight under Sir Marmaduke Langdale. When, in February 1645, they relieved the royalist garrison at West Yorkshire's Pontefract Castle, their undisciplined, licentious behaviour swayed former supporters from the cause. Indeed, this was one of the final royalist skirmishes near York. Having been with Charles during defeats at Naseby and Rowton Heath, they were returning north under Lord Digby and Sir Marmaduke Langdale. The cavalry attacked and defeated a parliamentarian garrison in Sherburn-in-Elmet, southeast of York, but the victory was short lived. A second parliamentarian troop with Colonel Copley counterattacked and routed them, the final engagement taking place in October.

The strategic importance of York as the primary northern stronghold of the royalists was thus ended. However, despite the problems caused by the Civil War, York eventually recovered its position, influence, and significance. Its strategic location was key to its importance, but its position on the navigable rivers, and its relative protection by rivers and extensive wetlands, were also critical.

Battle of Naseby

The wider Civil War conflict continued with a battle on 14 June 1645 regarded as a key turning point in the war. At this point, despite several victories, the parliamentarians had failed to achieve an overwhelming advantage. South of Leicester in a shallow valley near Naseby in Northamptonshire, the royalists occupied the higher ground. Then, as the parliamentary army moved from wet boggy terrain to a higher area, the Cavalier cavalry charged with considerable success. They employed a tactic acquired by Prince Rupert from his European campaigns, of massed horses close together called the 'thunderbolt charge'. This swept through the Roundhead army to great effect. However, instead of pressing home their advantage, the ill-disciplined royalists pursued the fleeing parliamentarian troops and the baggage train. When they returned to the field, the king's army had been routed by Cromwell's Roundheads, and Charles had fled the scene. This was an early encounter with Cromwell's New Model Army of professional cavalrymen and the royalist cause was effectively lost from then onward. Key decisive moments were initially the shifting of Lord Fairfax's parliamentary troops on the advice of Oliver Cromwell, off the wet, boggy ground, which triggered Rupert's nearly successful cavalry assault. Turning victory into defeat however, the cavaliers moved temporarily out of the conflict to plunder the baggage train. This folly allowed Cromwell to annihilate the remainder of the royalist army with twelve thousand Royalist forces beaten by fifteen thousand Parliamentarian

Cavaliers at Naseby, 1645.

soldiers. Defeat at Naseby ended any realistic hope of Royalist victory, though Charles did not actually surrender until May 1646. In this case, good knowledge of wetland terrain, a resulting change in tactics, and ruthless discipline, and the lack thereof, were key factors in the victory.

The First English Civil War took place in England and Wales from 1642 to 1646 and was followed by the Second English Civil War between February and August 1648 in England and Wales. Into the early 1650s, there were further conflicts as Cromwell sought to suppress the Irish and the pro-monarchy Scots. As in the first period, landscape and topography played significant roles in the major conflicts.

Topography and terrain on heath and common

When we consider the roles of heaths, moors, and bogs in wars and individual battles, it is clear that open ground enables certain types of military strategies to be played out in the flatland landscape. Significant barriers in the flat countryside might be rivers and river crossings and areas of marsh, fen, and bog which themselves are intrinsically dangerous and make movement through them problematic. Dry heath or common allow easy deployment of troops, both infantry and cavalry, but marshy or boggy areas offer defence against easy attack but are also hazards, especially when unseen. Furthermore, while open ground allows coordination and control of an army, the same openness can leave troops vulnerable to enemy attack. This applies across the board, whether using arrows in a medieval battle or artillery and tanks in modern warfare. Moreover, in expansive undrained wetlands, a local population of fighters can drift away into the swamp or to wet woodland, where a superior force may struggle to follow.

The Highlanders piping themselves back from the trenches, First World War.

British soldiers detonating unexploded shells, October 1917.

The Greek army in the Kresna Pass in Bulgaria during the Second Balkan War between Greece and Bulgaria, 1913; this image highlights the treacherous conditions of mountain warfare.

Chapter 8
Mountains and other barriers

Mountain ranges and lesser hills often mark territorial boundaries and historically separate communities. They delineate uplands from lowlands often with different cultures, and distinct tribal or national regions. Such rugged and often remote terrains also provide places to which indigenous people can retreat during threat of hostilities and provide formidable barriers to military incursions. Local knowledge and insight such as routes of safe passes and trackways can be hugely influential. In this context a relatively small group of indigenous fighters may hold off and outsmart a much larger force of invaders.

Medieval Spain and Islam

Expansive terrain and significant mountain ranges influenced the medieval conflicts in Iberia, between the European Christian cultures and the Islamic forces of

Italian Alpini lassoing an Austrian machine-gunner in the Alps, April 1916.

Austrian Alpine troops in the Dolomites, 1916.

North Africa and the Middle East. With much of southern Spain overrun by the Mohammedans in the early medieval period, the losses of significant strongholds spurred Pope Innocent III to mount a crusade to return the country to Christianity. In 1211, the various Christian powers set aside their own squabbles and gathered a force of around 13,000 Christian fighters to reclaim the lost territories. However, their passage through mountainous regions was difficult and blocked by the army of Amlohad caliph Muhammad al-Nasir. Mountains can form a significant barrier in themselves, but they also provide terrain within which fighters can be deployed to good effect. Nevertheless, the Christian force, led by Alfonso, negotiated the difficulties with the aid of a local shepherd who guided them through a hidden pass. They were therefore able to take their opponents by surprise. After days of negotiation and then fighting, the Christian army eventually prevailed, and the Moslem force fled after suffering heavy casualties. This victory proved to be a turning point in the Reconquista or reconquering of Iberia and the return to Christianity which was completed around 1500. The difficulties presented by mountainous regions were demonstrated but so too was the benefit of local knowledge of the terrain.

Bathhouse Chesters Roman Fort, Northumberland.

Carthage and the Romans

The Punic Wars between the Carthaginians and the Romans raged between 264BCE and 146BEC, as the rival civilizations battled for supremacy in the Mediterranean, North Africa, and southern Europe. Rome felt threatened by the growing imperial dominance of the Carthage city state in Spain, Sicily, and beyond. During the Second Punic War in around 218BCE, the Carthaginian army was led by Hannibal Barca in an invasion of Italy. In a strikingly brilliant and daring move Hannibal brought his army over the Alps, a barrier which the Romans had always assumed was impassable. The conflict swung in favour of the Carthaginians with a single battle costing 70,000 Roman lives, but ultimately, they lost as Hannibal hesitated and Rome countered with an invasion of Carthage.

In crossing the Alps, the mountain pass took its toll; most of the Carthaginians' war elephants perished. However, this case shows how misplaced confidence in topographic defences can lead to near catastrophic outcomes, and how a visionary commander can utilize terrain and topography to brilliant effect. Hannibal's bold move nearly paid off, but as is often the case with the Romans, they eventually won.

Hadrian's Wall following the natural topography to maximise visual and defensive impact.

The Roman invasion of Britain

The total conquest of Britain eluded the Romans, and while England was largely Romanized, the more remote areas remained stubbornly intractable to its influence. The zones were remote, often mountainous, frequently forested, and sometimes very wet. Transit was often difficult, and the terrain generally favoured the indigenous peoples. One stratagem was to establish roads and forts in key locations. Another ploy was to develop supply routes for supplies and troops to move quickly either around the coast or along canals cut through the vast swamps and wetlands of the time. Combined with long-distance beacon signalling from signal posts around the shoreline and on significant high points across the countryside, this approach enabled the conquest of much of the territory and very nearly the capture of the whole area by the Roman General Agricola.

However, at a key point in the campaign, Agricola was recalled to Rome, his legions were largely withdrawn, and the opportunity was squandered. In their attempts to subdue the native tribes, topographic barriers such as expansive hills and mountains were critical, but so too were extensive wetlands with fens, bogs,

Emperor Constantine at the Battle of Miliran Bridge, between the Roman emperors Constantine I and Maxentius, an important route over the Tiber, 28 October, AD312.

marshes, and dense areas of forest. In all these situations, relatively small groups of untrained and disorganised warriors could hold out and fight guerrilla tactics with a degree of success. If the trained legions could coax the tribes into direct head-on battle on flat, dry ground, then the overwhelming advantage lay with the Romans. Some of the indigenous combatants quickly learned this and adapted their own tactics to avoid full-on conflict. This situation was similarly described in another chapter with the war between Napoleon and the Russian Empire.

The Cumbrian Mountains in northwest England

Roman Cumbria was an area that lay on the northwest frontier of Roman Britain, and indeed of the Roman Empire itself. The regional term 'Cumbria' is a much later designation that the Romans would not have used. Interest in the Roman occupation of the region lies in this frontier context and leads to some key questions concerning their strategic viewpoint. For example, why did the Romans choose to occupy the northwest of England, and why build a solid barrier in the north of this region (Hadrian's Wall)? Furthermore, why was the region so heavily militarized and to what extent were the native inhabitants Romanized compared with their compatriots in southern England?

The decision to conquer the area was taken by the Romans after the revolt of Venutius threatened to turn the Brigantes and their allies, such as the Carvetii, against Rome, having formerly been pro-Roman tribes. After a period of conquest and consolidation, based on the Stanegate line, with some coastal defences added, Hadrian decided to turn the previous turf wall into a solid, largely stone-built one. Although abandoned briefly in favour of the more northerly Antonine Wall, the

Hadrianic line was fallen back upon and remained for the rest of the Roman period in Britain. When we examine Hadrian's wall, one of the outstanding features of this extensive and complex, often multi-layered, structure of walls, banks, and ditches, is how it maximizes topographic impact and utilizes the potential defensive nature of the terrain. The wall often follows dramatic and precipitous rocky escarpments and outcrops to give enhancement to the defensive nature of the construction but also visual impact to any British tribes approaching from the north. What we have here is a clear statement of Roman civilization, power, superiority, and law. The wall ends on the south banks of the huge Solway Firth. To the north lie the largely unconquered, and to the Romans, uncivilized, lands of the Scots and the Picts. Heading eastward the wall joins the Solway to the Tyne to form an obvious political and topographic barrier separating Roman rule from the tribes beyond.

The issues for Cumbria as a region relate to its geographic location on the edge of empire, but are further complicated by the Romans' need to maintain pre-Roman tribes in the quasi-independent sub-kingdoms. One of the most powerful British tribes in northern England was the Brigantes; Venutius was their first-century leader at the time of the Roman conquest. He may have been one of the Carvetii tribe that was part of the wider Brigantes confederation. His significance also comes to the fore around AD51 as the husband of Cartimandua, queen of the Brigantes. It is documented that the British resistance leader Caratacus was defeated by Publius Ostorius Scapula in Wales and fled north to seek sanctuary with the Brigantes. However, Queen Cartimandua simply handed him back to the Romans. Although the Brigantes were an independent kingdom, the Roman writer Tacitus stated that Cartimandua and Venutius were loyal to Rome. Within the politics of the time, this meant they were, to an extent, defended by military Roman power against other warlike neighbours and tribes.

Nevertheless, with Caratacus gone, Venutius became the most prominent leader of British resistance to the Roman occupation. The situation was complicated since Queen Cartimandua, apparently tiring of him, had married his armour-bearer, Vellocatus. The latter was then made king of the Brigantes in place of Venutius. Initially, Venutius's objective was to overthrow his ex-wife, but this grew into open revolt against the Roman occupation and Queen Cartimandua's Roman protectors. Venutius did achieve a degree of success; fighting from remote mountain strongholds always carries advantages. However, with this affront to their power, the Romans defended their client queen and during the governorship of Aulus Didius Gallus (AD52–57) the revolt of Venutius was put down by General Caesius Nasica.

This sort of tribal unrest tended to be associated with these remote and often mountainous regions. Disturbances might be triggered by temporary incursions from tribes north of the wall raiding south, and sometimes due to changing politics within the empire itself affecting the Roman legions in and around Cumbria. While resistance was maintained in the mountainous heartlands, and was difficult to totally eradicate, around the major Roman settlements like Carlisle along the Wall itself, and around the numerous forts, many British tribes became significantly Romanized. In the west of Cumbria, the Romans moved troops and goods by ship through major centres with ports, such as Ravenscar. Throughout the mountainous interior, the major passes were occupied, with Roman forts established along these arterial routes to keep law and order.

Roman Wales

The Welsh kingdoms were troublesome and problematic for the Romans. These were very independent tribes in difficult, rugged, remote terrain and while access by sea helped, the inland zones were difficult to penetrate and to hold militarily. Certain key locations were important, such as the major legionary bases at Chester in the north and Caerleon in the south. With a strongly Romanized presence in these centres, a degree of regional influence and control might be exerted. However, parts of Wales held particular significance to the Britons across the country because of the Druidic influence, and its stronghold in Anglesey. This island off the northwest coast of Wales, was a major centre of Celtic pagan traditions; it was here that many druids retreated from the Roman onslaught. Determined to destroy Druidic practices and their influence over the British Celtic tribes, the Romans moved inexorably toward the island. The destruction of the Druids by the Romans through the occupation of Anglesey took place in AD77 and effectively ended their wider influence.

The Isle of Anglesey (Mona to the Romans) is a windswept island located in the northwest of Wales, bordering the Irish Sea. Megalithic burial chambers and standing stones mark the island's habitation by late Neolithic and early Bronze Age peoples. It is 261 square miles (675 square kilometres) in area with low and fertile valleys running northwest to southwest and was an early centre for cultivation of grain and rearing stock. However, by around 100BCE, the islanders spoke Celtic languages and associated customs were adopted as the community grew to become the most significant Druidic stronghold in Britain.

The Romans first came across these native holy men during Julius Caesar's brief visitation in 55BCE. However, it took over a century for them to conquer Anglesey and destroy most of the sacred Druidic traditions. Across the Roman Empire, druids were largely known for their savage rituals, ceremonies, and human sacrifice, though

Modern-day Druids celebrating at Stonehenge in the 1970s.

some of this was perhaps Roman propaganda. The most famous of these sacrificial events was the burning of a wicker man, with victims tied to wooden effigies and set alight to burn to death. There was also the triple death whereby the victim was strangled, drowned to the point of near death, and then stabbed. There were various levels of druids with ranks marked by different coloured robes: standard in white, sacrificers in red, bards in blue, and junior recruits wearing brown and black. The Romans' attitudes, documented in their writings from the time, suggested they saw druids as distortions of nature, to the extent that their absolute destruction was the only solution. However, coming from the culture that killed hundreds of people and animals in amphitheatres for mass public entertainment, such criticism seems a little rich. Indeed, it is likely that the image was much exaggerated as part of the justification across the wider empire of the brutal colonization of Britain. Other north European tribes would have had connections to the Celtic Druidic beliefs too.

Romanization

The build up to the conquest of Anglesey in AD59 took over a hundred years while the Romans tried to absorb Britain into its wider empire. This process began in 55BCE, when Julius Caesar crossed what is now the English Channel with two legions. As the Roman fleet approached Dubris, now the 'white cliffs of Dover', they found the shoreline lined by massed Britons brandishing spears. Caesar decided to move on down the coast to land at Pegwell Bay. This was to be a brief foray and the Romans quickly returned to Gaul. Then, in 54BCE, Caesar returned, this time with five legions amounting to 2,000 cavalry, and 27,000 men in 628 ships. The landing was unopposed following prior political negotiations. Indeed, the English chieftain Mandubracius of the Trinovantes had sent an envoy to Rome with promises of allegiance if he received assistance in retaking his throne from his bitter rival Cassivellaunus of Catuvellauni. The latter, understandably intimidated by the mass of the Roman force which had come ashore, avoided direct confrontation. Instead, the Britons engaged in a guerrilla warfare which made use of their 4,000 highly mobile charioteers. Nevertheless, the Roman army pressed on to cross the Thames River and capture Cassivellaunus's capital, installing Mandubracius on the throne but clearly now as a Roman puppet.

Over the next almost hundred years, from 54BCE to AD43, the Romanization increased to generate a power base in southeast Britain, overseen by British elites who adopted the Roman culture and lifestyle. With four main trading routes established, the wilder western and northern regions of Britain were sources of trade and slaves. This uneasy situation was maintained until, in AD43, a British tribal leader called Caractacus began to expand his influence and foster anti-Roman sentiment. This resulted in Emperor Claudius despatching legions commanded by Aulus Platius to bring Caractacus into line and further expand the Roman territory. From AD43–47, as the forces sent by Claudius moved across England, and then westward toward Anglesey, most British tribes capitulated. Indeed, a century of Roman rule with their imports, culture, and conventions now adopted by many natives, had softened the opposition. This first phase of subjugation was relatively smooth.

The subjugation of Anglesey

Then, from AD47–60, the Romans looked westward and ultimately to the spiritual centre of resistance in Anglesey. Finally, in AD59, a Roman legion commanded by Suetonius Paulinius, approached the Penmon Peninsula on the Isle of Mona (Anglesey), and was appalled by the spectacle before them. On the island's beach were huge numbers of druid men and women shouting, chanting, and waving their arms so wildly that the legionaries were perplexed and bewildered. However, once their nerves had settled, they set about destroying the druids and their sacred groves. Although most Druids were annihilated by the attack, some managed to escape across the sea to the then little-known island of Ireland. One reason for some druids escaping was that the Romans had received news that in southeast England, Queen Boudicca had rebelled and was advancing on the Roman centres of Colchester and St Albans.

However, the Roman legions returned to Anglesey in AD79, triggered by the massacre of an auxiliary squadron by the north Wales Ordovices tribes. Gnaeus Julius Agricola, a junior officer in the AD59 campaign, and now a senior Roman commander, undertook a further brutal invasion of Anglesey. This time, with the help of native auxiliaries well acquainted with the region's geography, it was reported that Agricola led a surprise attack as his soldiers swam the Menai Straits (The Narrow Water) that separate Anglesey from the mainland. Whether or not this is true is questionable as the crossing is notoriously dangerous with strong and variable riptides. It is possible that the sea level was lower than today, and there is a narrow section of the strait across which cattle were formerly driven between the island and the mainland, so perhaps at low tide it could be crossed. However, it was suggested that the Druids had expected to see a fleet of ships and were taken aback by the sudden appearance of the legionnaires on shore. The Druids were wiped out, and Agricola went on to similarly subdue the other warlike tribes of northern England. The persistence of the Druids throughout the early period of Roman settlement was down to the remoteness of their spiritual centre and then the specific topography of the Menai Straits and Anglesey itself. Their downfall can be in part perhaps due to an over-confidence in the security of their terrain, and the unexpected arrival of legionnaires but without ships.

Contested spaces and landscapes in post-Roman Britain, the case of Wales

Following the fifth-century departure of the Roman legions from Britain, the remaining Romano-British came into conflict with successive of invading tribes from Europe. The resulting wars were battles between the Anglo-Saxons, who later formed into the Kingdom of England, and the Britons, the pre-existing Brythonic population of Britain south of the Antonine Wall, who came to be known later by the English as the Welsh. This was along with conflicts between the English and Welsh in subsequent centuries. The main military engagements followed from around AD446, when the Anglo-Saxons are said to have arrived in Britain, to the late Middle Ages when England annexed the whole of Wales in 1535. The so-called Welsh were pushed back to the region's most remote area from southeast England, essentially from where the Angles, Saxons, and Jutes were most dominant. These remote areas included Wales itself and by the medieval period were separate tribal areas ruled by Welsh princes with on-going issues of Anglo-Saxon or English overlords wishing to control them. However, throughout much of Wales the mountainous topography

The sack of Bath by the Saxons.

aided independence of culture and thought. The conflicts ebbed and flowed with further complications arriving with the Viking onslaughts in the AD800s which brought the Welsh and Saxons together against a common enemy, for a while.

The eleventh century gives a good idea of the military and political fortunes of the kingdom. A united England emerged and even the Welsh were, for a time, unified under Gruffudd ap Llywelyn. However, Gruffudd was killed during ongoing conflicts before the Norman conquest of England. Saxon incursions into Wales preceded savage assaults on the country by the newly established Norman overlords of England. Some important moments are highlighted below and many of these hinged on the inaccessibility and remoteness of the mountain terrain and topography across the principality.

1. 1039: Battle of Rhyd y Groes where Gruffudd ap Llywelyn, recently crowned King of Gwynedd, ambushes and destroys a Mercian army led by Leofric of Mercia in Brycheiniog.
2. 1052: Gruffudd ap Llywelyn invades Herefordshire and sacks Leominster.
3. 1055: Gruffudd ap Llywelyn allies with the exiled Ælfgar, Earl of Mercia, and ravages Herefordshire.

The iron grip of the Norman-English subjugation of Wales; Harlech Castle as built in the 1300s.

4. 1062: Harold Godwinson, Earl of Wessex, and his brother Tostig start a series of campaigns on behalf of the English crown against Gruffudd ap Llywelyn in retaliation for many years of border raiding, Gruffudd is killed.
5. 1066: Battle of Hastings and the Norman defeat of the Saxons.
6. 1067: Bleddyn and Rhiwallon ap Cynfyn, co-rulers of Gwynedd, invade Herefordshire to support Eadric the Wild, an English rebel resisting the Norman conquest of England.
7. 1067: Having utterly conquered the whole of England in under two months, the Normans invade the Kingdom of Gwent and drive King Caradog ap Gruffudd into exile.
8. 1073: The Normans invade Gwynedd and occupy Arfon.
9. 1085: The Normans launch a wholesale invasion of Gwynedd and Powys.
10. 1091: The Normans seize lowland areas in the kingdom of Morgannwg (formerly Glywysing) driving Iestyn ap Gwrgan into exile.
11. 1093: The Normans and their English subjects advance into Brycheiniog and kill Rhys ap Tewdwr, the King of Deheubarth.
12. 1094: Aber Llech is the culmination of a national uprising across Wales that largely drives the Normans back into England. Deheubarth makes territorial

Conway Castle, North Wales, 1970s.

gains at the expense of other southern realms.

13. 1095: The Normans return but fail to draw the Welsh into battle.
14. 1098: The Normans occupy Gwynedd and Anglesey but withdraw within the year.

For any conquering force entering Wales, terrain and topography combined with relative remoteness to make life very difficult. First, there was the problem of penetrating deep into mountainous heartlands and subduing the native tribes. However, even if this was achieved, there was then the more difficult task of holding on to these gains and supplying fortresses with men and provisions. This proved to be an ongoing challenge for the post-conquest English. The new king of England, William I set about establishing his English domain with earldoms imposed along the Anglo-Welsh borders at Chester, Shrewsbury, and Hereford. From these bases the newly arrived Norman overlords began to make inroads westward into Wales itself. In 1081, William personally took an army into south Wales as far as St David's and during the 1080s and 1090s, the Normans conquered and settled the Vale of Glamorgan in south Wales through to Pembrokeshire. During the reign of William's youngest son, King Henry I, Norman settlement in south Wales was further encouraged and is reflected in the construction of royal castles such as Carmarthen in 1109. Nevertheless, the Welsh princes refused to submit to Norman rule and retook some of the lands after Henry's death in 1135.

Welsh resistance was significantly strengthened by Llewelyn Fawr (Llewelyn the Great) who became Prince of Wales in 1194. His armies drove the English from north Wales in 1212, and in 1215 Llewelyn even went beyond the principality to take the English town of Shrewsbury. This long-serving Welsh leader reigned until 1240 and defeated numerous attempts at reconquest by armies of the English kings (now Henry III). After his passing, Llewelyn's son Dafydd was Prince of Wales

The impressive natural topographic defences of Harlech Castle in North Wales pictured in the 1970s.

from 1240 to 1246, and Llewelyn II (his grandson ap Gruffydd) reigned from 1246. Fierce nationalism, a strong leader, and the rugged mountainous terrain, clothed by extensive forests and peat bogs, proved a mix powerful enough to preserve Welsh nationalism.

However, a key turning point was in 1272, when, following the death of King Henry III, his son Edward I became king of England. Edward had a justifiable reputation as an astute military campaigner but also one with vicious, brutal tendencies, and expansionist aims. Disdainful of the Welsh and the Scots, his intention was to totally subjugate them, and it was said that he had a particular dislike of the Welsh prince Llewelyn ap Gruffydd. Through three major military campaigns on a scale the Welsh could not hope to match, Edward attained his desired subjugation of Wales. In 1277 the first invasion was along the north Wales coast by a huge English army with heavy cavalry. With limited ability to resist, Llewelyn accepted the humiliation of Edward's peace terms. However, in 1282, led by Llewelyn's brother Dafydd, the Welsh were pushed to the point of rebellion throughout northeast Wales and Edward reacted by leading another invasion. One result was that on 11 December 1282, at the battle of Irfon Bridge, Llewelyn was killed. Welsh resistance continued into 1283, under the leadership of Dafydd, and through into the following year. Unfortunately, in June 1283, the Welsh handed him over to Edward and he was tried and executed.

Conwy Castle, North Wales, pictured in the 1970s showing the massive medieval walls and towers overlooking the Menai Straits. It was built in the 1300s as part of Edward I's suppression of Welsh independence.

With the Welsh ruling dynasties in shreds, Wales was in effect an English colony, as ratified by the Statute of Rhuddlan in 1284.

To hold the lands and influence gained, the Normans constructed massive stone-built castles across the country at key strongholds. This imposed Norman-English rule but did not fully sway the rural communities in more remote areas. As in many cases throughout history, and around the globe, there is a big difference between merely defeating a tribe or country into subjugation and maintaining control over the longer term. Supply lines can be stretched and vulnerable, and mountain and forest provide endless places where indigenous fighters can slip away and hide. To guard the independently minded Snowdonia region, following the first invasion, Edward built Flint, Rhuddlan, Builth, and Aberystwyth castles and after the second, Conwy, Caernarfon, and Harlech. Finally, after the Welsh rebellion in 1294, and over a thousand years since the Roman conquest, Beaumaris Castle was constructed to hold the Isle of Anglesey.

A final line in the history of Welsh resistance relates to the 'uncrowned prince of Wales', Owain ap Gruffydd (c.1359–1416) otherwise known as Owain Glyndŵr or Glyn Dŵr (Owen Glendower). He was a Welsh nobleman, connected to the former

Harlech Castle, North Wales, viewed in the 1970s.

Princes of Gwynedd, Powys and Deheubarth, supposedly a descendant of Llewellyn the Great, and became a military leader. The lord of Glyndyfrdwy, he rose to lead ten years of Welsh resistance during the Late Middle Ages. Glendower was the last Welshman to claim the title Prince of Wales and at the peak of the rebellion, between 1403–1406, Owain controlled most of Wales, including significant English castles. With a national parliament at Machynlleth, the uprising was the final throe of the Welsh independence movement, but the end came swiftly when, by 1407, the English retook Anglesey and much of south Wales. In 1408, they seized Aberystwyth Castle, and then Harlech Castle in February 1409; Wales was formally annexed to England by the Laws in Wales Acts of 1535 to 1542. Even today, the often remote and rugged landscape is imbued with a sense of cultural, if not political, independence. Mountains, deep narrow valleys, forests, and peat bogs protected Welsh independence for centuries, but ultimately politics and economics won the day.

The case of Scotland in northern Britain

While the Romans did get north into Scotland and established the Antonine Wall in AD142, running east to west from the River Forth to cut Scotland in two, and with southern areas under Roman influence, this was a short-lived venture. They fell back to Hadrian's Wall in the south. The strategy of Agricola was to establish forts along major routes and passes through the countryside and especially the Highlands, and to move troops and supplies most effectively around the coastline by ship which avoided many areas of difficulty and speeded movement and communication. This strategy could have worked but was stretched to breaking point by remoteness, difficult terrain, and warlike, fiercely independent tribes. The more southerly areas which were inherently less remote and less rugged, were probably more amenable to Romanization and trade. Overall, this was perhaps a step too far for the Romans and problems at the core of the empire, meant the withdrawal of military resources at the wrong time for the initiative to be successful.

The people north of Hadrian's Wall were regarded by the Romans as uncivilized and barbaric and generically described them as Picts. Probably originating from Scandinavian tribes there is little known of these people or their history, because apart from a few Roman writings, nothing was recorded. They left some art works and inscriptions but little else, and ultimately, they probably merged into the southern Scots' cultures. One claim to military fame is that despite numerous violent engagements, the Picts held their territory against the invading Romans. While they lost individual battles, they 'won the war' and in this sense the Scotland of the Picts holds the distinction of never falling to the invading might of the Roman Empire. The Picts were mentioned in written records from AD297 until c. 900 when there is no further account.

Testing tactics at the Battle at Mons Graupius

The most significant incursion was in AD79–80 when the Roman governor of Britain, Julius Agricola, invaded Scotland. By AD82, his legions had established fortifications on a line between the Clyde and Forth rivers. Following the setting of this bridgehead, in AD83, Agricola invaded northern Scotland where he faced the Pictish tribal leader Calgacus at Mons Graupius. Roman historian Tacitus recorded details of the battle though it is unclear how much was true and how much was invented. Mons Graupius was an example of the Pictish tribes setting aside their rivalries and coming as one under an overall elected leader when threatened by an external force. It was suggested that Calgacus had a force of around 30,000 men facing 11,000 Roman soldiers of the 9th Legion from York and Malton. The Picts attacked the Romans in a style customary of their tribal warfare which was essentially a headlong rush at the opponent followed by fierce hand-to-hand fighting. The Roman legion held firm in their disciplined formation and withstood the assault.

They then counterattacked and the Picts scattered before them into small bands and disappeared into what Tacitus described as their 'far and trackless retreats'. The apparent rout was in fact a tactical manoeuvre as they 'had retreated back into the forests and mountains', and this is where the landscape and detailed knowledge of topography and terrain come to the fore. Calgacus was in reality testing the Roman tactics and power.

The legion had won the battle with the possible slaughter of up to 10,000 Pictish warriors, but they couldn't win the subsequent war. With their tribal society based on scattered small settlements in remote, mountainous, and forested countryside, there were simply no towns or cities to capture. This landscape, and the social order it supported, did not suit the Roman style of battle and conquest, followed by occupation, because essentially, there was nowhere to take and hold. Rather than being focused on a single major settlement in a particular region, the Pictish tribal system meant they lived off the land, and they could move quickly from one place to another. There were no towns to conquer, farms to burn, or other resources to capture and control. Furthermore, after the experience of the battle at Mons Graupius the Picts had learnt their lesson and avoided full-on confrontations. Instead, they fought a guerrilla campaign from the mountains and forests, where they could attack, harry, and disappear from whence they had come. Essentially the Picts, fighting on their home turf and knowing the lie of the land, were unconquerable by the Romans because they had an effective strategy implemented by appropriate tactics. This was all new to the Roman legions who failed to adapt. They were unable to subdue the enemy that lived, moved, and fought unlike any others they had faced. It would later also prove successful for the Germanic Goths under Athanaric resisting the Roman invasion of their lands around AD367–369. In many ways this has parallels to the American Seminoles in the Everglades wars of the 1800s.

One response by the Romans was to accept that the Picts were unconquerable; this was established in the countryside by an imperial demarcation. In AD122, Emperor Hadrian ordered the building of his now-famous wall running over seventy-three miles (120km), from coast to coast. This was sometimes a ditch with a turf wall, but often a stone wall of up to fifteen feet or more, with mile-forts and occasional major settlements. The Romans went further under the reign of Antoninus Pius and in AD142, constructed the Antonine Wall further north. These walls did not physically stop the Pictish raids, but they were important psychological barriers, marking as they did the boundary of empire. The walls provided demarcation between the southern lands under Roman civilized rule and the uncivilized Pictish barbarian wilderness to the north. The same ploy was used in North Africa where recently discovered

The medieval stronghold of the Campbells of Glenorchy: Kilchurn Castle, Loch Awe, Argyll, Scotland in the 1980s.

boundary posts have been found under the shifting desert sands and again mark the separation of empire from the lands beyond.

For Scotland and the Picts, the countryside they occupied with its mountains, glens, and forests, combined with the way they lived and were organised, created a situation that the sophisticated military might of Rome was unable to overcome. This was almost a blueprint for guerrilla warfare and resistance throughout history. While the first and only frontal attack on the legions resulted in defeat and massive loss of life by the Picts, their strategic and tactical responses won the war. This was a battlescape of rugged hills and mountains, with great rivers, bogs, marshes, and forests. Furthermore, the Scottish coastline boasts innumerable islands and sea lochs to which and through which a mobile force can retreat, manoeuvre, and hide. This countryside becomes the ideal landscape of resistance and a formidable terrain for any would-be conqueror however sophisticated their military machine.

Mountains and hills as topographic resistance

Topography, especially mountains or hills, have often tipped a conflict one way or the other. This was the case in the eighteenth-century wars between Austria and Prussia and indeed with numerous conflicts throughout eastern and central Europe in the medieval and early industrial periods.

With mountains, vast forests, and extensive peat bogs and marshes, Poland has been a landscape for warfare since time immemorial. Sandwiched as it is between European powers such as Germany and Russia, this has been a region contested by vying interests both within Poland and beyond. In the mid-1700s, with ongoing conflicts across the European continent, Prussia was under severe pressure from a coalition force of Russia, France and Austria. So, in late 1757, King Frederick II (later 'The Great') of Prussia took the fight to his enemies; in November he marched against a Franco-Austrian force which he routed at Rossbach. His troops then turned to meet the army commanded by Charles of Lorraine which had recently captured Breslau in Silesia. The Austrian army numbered around 66,000, about twice that of the Prussian force. However, at the time, the latter were considered the best-trained and most-disciplined military command in Europe.

With precise tactics Frederick feigned an attack on the right of the Austrian army while cunningly from a battlescape context, moving his main force behind a range of low hills that masked the ploy. The manoeuvre enabled the Prussians to launch a surprise infantry attack on the Austrian flank with the full support of artillery and cavalry. The ruse was dramatically successful with fierce combat effectively rolling down the Austrian lines from the side resulting in a resounding victory for Frederick, establishing his reputation as one of the greatest military tacticians of the era. The Austrians suffered around 22,000 casualties to the Prussians 6,000. Something like one in six of the troops taking part were wounded or killed and Frederick went on to capture Breslau (modern-day Warsaw). This European example shows clever military tactics and knowledge of local terrain used to great advantage to achieve a notable victory. Furthermore, knowledge of the battlescape enabled them to use topography to conceal a military manoeuvre and this proved very effective.

The European wars in Canada

At around the same time as Leuthen played out in Poland, European powers were in conflict around the world as they pursued competing claims for expanding empires. In this context, Britain and France were at war over the conquest of the New World, and in the case that follows, the battle for Quebec in Canada is a good example of where extreme terrain and the assumption of impregnability can prove decisive.

By 1759, in what is regarded as the world's first global conflict, Britain was at war with France and the French Canadians over control of the French North American colonies. British General James Wolfe took his troops up the St Lawrence River to launch an assault on Quebec, at the time the capital of New France. Landings to the east of the city failed because of fierce resistance from entrenched French soldiers and, fearing the onslaught of extreme winter weather, Wolfe decided to try an alternative, and very bold approach. If he held back too long, the winter ice in the river would necessitate withdrawing until the following year, and the alternative was to scale the rugged west of the settlement. Protecting that side of the city was a

The Citadel of Quebec as stormed by the British army, 1780s.

117-foot (fifty-four-metre) high almost sheer cliff that was considered by the French defenders to be unassailable and therefore only lightly guarded. Once again, we see the perception of topographic invulnerability put to the test.

On the night of 12 September 1759, having climbed the cliffs as quietly as possible and under cover of darkness, the 4,000 British redcoats surprised the French garrison and were able to assemble on the Plains of Abraham. It was onto this position that the French commander, Montcalm, marched, supported by cannon-fire. Having lain flat on the plain to avoid the worst of the cannon volleys, the redcoats stood up to face the French infantrymen with controlled musket-fire. The impact was so great that the French troops broke and fled, pursued by the redcoats. Although victorious, the latter took a heavy toll from muskets and Wolfe himself was killed, becoming a British national hero with the fall and capture of Quebec. Montalm was also fatally wounded.

In this case, the terrain, with protection from assault by both river and cliffs, helped the initial defence of Quebec. However, the assumption that this natural topography was impregnable was the undoing of the French garrison and the decision to use the topography to his advantage won the day for Wolfe. Triggered by the threat of a long winter and inclement weather delaying their progress, Wolfe took the bold decision to scale the cliffs. Victory was the result but with a huge loss of life, including his own and that of the French commander. The ongoing conflicts in the New World continued with the American colonies seeking independence; in many of these battles the natural landscape, terrain, and forest cover were to prove decisive often guided by knowledge and insight from native American scouts.

American War of Independence and the Battle of Saratoga

The Battle of Saratoga was a battle that the British should not have fought since so many factors turned against them, contributing to a very demoralizing defeat. Following the American 1776 Declaration of Independence from British colonial rule, Britain was seeking to reassert power and control. The British General John Burgoyne marched an army south from Canada with the intention of taking New York. However, following a failed attack on an American garrison en route, with Native American auxiliary forces having deserted, and now short on supplies, the expedition was going badly. Furthermore, US General Horatio Gates had fortified his position close to the Hudson River at Bemis Heights, a position that now blocked the route south for the British. Burgoyne decided to attack but his troops were being sniped at by US riflemen hidden in the adjacent woods. Though they suffered heavy losses, the British held their position and attempted further attacks, but to no avail. Eventually the British fell back north to Saratoga and ultimately surrendered.

Burgoyne's troops mixed British regular redcoats with so-called Hessians, highly trained German soldiers who fought with massed musket shots before advancing into enemy lines with bayonets fixed. Gates also took a European view of tactics whereas his second-in-command, General Benedict Arnold, favoured a less-formal, more partisan tactic suited to the US troops who had less training and were recruited from farmers and other frontiersmen but who knew the terrain. The US fighters were experts at exploiting forest cover and were excellent at sniping from concealed positions. The effective use of forest cover and high ground, together with tactics to make the best of the terrain and topography, carried the day and ultimately were perhaps major factors in winning the war. Remarkably, considering the outcome, General Arnold was relieved of his command for insubordination at the point where he drove a wild charge at the British force that successfully turned the battle. This tactic was achieved at some cost, including injury to himself, but his insight into the landscape and knowledge of appropriate tactics for wilderness fighting were the key.

European conflicts exported to North America

In the late 1700s, the Napoleonic Wars were engulfing the European continent and at around the same time, these imperial powers were contesting the global new worlds in America, Africa, and Asia. From North American forest fighting in Canada, we move south to the United States. Some conflicts in this globalizing world were between European imperial superpowers (as discussed above), whilst others were between them and the indigenous peoples they sought to displace or subjugate. From the earliest European visitors in the westward expansion of the United States, white settlers often encountered Native Americans or 'Indians'. While many contacts were peaceful, the cultures frequently clashed as the Europeans were taking the land and resources away from the indigenous people. This situation resulted in conflicts with hundreds of battles and skirmishes between the Indians and the pioneers who were encroaching on their territories, as well as between indigenous tribes and the US Army. The Indian Wars are regarded as taking place from 1866 to 1890 and are the most long-lived American war to the present time. More accurately the conflict ran from around 1775 until 1924, a 250-year period of North American history resulting from Europeans seeking to seize and control Native American land.

With European settlers moving ever westward after 1780, there was an increased size, duration, and intensity of armed conflicts between settlers and Native American Indians climaxing in the War of 1812. The inevitable outcome of this conflict was the defeat of the main Indian resistance in both the Midwest and the South. In future, conflict with settlers would become far less common. Overall, the landscapes of these wars varied dramatically from open prairies to mountainous regions, and dense forests. These factors certainly help explain some historic differences between the northern-US and Canadian experiences, and the fates of the indigenous people in the south and western regions. Furthermore, there were indirect implications to European settlement and expansion across the prairies, especially by the later 1800s with the expanding railway networks. Associated with the colonization was the mass slaughter of the huge, roaming herds of bison on which many of the native American plains tribes depended. Displacement then resulted in annihilation of many tribes through brutal one-sided conflicts, and for those who remained, starvation. Disease was also a major factor in the outcomes of the meetings of Old World and New.

Although some of the greater battles are known, such as the Battle of the Little Bighorn in June 1876, many of the conflicts were small-scale skirmishes, essentially mobile affairs, and hardly documented. The one factor in favour of the resident peoples was their knowledge of the land, the terrain and topography, and other natural factors. Some of the landscapes being contested were extremely arduous (Death Valley Arizona having summer temperatures well over forty degrees centigrade), and even to survive there required good local knowledge. Indeed, in some cases it was this deep understanding of the landscape that enabled the vastly inferior native forces to hang on and resist the incursions for so long.

Geronimo

Most famous of the resistance leaders toward the latter stages of the war, was a warrior called Geronimo who was born in 1829 and died in 1909. He was a significant leader and medicine man for the Bedonkohe band of the Ndendahe Apache tribe, not a chieftain, but a spiritual leader or shaman. From 1850 to 1886, allied with members of three other Central Apache bands, the Tchihende, Tsokanende, and Nednhi, Geronimo led raids against the Europeans and fought against both Mexican and US forces. These campaigns ranged across the rugged landscapes of northern Mexico and the southwestern American states of New Mexico and Arizona. This was a part of the ongoing struggle by the Apache tribes following the invasion of their territories after the end of the Mexican war in 1848. Forced into Reservations, the Apaches bitterly resented the imposed changes to their free-roaming lifestyles and traditions. Geronimo and his braves now undertook raids beyond the reservations and tried to reinstate their former nomadic way of life. In the final phase of Geronimo's war against American oppression (1876–1886), he was forced to surrender three times and ultimately adopted settled reservation life.

Geronimo (1829 to 17 February 1909) pictured here in 1885.

During the struggle Geronimo proved to be a superb leader of raiding parties of between thirty to forty braves and their associated guerrilla warfare. Eventually, it was largely the arduous landscape and conditions in the remote mountain and desert areas that took their toll. In 1886, following an intense pursuit by American forces across north Mexico after their third reservation breakout in 1885, Geronimo surrendered to Lieutenant Charles Bare Gatewood. When he gave up for the last time, he and his band had been reduced to a half-starved motley crew. Along with twenty-seven Apache warriors, he was despatched east to join others of the Chiricahua tribe already exiled to Florida. Following years of exploitation by the American authorities as an exhibit at fairs and other events, he died a prisoner of war at Fort Sill hospital in 1909.

The Sioux and the Nez Perce Indians

So, in the mid- to late-1800s, the conflicts endured as a series of greater and lesser confrontations, with occasional but notable victories such as that by the Sioux Chief Red Cloud over the US Cavalry on the northern Great Plains in 1867. However, it was increasingly clear that military defeat of the US Americans by the Native Americans would never be permanent as simply more and more would come. The consequence of this realisation was that negotiations would be necessary, tempered by an understanding that the US government, and its representatives, could not be trusted. This situation was compounded by the potential to weaken native American resolve by the lure of drink and gambling. By about 1870, the result was that the settler American population had grown to around forty million and was still growing, while the Native Americans were at about half a million with their numbers falling.

Against this context, the Nez Perce Indians are an interesting study because they lived away from any goldfields and thus mass, uncontrolled immigration, in an area between Idaho, Oregon, and Washington State. They lived north and inland, protected from the Great Plains by rough country and from the open plains of Montana by the Bitterroot Range of the Rocky Mountains. In this barren, remote countryside the Nez Perce Indians continued to exist with reasonable independence and avoided some of the disastrous events that overtook tribes on the open plains, in areas where white settlers wished to establish themselves.

However, as settlers pushed into ever-more remote areas and tensions rose, conflict became inevitable. The sentiment of the Native Americans was expressed by one of the chiefs summoned to a parley, and which was along the lines of 'Leave us alone, we are living peacefully here'. The US government was forcing all the tribes to sign treaties that confined them to designated reservations, and this now included the non-treaty Nez Perce tribes. The government wanted all tribes to be subject to the treaty to which some but not all had signed up. The view of the non-treaty tribes was that they were autonomous, had not given up their lands, and that nobody could give them up on their behalf. The US government negotiator agreed with their sentiments and felt that the area was high and cold and only good for raising stock and fishing;

the latter was important to the natives. Sadly, the scene was now set for a protracted and bitter conflict. Ultimately, the Indian chiefs decided the only option was to move north where they might still be free, across the border into Canada. The Nez Perce utilized the rough terrain and their superior knowledge of the mountainous countryside to best advantage and to wage guerrilla warfare against their technically superior foe. Sniping from boulder-covered hillsides and around narrow canyons, the Nez Perce continued their struggle until 1877. By this time, heading north to escape with their women and children across the border into Canada their trek covered 1,500 miles over a period of around ninety days. Nevertheless, the US military had the objective of rounding the tribes up as prisoners and confining them to the designated reservations. The tribes came within a few miles of the border when they were finally overwhelmed. The 418 Nez Perce that survived the trek were described as emerging from their jagged holes on the windswept plains of northern Montana, now reduced to freezing, starving people, with wounded warriors, women and children, and old men. With much increased respect following the way the chiefs and their tribes had conducted themselves throughout the war, the leaders were promised that they could go back to their homeland.

In terms of military tactics, it was noted that the natives fought with almost scientific skill, using advanced and rear guards, skirmish lines, and field fortifications. The US cavalry was impressed. What was described as their 'great retreat' was also something that began to change American attitudes to the native people. However, at the start of the war, a quasi-religious movement had emerged in the northwestern US, initiated by a prophet called Smohalla. He asserted that communication with God was through dreams and not prayers, and indeed, that the true deity was Mother Earth. Furthermore, the 'Dreamer' philosophy held that the white settlers desecrated the Earth through mining, agriculture, and the dividing up of the land. Beyond this, if the Native Americans returned to their traditional ways, the Whites would disappear. The Dreamer idea was a real threat to US governmental ambitions because being a pan-tribal philosophy it could unify groups to a coordinated uprising. This never happened and it is clear from reading accounts that some tribes like the Cheyenne worked for the government, and during the great retreat, these tribes took part in the slaughter of the Nez Perce. Others, such as the Sioux, had battle-hardened warriors close by but failed to come to the aid the Nez Perce tribes.

The US government once again broke its word, and the Nez Perce were despatched to Indian Territory in Oklahoma where many of the survivors died of malaria or malnutrition. Late in the day, following protests from the Presbyterian Church, the remainder were returned to Idaho.

Chief Sitting Bull (1831 to 15 December 1890) Hunkpapa Lakota leader.

Soldiers in the British Indian Army, 1800s.

The latter stages of the Indian War

During late 1890 and early 1891, the last major conflict with the Sioux tribes took place with the Pine Ridge Campaign involving around half the regular infantry and cavalry of the entire American Army. At the Wounded Knee Massacre, Chief Sitting Bull's half-brother Big Foot was killed, and around 200 Sioux braves were slaughtered by the US 7th Cavalry. This followed the killing of Sitting Bull and his son Crow Foot at Standing Rock Agency during a gun battle with Indian police sent by the American government to arrest him; the outcome in late January was that the tribes returned to their allotted reservations. The final act of the Indian War was probably in 1898 with the Battle of Leech Lake when the Chippewa tribe rose in protest over an arrest on Lake Leech in northern Minnesota.

The struggle of the Native Americans against numerically and technologically superior invaders, mostly from Europe, was always going to end badly for the indigenous people. This was despite the native American warriors being regarded

British Indian Army Punjabis, 1800s.

British Indian Army Punjabi regiment, 1800s.

as some of the bravest and most accomplished hand-to-hand fighters in the world. However, the natives were fighting for their land, and with it for their survival, and they knew the terrain, the topography, and the conditions.

However, the outcomes of the prolonged wars were the removal of the native peoples from their traditional lands and their customary lifestyles, and the imposed limitations of reservation occupancy. The way the campaigns played out varied dramatically according to terrain and the geographical character of the countryside. The native people varied in lifestyles from the nomadic plains Indians to the forest tribes of the north, and the more settled communities in some of the southern areas. The northern high mountains, lakes, and forests lent themselves to guerrilla warfare and local resistance against superior forces with better weapons. This seems to be associated with a much stronger level of native resilience and a degree of resentment of the natives by the settled Europeans even today.

For the nomadic plains tribes their fates were generally sealed by dependence on the natural resources that the newcomers either took from them or drove to near extinction. A few resistance leaders like Geronimo held out through sound knowledge of topography and terrain, able to operate guerrilla raids and then retreat into the landscape. This echoes the Seminole tribes in Florida. Rugged, remote terrain and topography and often harsh conditions of extreme temperatures, high and low, and drought, made conquest by superior forces and more advanced technology problematic and long-winded. These were similar issues to those in the mountainous battlescapes of Old-World Afghanistan discussed below.

The Afghan Wars

Afghanistan has a landscape of irrigated land, with small but fertile river valleys, deep gorges, deserts, high plateaux, and snow-covered mountains. The eastern part of the country is divided by towering mountain ranges called the Hindu Kush and Pamirs, whose peaks rise to around 24,000 feet. The climate is extreme with cold, snowy winters and hot, dry summer and major temperature changes between night and day, season to season, and place to place with summer highs of around forty degrees centigrade and winter lows down to well below freezing. Much of the region is dry and so fresh potable water becomes a problem for any invader.

The Anglo-Afghan Wars, or simply the Afghan Wars, were three conflicts: 1839–1842, 1878–1880, and 1919. From its imperial base in India, Britain's objective was to extend influence and control its hostile neighbour, Afghanistan, and neutralize Russian influence. With such a complicated region and a long history of conflicts, neither the historic complexity of Afghanistan, nor the more recent conflicts and interactions with Russia or the US and its allies, are considered here. The first widespread use of the word Mujahideen, or Mujahidin, referred to the guerrilla militant groups led by the Islamist Afghan fighters in the Soviet-Afghan War. This has since been usurped by other militant Islamic fighters, notably the Taliban.

After a long civil war from 1816, the Bārakzay clan assumed control of Afghanistan, with Dōst Moḥammad Khan taking the throne in 1826. However, with Britain and Russia competing for political influence, Dōst Moḥammad had to balance his power play between the two imperial influences; the British believed that either he was directly hostile to their interests or was at least not resisting Russian overtures. Because of this perception, the British took direct action, first through negotiations, and then when these failed, through an invasion ordered by the governor-general of India, Lord Auckland. The intention was to restore to the throne the exiled former ruler Shah Shojāʿ.

In April 1839, the British army entered Kandahār and Shojāʿ was crowned shah.

Ghazna (Ghaznī) was captured in July, and in August, Shojāʿ took his place at the capital, Kabul. The Afghans quite reasonably took a dim view of both the foreign invasion and a ruler forced on them by a foreign power. Having escaped first to Balkh and then to Bukhara where he was re-arrested, Dōst Moḥammad broke out of prison to lead his Afghan partisans against the British and the shah. Following a battle at Parwan in 1840, Dōst Moḥammad surrendered to the British, and was deported to India with most of his family. However, insurrection was ongoing, and with terms for the withdrawal discussed with Akbar Khan (Dōst Moḥammad's son), the British retreated to India. However, Sir William Hay Macnaghten, the British political agent, was killed during a parley with the Afghans. Then, on 6 January 1842 when around 4,500 British and Indian troops with 12,000 camp followers left Kabul, with groups of Afghan fighters following them, their exit became a bloodbath. Shojāʿ was killed after the British abandoned him and the city. Later that same year, British forces reoccupied Kabul but Lord Ellenborough, the new governor-general of India, chose to evacuate Afghanistan, and by 1843 Dōst Moḥammad returned to Kabul as head of state.

In November 1875, British Prime Minister Benjamin Disraeli made Lord Lytton the new governor-general of India and with Russian influence again on the rise, a key issue was India's relationship with Afghanistan. Lytton came with orders to counteract the Russian threat or at least to ensure a strong frontier, if necessary, by force. Therefore, on his arrival in India, he informed Shīr ʿAlī Khan, the third son of Dōst Moḥammad, who had succeeded to the throne after his father's death, that he was sending a 'mission' to Kabul. Lytton was furious when entry to Afghanistan was refused but did not take direct action until 1878 when Russia's General Stolyetov was given access to Kabul. The Second Anglo-Afghan War began on 21 November 1878. Shīr ʿAlī fled Kabul and died in exile in early 1879. With the British army occupying Kabul, a treaty was signed at Gandamak (Gandomak) on 26 May 1879, accepting Shīr ʿAlī's son, Yaʿqūb Khan, as the new emir. This recognition came with conditions, namely that he agreed to a permanent British embassy in Kabul and conducted his relations with foreign states in accordance with the wishes and advice of the British.

Once again this was a short-lived situation: on 3 September 1879 Sir Louis Cavagnari, the British envoy in Kabul, was murdered along with his escort. In response, the British army was sent to occupy Kabul and the Afghans, now commanded by Ayub Khan, met with British-Indian forces at Maiwand on 27 July 1880 and were victorious. This was a strategically significant step to maintain national unity and identity. Defeat for the British meant retreat from Kandahar. Ayub Khan laid siege to Kandahar but the ploy against the better-armed British failed, and on 1 September, the Afghan force was routed by General Frederick Roberts at the Battle of Kandahar.

The trek to Kandahar

Roberts' trek from Kabul was the stuff of legends; his army marched in the intense summer heat over difficult terrain in full battle kit. Each day of the march around five hundred or more soldiers fell ill. Roberts himself had to be dragged on a litter for the final few days of the ordeal. On reaching Kandahar on 31 August, his 11,000 troops had forced-marched about 300 miles (483km) in three weeks under intolerably harsh conditions with baking sun, temperatures of nearly forty degrees centigrade, and over rough, rocky terrain, with almost no shade. The battle began almost immediately with an artillery bombardment of the Afghan force followed by the 92nd Highlanders and 2nd Gurkhas driving northward village by village. This was combined with a movement southward by the 72nd Highlanders and the 2nd Sikh regiment. The two-pronged attack met at the Afghan camp at midday with support from the 3rd Brigade. This direct assault triggered a massive retreat by the Afghan forces who melted away into the hills of Herat. They left their artillery and most of their supplies behind. Losses in the actual battle, rather than the march, amounted to 250 casualties from 11,000 British, and 1,500 Afghans from their 13,000 troops.

This decisive British victory relieved Kandahar and restored the prestige of the British Empire, making Roberts a national hero and ending the Second Anglo-Afghan War. After Yaʿqūb abdicated in July 1880, ʿAbd al-Raḥmān, nephew of Shīr ʿAlī, became emir. During his reign, the modern boundaries of Afghanistan were established and recognized by both the British and the Russians.

During the First World War, there was considerable support in Afghanistan for the cause of the Ottoman Turks against the British. However, the incumbent emir, Ḥabībullāh Khan, kept a non-involvement policy until assassinated by individuals of the anti-British movement on 20 February 1919. Ḥabībullāh's son, Amānullāh Khan, succeeded to the throne and declared total independence from Great Britain which, in May 1919, led to the Third Anglo-Afghan War. This was indeed a limited affair with just a few skirmishes between the British Indian Army and the Afghans before independence was recognized and accepted. Direct British interests ended, and the Afghans signed a treaty of friendship with Bolshevik Russia becoming one of the first states to formally recognize the Soviet government. This ensured a special relationship between the two countries until the Soviet invasion of Afghanistan in December 1979, resulting in the Soviet-Afghan War (1979–1989).

Landscape and terrain have proved problematic for many would-be invaders and combinations of remote valleys, rugged mountains, and fiercely warlike indigenous tribes make conquest and retention very difficult. This has been the case with the Afghans situated at the eastern end of the great Himalayan mountains. Over the

British Army rescuing the wounded.

centuries, the region has been contested by various invaders from the north and east, from Asia such as the Mongols, from the immediate east from India and the Sikh Empire, and from European Greek empires. The Parthan Empire extended across this rugged landscape in the early centuries of the first millennium with a culture of independence and military strength. This continued through hundreds of years into the nineteenth and twentieth centuries with British and Russian invasions too. With their ability to resist foreign invasion, the Afghanistan region became known as the 'death of empires'. Rugged terrain was compounded by very hot summers and bitterly cold, harsh winters. This is not a landscape for the faint-hearted, and it breeds a tough, unforgiving, tribal society.

Soviet-Afghan War

The latter was a conflict between insurgent groups and tribes known collectively as the Mujahideen in independently minded parts of the country, together with smaller Maoist groups. This alliance fought a nine-year guerrilla war against the military occupation of the Soviet Union and their satellite state, the Democratic Republic of Afghanistan (DRA). This took place during the 1980s and was mostly across the Afghan countryside.

In recent decades, the country has again been engulfed by cataclysmic wars and bitter in-fighting between internal factions. However, it still seems that the topography, terrain, and the people of Afghanistan combine to make the country a battlescape that is the death of empires old and new. As so often the case in harsh, remote, independent domains, the battlescape of perilous mountains and ravines, extreme weather, and shortage of resources such as potable water, combine with sheer bloody-mindedness of the indigenous tribes to make it almost impossible for an external power to conquer and hold. The situation in Afghanistan continues to this day.

The European Napoleonic Wars and the Battle of Austerlitz

Fought in the modern-day Czech Republic, the Battle of Austerlitz, or the Three Emperors, was fought between France and Britain's allies, Austria, and Russia. In this conflict, one of the issues for Napoleon was the sheer vastness of Russia and the central European landscape. This meant difficulties in maintaining supply chains, and potentially facing the extremely arduous winter conditions. In 1805 Russia and Austria joined with Britain in the Third Coalition against Napoleonic France. When Austria declared war, Napoleon was camped at Boulogne and preparing to invade Britain. Instead, he decided to lead his Grand Armée from their encampment to south Germany, and by October was in Ulm, where he received the surrender of the entire Austrian army. French soldiers then occupied Vienna, which triggered Russia to move in aid of the Austrians; together they amassed a force of around 90,000 men which assembled northeast of the city. Now acutely aware of the dangers of winter disruption to supplies, and the sheer impact of extreme weather on his army, Napoleon was reluctant to contemplate retreating. He gambled on drawing his opponents into an early battle. To this end he advanced his force of about 70,000 men to Austerlitz where they appeared to take up a potentially weak position with the nearby strongpoint of the centrally placed Pratzen Heights unoccupied. The Russian General Mikhail Kutuzov had realized that one way to defeat Napoleon was to avoid direct conflict and simply keep skirmishing. Given time, the extreme weather and lack of supplies would do the rest. However, the Russian emperor, Tsar Alexander I, overruled this enlightened military view and took personal command of the joint Austro-Russian force. What followed, while a very risky stratagem, which was always Napoleon's way, was that the allies attacked the weaker French right flank as Napoleon had hoped. Having massed his main force in the centre and left he was able to counterattack, but now found his troops on the end of unexpectedly strong resistance from the Russians. The allies nearly broke the French right and made a strong fight on the French left. However, the French infantry and the Imperial Guard Cavalry in the centre ultimately won through.

The Italians hauling a heavy gun in the High Alps, First World War.

Wetland also influenced the conflict; the Goldblach stream and marshy ground in that area of the battlefield had unexpectedly hindered the Austro-Russian advance on the French right wing. This compounded the other issues. The French Imperial Guard finally took the Pratzen Heights; their infantry had emerged from thick fog to surprise and overwhelm the Austrian troops defending the plateau. Napoleon's gamble paid off. With far fewer troops, and taking a deliberately weak position in the landscape, he won a resounding victory. The combined Russian and Austrian armies had lost about a third of their men killed, wounded, or taken prisoner.

The outcome of this battle was the consequence of particularly bold tactics, clever use of terrain and topography, and a little luck with weather conditions in taking the heights. However, the other factor, which was later to prove Napoleon's undoing, was the threat of harsh winter weather in the inhospitable terrain of central Europe without the necessary clothing. Ultimately, Napoleon's Grand Armée was to fall prey to extreme weather and the Russian persistence in leaving towns and countryside stripped bare as they retreated, while Napoleon advanced.

The Eastern Front in the First World War

From a western-European and British perspective, the main conflicts of the First

Loading fodder for the horses of the Italian troops in Tripoli 1911.

The Italians repulsing Austrian troops in the Alps, April 1916.

World War were those on the Western Front. There is perhaps less general recognition of the horrendous conditions of the war taking place in the east: the Alpine conflict between the Italians and the Austro-Hungarian Empire. This was an especially grim conflict often fought in very extreme conditions.

During the Italian-Turkish War in Libya (1911–1912) the Italian forces had experienced serious problems with equipment and munitions. These issues were still unresolved when Italy joined the Allies in the First World War; their entry into the war was in part an attempt to resolve these long-standing territorial claims with Austria. From the outset, the Austro-Hungarian forces held and fortified the higher ground of the Julian Alps and Karst Plateau against the Italian troops who had a numerical advantage of about three to one.

The Italian or Alpine Front of the Great War was a series of battles and military encounters along the Austrian-Italian border that took place between 1915 and 1918. With agreement from the Allies, 1915 Treaty of London, Italy joined the conflict with the intention of annexing Austrian Littoral, north Dalmatia, modern-day Trentino, and South Tyrol. The hope was for a surprise assault leading to swift annexation, but

Italian position in the High Alps, First World War.

the situation quickly descended into trench warfare. It bore similarities to the Western Front in France, but with a major environmental difference in the battlescape: high altitudes and extremely cold winters.

However, it was an offensive much farther east that helped tip the balance, both here and on the Western Front. The biggest and most bloody conflict during the Great War was the Russian Brusilov Offensive that, because of its intensity, helped relieve German pressure at the Battle of Verdun and the Austro-Hungarian pressure on the Italians. Indeed, the result of the Russian advance was that the Austro-Hungarian army was so weakened they had to rely on German aid to continue. Romania also entered on behalf of the Allies but for the Russians the impact of their assault was a major factor in triggering revolutions within Russia itself.

The Battles of the Isonzo

An Italian attack intended to cross the Isonzo River, capture the fortress town of Gorizia, and gain access to the Karst Plateau. This involved the first Battles of the Isonzo starting in June 1915. However, despite numerical superiority, the Italian force failed to break the strong Austro-Hungarian defensive lines in the highlands of northwest Gorizia and Gradisca. Occupying the high ground in this alpine landscape, the Austrian army had a huge advantage, and the Italian force struggled with its assault and with the need to climb in this montane terrain. Most of the Italian troops were not used to, or trained for, alpine conditions. The battle ended in early July with the Italian troops having struggled to get over the river.

The Italians had professional officers, but their troops were poorly equipped and had limited training. Furthermore, there was a deep disquiet over their commander General Luigi Cadorna, and generally a serious lack of morale. The ongoing shortages of equipment and munitions were problematic and, like many armies of the time, was compounded by ineffective supply chains. Horses were mostly used to carry necessary supplies, but they struggled badly in the rough mountain terrain. By the time the war moved into the winter months the ill-supplied Italians, many recruited from the lowlands of northern Italy, were unequipped and untrained for an alpine conflict in snow-bound icy conditions. With temperatures mostly sub-zero and heavy snowfall, the situation was dire for troops often untrained and unsupplied in terms of suitable clothing and footwear.

Then, in mid-July, in the Second Battle of the Isonzo, the Italian military tried a further frontal assault on the Austro-Hungarian trenches, this time with greater artillery support. The battle continued in a stalemate as both sides exhausted their ammunition, but the Italians managed to take Mount Batognica over Kobarid which had strategic significance in a later conflict. By now the war had pushed out significant numbers of local people from the area, thousands of these civilians died from the resulting malnutrition and illness. With Allied victory at the Battle of Vittorio Veneto came the collapse of the Habsburg Empire and Austro-Hungary was no longer a unified entity. In November 1918, the capture of Trento and Trieste by the Italians concluded the military operations with the armistice of Villa Giusti. For Italy, this was the Fourth Italian War of Independence and was the final step in Italian unification.

In terms of wider awareness of the Great War, the Alpine Front is often forgotten, but the cost in lives and in human suffering was appalling. The terrain and extreme conditions, especially in winter, took a massive toll on mostly unequipped and untrained soldiers, from both sides, but especially the Italians. Soldiers recruited from the lowland towns and cities of northern Italy were without adequate clothing and had limited training, in winter they were described as freezing to death overnight at their posts. With treacherous and precipitous terrain, the Austrians and Germans especially made clever but deadly use of the snow and ice-bound conditions to wreak havoc on their enemy. One ploy was to fire artillery onto the snowbound mountains above the Italian positions to trigger catastrophic avalanches. These slides of ice, snow, and rock swept downhill devastating all before them. To fight effectively in the alpine situation requires specially trained troops, preferably mountaineers, with the necessary equipment and clothing to survive. To send soldiers to the front without these basics is almost a one-way ticket. The Italian Front demonstrated very clearly the importance of mountainous terrain in the European arena

Yugoslavia and the Balkans in the Second World War

Extensive massifs form physical barriers to invaders and offer places of retreat for those under attack. Mountain chains as battlescapes are often landscapes of resistance. In the 1940s, this was shown in the region of wider Yugoslavia. The areas formerly incorporated into Yugoslavia had long been disputed territories with a complex overlayering of different ethnic groups, contrasting religions, and competing imperial ambitions.

Prior to the outbreak of the Second World War the government of Milan Stojadinović (1935–1939) sought neutrality with the Axis Powers and the Allies, with a non-aggression treaty with Italy and one of friendship with France. However, the region had long had internal tensions, such as Croatian leaders demanding increased autonomy, and this led to the removal of Stojadinović from government. Tensions increased between pro-fascist Ustaše, seeking an independent Croatia close to the Axis countries; Serbian civilians and armed forces wanting an alliance with the Western powers; and the communists turning to the Soviet Union as a natural ally. This created a split within the Yugoslavian resistance, with on one side the partisans, a communist-led movement propagating pan-Yugoslav tolerance with left-wing and liberal republican elements. On the other side were the Chetniks with a conservative royalist and nationalist grouping having an almost exclusive Serbian support base. This situation meant that from the outset, up to 1943, the Chetniks fought under the name of London-based King Peter II's Yugoslavian government-in-exile with recognition from the Western Allies. On the other hand, the partisans were supported by the Soviet Union.

Partisans and mountains

At the outset, the partisan forces were relatively small, poorly armed, and without any infrastructure. But they had two major advantages over other military and paramilitary groups in former Yugoslavia. The first and most immediate advantage was a small but valuable cadre of experienced veterans of the 1930s Spanish Civil War. Unlike some of the other military and paramilitary formations, these veterans had experience of a modern war fought in circumstances like those faced by Yugoslavia in the Second

Serbian troops.

World War. Much of the Spanish war had been fought in mountains and remote countryside. In Slovenia, the partisans drew on the experienced TIGR (Trst, Istra, Gorica, and Reka) members to train troops. They were the revolutionary organization of the Julian March TIGR, a militant, anti-fascist, insurgent organization responding to fascist Italianization of Slovene and Croat peoples in former Austro-Hungarian territories subsumed into Italy after the Great War.

Preparations began in the early 1930s, with the Soviet Union training communist volunteers for guerrilla warfare in Yugoslavia. As war broke out, hundreds of people, who would become prominent Yugoslav communist leaders, undertook partisan courses led by Soviet military intelligence. Significantly, the partisan resistance was founded on communist ideology not ethnicity which had long been a major issue across the region and remains so today. They therefore attracted support across national lines and recruited from all parts of the country. Other paramilitary forces at the time were linked to, and thus limited by, territorial factors and ethnicity of Croat, Serb, or others.

Occupation by the Axis powers

The various sub-countries of the time making up greater Yugoslavia each had strong cultural identities though often with varying mixes of ethnic and religious background. It was into this largely rural and often forested and mountainous landscape that a mixture of Axis powers sought to impose their rule. Germany had tried to persuade Yugoslavia to join the Axis and there was considerable pressure when Bulgaria, Romania, and Hungary joined, along of course with Italy and Italian-controlled Albania. Indeed, all Yugoslavia's land borders (Austria, Bulgaria, Romania, Hungary, and Italy, with Albania), were part of the Axis, and they had strategic control of the Adriatic Sea, Yugoslavia's only coastline. So, in March of 1941, Yugoslavia's prince regent and the government decided the country would join, but the Yugoslavian military opposed this. The invasion began on 6 April 1941, when the Germans launched a massive air assault on the Yugoslav capital, Belgrade. The impacts and effects varied between Germans and Italians, Bulgarians, and Turks. However, whichever nation was involved, the indigenous peoples resisted strongly.

Resistance

The first armed anti-fascist resistance unit in 1940s-occupied former Yugoslavia began active service almost as soon as it was formed. The tactics employed included sabotage and diversionary attacks on infrastructure such as key railway lines, telegraph connections, and municipal buildings in villages. They seized arms and ammunition and began to generate communist propaganda. At the same time, the Provincial Committee for Serbia of the Communist Party of Yugoslavia launched armed insurrection in Serbia with its Supreme Staff of the National Liberation Partisan Units of Yugoslavia chaired by Josip Broz Tito, later to become president of liberated Yugoslavia. On 4 July 1941, the uprising began and three days later, the partisans killed two gendarmes who were enforcing the ban on political rallies following German occupation. Known as the Bela Crkva incident, this signalled the start of the major uprising against Nazi occupation in Serbia. Other acts of insurrection followed, and while the occupying Germans managed to suppress many of these, a broad movement was emerging. Over the period, various smaller resistance groups joined with the partisans.

A separate organisation emerged called the Chetnik movement, the Yugoslav Army in the Fatherland or JVUO. This was initiated in mid-May 1941, by former Yugoslav soldiers after the surrender by the Royal Yugoslav Army and was coordinated in western Serbia by Colonel Draža Mihailović. Unlike the communist partisans, Mihailović's forces were almost exclusively ethnic Serbs, which would cause friction. With a common enemy and purpose, the partisans and Chetniks tried to collaborate in the early stages of the uprisings, but this did not last. Following lengthy but unsuccessful negotiations, the Chetnik leader, General Mihailović, decided that the partisans were the primary foe. He claimed his rationale was humanitarian and would limit German reprisals on the Serbian population. In this volatile climate, the Chetniks turned on the partisans and were supported with supplies and cooperation from the German and Italian occupational forces. At this point, despite advice from their people on the ground not to do so, Britain was still supporting the Chetniks. But then in December 1941, the partisans began to operate more-or-less nationally across Yugoslavia rather than on the previously parochial level.

However, by April 1941, the country had been overrun by the Axis powers and control was split between Germany, Italy, Hungary, Bulgaria, and the internal client 'puppet' regimes. The latter included the Axis-allied Independent State of Croatia and the Government of National Salvation in German-occupied Serbia. Then, after the June 1941 Nazi invasion of the USSR, the communist-led republican Yugoslav partisans were commanded by Soviet Moscow to start guerrilla warfare to resist the Axis forces. The resulting National Liberation War involved Yugoslavian communist partisans and a wide range of pro-Soviet or pro-Axis forces in a complex mix of spatially and ethnically orientated resistance movements. With support and allegiances ebbing and flowing, the resistance movements fought together against a shared enemy but also against each other and in alliance with the occupying armies. The pro-Soviet partisans were staunchly anti-Nazi, as were the Chetniks until they changed sides and became pro-Italy; when the latter capitulated, they collaborated with German and Ustaše military. With major offensives launched against the partisans by the Axis occupying armies, the resistance was almost annihilated but hung on in the densely forested and inaccessible mountain areas.

The influences of terrain and topography in national identity and resistance

Clearly, the terrain and topography of former Yugoslavia were central to the historical and ethnic identities of the separate regions of this extensive country, and this carried through into the late twentieth-century civil wars. It was also this landscape of resistance that allowed the partisans and other groups to wage what would become a successful guerrilla campaign against overwhelming occupying forces. Eventually the partisan movement was recognized by the Western Allies and their dominance contributed to the defeat of the Axis, and post-War to the emergence of the socialist state of Yugoslavia. The 1940s occupation was ended with supplies and aerial support from Western Allies and Soviet troops on the ground, which through the Belgrade Offensive meant partisan control of the entire country.

The Second Enemy Offensive and escape routes through the mountains

There had been several major military campaigns fought by the Axis troops including the so-called Second Enemy Offensive against partisan forces in eastern Bosnia in January 1942. This was almost successful but, having avoided being encircled near Sarajevo, the partisans were able to escape over the Igman Mountain plateau in central Bosnia and Herzegovina. This area is part of the Dinaric Alps, located southwest of Sarajevo and close to the Bjelašnica mountain range in the south and west, the Hadžići and Ilidža in the north, and the Željeznica River in the east. The mountains rise to almost 5,000 feet (1,500m) and are covered in forest. There were subsequent Axis assaults, but each time, the partisans were able to elude them, and their guerrilla campaigns against the Axis occupiers and their local allies became increasingly successful.

The Fifth Enemy Offensive followed by the capitulation of Italy

However, in May and June 1943, the Fifth Enemy Offensive, the Battle of the Sutjeska or Fall Schwarz, achieved its objective of surrounding the partisan forces in southeastern Bosnia and northern Montenegro. Nevertheless, by this time, the partisan forces included around 150,000 fighters, mostly men with perhaps five per cent women, plus tacit support of several million indigenous peasants. Furthermore, support for the resistance movements was increasing rapidly.

There was also the Croatian Home Guard with 130,000 men in 1943 which included its own air force made up of five hundred former Royal Yugoslav Air Force officers, 1,600 NCOs, and 125 planes; by 1943 this had grown to 9,775 personnel and 295 planes. In September 1943, when the Italians agreed an armistice with the Allies; they still had seventeen divisions in Yugoslavia, the commanders of which refused to join the Germans. In Montenegro at least two Italian infantry divisions simply joined the partisans as complete units, and another in Albania did the same. Some Italians surrendered to the German forces and were imprisoned in Germany or in some cases faced summary execution. Other Italian troops surrendered to Croatian forces, or the partisans, or trudged cross-country to Italy or escaped by ship across the Adriatic.

The partisans as a growing force of resistance

Over this period, in the extensive mountain landscapes of Yugoslavia, the partisan forces grew to be the biggest such movement in Axis-occupied Europe. Ultimately, there were 800,000 soldiers in four field armies that won through in conflicts

Serbian troops behind earthworks near Adrianople, Turkey, in the war between Turkey and Bulgaria, 1912.

Russian military transport in the Carpathian Mountains.

against the various occupying forces. This largely guerrilla troop became the official army of the emerging Democratic Federal Yugoslavia state which was later the Socialist Federal Republic of Yugoslavia and remained so until the death in 1980, of the wartime leader, Tito. The latter was the country's premier from 8 March 1945, with the slogan 'In combat they are forging a free and fraternal nation'.

The closing stages of the Yugoslavian conflict

It is estimated that the occupation cost more than a million lives and that the death toll involved large numbers of civilians including the bulk of the Jewish community, many of whom were killed in extermination camps by both puppet regimes and the occupying Axis forces. The Ustaše regime in Croatia for example, mostly Croat and Muslims, undertook genocide of Serbs, Jews, Roma, and anti-fascist Croats. The Chetnik Serbs, and Montenegrins acted similarly toward Muslims, Croats, and pro-partisan Serbs. The occupying Italians used violence and ethnic cleansing with Slovenes and Croats. German Nazis responded to the rural guerrilla warfare with mass civilian executions in villages supporting the resistance; the German SS massacred civilians and prisoners of war. Hungarian Axis forces murdered Serbs and Jews for their connections with the resistance fighters.

As the war wound down, the Yugoslavian communists, specifically the partisans, retaliated as the Axis and their collaborators collapsed. The brutal reprisals included forced marches, deportation of German and Italian communities from Yugoslavia, and the execution of thousands of military prisoners and civilians. These atrocities included violence and killing of Istrian Italians, and purges of Hungarians, Germans, and others linked to the fascist Axis occupiers. The levels of casualties were particularly high.

When modern Yugoslavia broke up in the 1990s, following Tito's death, the separate nations of what was essentially a federation went through a further period of appalling conflict. Simmering retributions and discontent perhaps harboured in often remote, rural, and mountainous countryside emerged once again and as the seismic geographic splits between and within countries and communities appeared once more. Viewed from outside, these appear to be the long-term consequences of complex histories and over-layering of conquests and subjugations over centuries and influences by the zones of identifiable terrain and topography of this turbulent region.

The topographic barriers formed by mountains and even by ranges of lesser hills become significant in defining territories and in influencing tactics and strategies. This applies to wider wars and in individual battles. Often combined with other terrain factors such as rivers and wetlands, this impact of topography may help direct invaders toward certain strategic decisions and often provide sanctuary for indigenous communities in the face of aggression. Particularly when the mountains are forested, these battlescapes favour indigenous guerrilla warfare, and this was the case in countries like Afghanistan and Yugoslavia too.

Finnish sharpshooter regiment, March 1894.

French legions in Tunisia, 1881.

Chapter 9
Deserts and plains

Deserts and plains offer significant barriers for aggressive invaders, but opportunities too. Open land allows deployment in the field and the use of cavalry, or in modern times, heavy, mobile weapons like tanks. On the other hand, negotiating these spaces can be fraught and local knowledge and adaptation bring great advantages. From the great plains of central Europe and Asia to vast deserts like the Sahara, such lands were historically the domain of mobile, nomadic people with grazing animals and tribal territories. Lack of water, or at least very limited supplies of potable water, are significant constraints in these places; they also vary from the searing heat of the Sahara to the bitter cold of the Gobi in Mongolia. Furthermore, even when the landscape is a hot desert, the nights can be very cold and so, these are indeed stressful landscapes.

A further factor that troubles invading forces even today is the mobile nature of

A British tank on the Western Front, First World War.

sand and active dune systems. Soft sand can be a death-trap as quick-sand or sinking sands, and the landscape is ever-changing rather than having fixed points from which to navigate. Additionally, the winds can whip up atrocious sandstorms too. Local peoples will be adapted to and knowledgeable about these challenges whereas newcomers can suffer badly.

Operation Eagle Claw

In terms of the inherent problems of a sandy environment, modern machines and vehicles must be adapted to the conditions if they are to function. Heavy machines and vehicles, from tanks to jeeps, simply sink into the sand and windblown sand clogs engines, vents and the like. A particular example of the problems and difficulties implicit in these situations, and especially with a failure to adapt to local conditions, was the abortive American mission to rescue hostages from Iran in the early 1980s. Operation Eagle Claw or Operation Tabas on 24 April 1980, was a failed attempt by the United States Armed Forces to rescue fifty-two embassy staff held captive at the United States Embassy in Tehran. Ordered by US President Jimmy Carter, this was one of Delta Force's first missions, and it experienced numerous problems. Of eight helicopters sent to the first staging area, Desert One, only five arrived in operational condition; one had hydraulic problems, another was caught in a sandstorm, and a third had a cracked rotor blade. During operational planning, although only four

British Camel Corps at the Battle of Omdurman, Sudan 1898.

helicopters were needed, the protocol was to abort the mission if fewer than six helicopters were functional. The field commanders indicated to President Carter that it was necessary to abandon the mission and it was subsequently aborted. However, things got much worse since the American team needed to withdraw from Desert One, and the one remaining helicopter crashed into a transport aircraft. The latter contained both troops and jet fuel, the explosion killed eight servicemen and wrecked the plane. The sheer ineptness of the events was widely portrayed as reflecting the President's period in office which was close to its end.

However, the real message of the failed Operation Eagle Claw was that in these harsh and often unforgiving environments, meticulous planning, and a capacity to address the stresses inherent within them, are the keys. Failure to anticipate possible problems and challenges can easily lead to catastrophe and such issues are likely to compound any existing problems associated with searing temperatures, melting components in machinery, and sand in the engines.

Boundaries and barriers

Vulnerability to invasion by people considered less advanced and less civilized, but more warlike, has long been a problem. This is particularly so when these potential invaders occupy vast, open territories from which their foe can emerge, strike, and then retreat. The tribes of Mongolia for the Chinese, and for the Romans the Picts in

Scotland, are such situations. One response to these threats is to build or otherwise create a barrier. Offa's Dyke between England and Wales, and Hadrian's Wall between northern England and Scotland, are typical examples.

The Great Wall of China

The Great Wall is an ancient series of walls and fortifications located in northern China, widely thought to date back 2,000 years to just after 221BCE, when China was first unified. It is worth noting that almost everything along the Wall that is as old as that, is no more than a mound of earth today. The modern idea of the Wall derives from the stone, battlemented structure built in the Ming Dynasty (1358–1644) and is no more than about 500 years old. Estimates of its length vary from 1,500 to 5,000 miles, but an archaeological survey carried out in 2012 by China's State Administration of Cultural Heritage suggested the Wall is more than double that length and it comes in at some 13,000 miles (21,000km) long.

Much of this structure is not actually a wall, although the Ming era sections around Beijing are. Farther west, brick and stone give way to earth which is sometimes moulded by the elements into gentle banks and ditches, and sometimes nothing is visible at all. In terms of the structure of the built sections, there is much more to the Wall than merely walls or banks. Like Hadrian's Wall there are fortresses, barracks, guard-towers, and beacon towers along the main route of the feature.

The original Wall was commissioned by the First Emperor of China who died in 210BCE, long before the emergence of the more widely recognized threat from the Mongols, around AD800. The threat at this earlier date was from the Xiongnu, who may have been the ancestors of the later Huns. The classic confrontation with the Mongols occurred from the late fourteenth century when they were chased out of China by the Ming rulers. However, the Great Wall was in many ways symbolic as it was easily overrun or avoided by northern tribes raiding into China; in 1449 the Mongols inflicted a significant defeat on the Ming Chinese south of the Wall. The Wall was only completed during a period of relative peace (1571–1644), and even when complete, was vulnerable. For example, it fell to the Manchus invaders in 1644 when a local Ming general opened the far eastern gate, Shanhaiguan, to the warlords.

Libya in the early 1900s

The complex politics and issues in North Africa, particularly Libya, continue today, but with their origins firmly rooted in the past. Its twentieth-century history was dominated by the relationships between colonial Italian ambitions and the native Libyan cultures. Italian colonization started in earnest in 1911 and continued up to 1943. This is tribal

Senussi elders.

country with perhaps seven main tribal groups with deep-seated connections and loyalties which have implications for conflicts and would-be conquerors. Indeed, in the early twentieth century, a significant part of the population was made up of largely nomadic tribes. The terrain of Libya mixes extensive, arid, hot desert with hostile, remote mountains and thus forms the sort of landscape from which guerrilla resistance can be effectively coordinated.

Italian troops advancing along a trench in Libya, 1911.

Caught between the Turks and Italy

Once the bread-basket landscape of the

Roman Empire, by the 1800s, Libya was part of the Ottoman Empire. Following the Italo-Turkish War in 1911, the region was mostly occupied by Italy and two colonies were established, as Italian Tripolitania and Italian Cyrenaica, but with ongoing resistance. The first Italo-Senussi War began in October 1911 when the Italians occupied Tripoli under the pretext of liberating Ottoman vilayats from the control of Istanbul. This triggered uprisings by the Arabic people in Libya but despite the local resistance, the Ottomans ceded Libya to Italy. So, from December 1912 onwards, the Italian military used Savari colonial cavalry troops raised from Arab-Berber communities and which, along with the Spahi (mounted Libyan police), became the Royal Corps of Libyan Colonial Troops. The result of the military incursions was that the Tripoli region was mostly under Italian control by 1914, though there were Arabic revolts in Cyrenaica and Fezzan with uprisings of the nomadic Senussi. The latter were led by Sheikh Sidi Idris al-Mahdi as-Senussi, who later became King Idris I, and these continued up until the Second World War. Following the 1911 Italian invasion, the anti-British Sheik Ahmed Sharif as-Senussi had abdicated as leader of the Senussi, and this paved the way for his cousin Idris to take control. Ahmed had previously led attacks on British military positions in nearby Egypt whereas Idris forged a strategic alliance with Britain. This situation led to an uneasy state of affairs between the Italian-established colonies, now republics, and with both the Italians and the British.

At the close of the First World War the Ottoman Empire found itself on the losing side with Germany, whereas Italy was one of the victorious Allies and this was to have ramifications for Libya. Turkey finally concluded an agreement to hand over control of Libya to the Italians. Nevertheless, Italy was itself mired in deep-seated problems with its economy, and major domestic issues of social, and political turmoil. Unwilling to drive through further military actions in Libya, the Italian government granted Libyans joint Libyan-Italian citizenship and each province had its own parliament and governing council. The Senussi and others were largely happy with this arrangement and Idris, now as Emir of Cyrenaica, personally took part in celebrations in Rome to mark the breakthrough. However, by late 1921, relations between the Senussi and the Italians had soured in part because of the refusal by Idris to disband his independent military capability.

In 1920, the leader of the Tripolitania Republic had died, and internal civil war between the tribal groups ensued. However, realizing that internal conflict reduced their chances of independence from Italy, the regional tribal leaders invited Idris to extend his rule from Cyrenaica into Tripolitania.

In 1922, the request was made formal, though Idris and his advisors were unsure whether to accept the offer because it would affect relations with Italy. Italian policy was against such a unification of Libya as a single entity as this would be contrary to their national interests but nevertheless, in November 1922, Idris accepted the proposals even though he worried that Italy, with its new Fascist leader Benito Mussolini, might retaliate militarily against the Senussi. Indeed, because of this imminent threat, the very next month (December 1922), Idris crossed into Egypt and exile. As expected, the rise of the Italian fascist dictator Benito Mussolini triggered a direct military response by the Italians. However, effective resistance by the Libyan people against the so-called 'pacification campaign' meant the Italian colonization of Tripolitania and Cyrenaica was limited in its initial success. It was not until the early 1930s, that Italy established full control of the country. This Second Italo-Senussi War eventually cost about 56,000 Libyan lives directly, and many others who starved, and this in a country of just a few hundred thousand people.

The Second Italo-Senussi War

By 1934, the two Libyan provinces merged into a single colonial entity named Italian Libya, and which from 1937 administered for Italy through four provinces. By 1939, the coastal provinces along the Mediterranean shoreline reflected the administration and architecture of metropolitan Italy. Effectively, subjugation continued until Libyan occupation by the Allied armies in 1943 as described later in this chapter. At the 1947 Paris Peace Treaty, Italy finally renounced its territorial claims in Libya.

The colonial government changed several times in response to armed Arabic opposition, mainly in Cyrenaica. During the period from 1919 to 1929, the Italian government kept separate colonial administrations for each of the two traditional provinces, and locally controlled devolved assemblies were established with limited independence. These were abandoned in 1927 and by 1929, Tripoli and Cyrenaica were joined into a single colonial province, but resistance continued. So, from 1931 to 1932, reacting to the Libyan partisans, Italian forces, commanded by General Badoglio, undertook a punitive pacification (or suppression) campaign. Worse followed as Badoglio's successor as field commander, General Rodolfo Graziani, was offered by Mussolini, the task of crushing Libyan resistance. His condition for acceptance of the role was that his operation was to be unfettered by any legal restraints from either Italian or international law. Mussolini willingly agreed to the use of illegal tactics and so the oppression intensified.

The Lion of the Desert

Despite the illegal oppression and fatalities, Libyans continued to fight back, the strongest opposition being from the Cyrenaica region. This continued resistance brought to the fore a Senussi sheik called Omar Mukhtar, later known as the 'Lion of the Desert'. From the early days of the Italian invasion, around 1911, he organized resistance and led Libyan military opposition to the Italians for nearly twenty years from the Cyrenaica region. Furthermore, continuing after his capture by the Italians and his execution on 16 September 1931, his example continued to encourage and inspire insurrection. Even today he remains a patriotic hero for the Libyan people.

By profession Mukhtar was a teacher of the Qur'an but he was also remarkably skilled in desert warfare strategy and tactics. Above all, he knew the local geography and terrain well. This aptitude was used to advantage in conflicts with the Italians unaccustomed to desert warfare. For nearly twenty years, Mukhtar led his small, highly aware guerrilla bands in raids against the Italians with great success. After each attack the Libyans simply melted away into the desert and mountain terrain. Mukhtar's small force targeted Italian outposts, cut supply lines and communications, and ambushed troops in remote countryside. The Italian Royal Army was both embarrassed and surprised by the success of Mukhtar's guerrilla tactics.

Mukhtar operated in eastern Libya around Benghazi and in the mountainous region of Jebel Akhdar or the Green Mountain. However, in 1924, the Italian governor Ernesto Bombelli established a counter-guerrilla force which, in April 1925, triggered a major setback to the Libyan guerrillas. Nevertheless, Mukhtar soon adapted his own tactics to counter the Italians and, being based in the east, received continued aid from Egypt. In 1927, despite the increasing controls under Governor Teruzzi, Mukhtar was still successful and in 1928 reorganized his Senussi band to meet new challenges. They were constantly hunted down by the Italian army and had to be ever alert and adapt as necessary to a fluid situation.

General Teruzzi acknowledged Omar Mukhtar's qualities of 'exceptional perseverance and strong willpower'. In 1929, Governor Marshal Pietro Badoglio negotiated a compromise with Mukhtar, which the Italians claimed was a total submission. However, by late October 1929, Mukhtar felt the situation was a charade and re-formed his resistance forces and prepared for an ultimate showdown with the Italian military commander, General Graziani.

In June 1930, a major offensive against Mukhtar's troops had failed to have the desired impact. This led General Graziani, with support from Governor Badoglio, Italian Minister of the Colonies Emilio De Bono, and Benito Mussolini, to prepare and initiate a plan to finally end Libyan resistance. The population of Jebel Akhdar, about 100,000 people, would be forcibly relocated to coastal concentration camps, and the Libyan-Egyptian border was to be fenced to break connections and supplies to the fighters from Egypt, as well as connections to the native population. This strategy, initiated in early 1931, had an immediate impact on the Senussi resistance. Mukhtar's men, without support or reinforcements, were being watched closely, attacked from the air by Italian aircraft, and on the ground by the Italian army. The latter were guided by informers and collaborators, but nevertheless, in the often remote and difficult landscape of arid mountains, deep, hidden valleys, and unbearably hot desert, resistance continued despite the hardship and risk.

Mukhtar's final opponent was Italian General Rodolfo Graziani who described his foe as 'of medium height, stout, with white hair, beard, and moustache, Omar was endowed with a quick and lively intelligence; was knowledgeable in religious matters, and revealed an energetic and impetuous character, both unselfish and uncompromising. Ultimately, even though he was one of the most important Senussi figures he remained very religious, poor, and true to his beliefs. Eventually, on 11 September 1931, Mukhtar was ambushed and taken prisoner, a struggle of nearly twenty years ending as he was wounded in battle and captured. After a mock trial ordered by the Italian court, five days later, Mukhtar, aged 73 years, was hanged before his followers in the Suluq prisoner of war camp. It was reported that he uttered the words 'From God we come, and unto God we shall return'. The Italians hoped that Libyan resistance would die with him, but his inspiration lived on.

Italian war crimes

Even without Omar Mukhtar the Libyan resistance across this large country and its mix of shifting sands and remote mountains, continued. As noted with other examples, in country such as this conquest is one thing but subduing native resistance in the long-term is a totally different proposition. Following a troublesome truce in 1932, the Italians moved the situation to full-scale war and their responses were violent and punitive. Operations included a fence of barbed wire extending from the Mediterranean coast to Jaghbub Oasis and intended to cut supply lines critical to the resistance. The next step was the mass deportation of communities from the Jebel Akhdar to remove local support of the insurrection. This forced migration saw over 100,000 people driven to concentration camps in Suluq and El Agheila. Thousands of Libyans died in the squalid conditions, and it was calculated that at least 80,000 perished in the fighting or through starvation and disease. This was around a third of the total population of Cyrenaica.

In this bitter conflict Italy was guilty of serious war crimes with illegal chemical weapons, refusal to take prisoners of war (executing combatants who surrendered) and mass executions of civilians. Ethnic cleansing involved the forced expulsion of

100,000 Bedouin Cyrenaicans, amounting to about half the Cyrenaica population. Italian soldiers bombed civilians, killed unarmed children, women, and the elderly, and raped and disembowelled women. They were accused of throwing prisoners out of aircraft in flight, running over people with tanks, and daily executions of civilians. From 1930 onwards, tribal villages were attacked with mustard gas bombs, and the Italian occupying force also deliberately reduced livestock numbers by killing, confiscating, or driving animals from pastoral lands to degraded desert areas. This caused further starvation as sheep numbers dropped to 98,000 in 1933 from around 810,000 in 1926. Goats reduced to 25,000 from 70,000, and camels to 2,000 from 75,000.

The concentration camps

During 1930 and 1931, all the nomads of northern Cyrenaica were relocated to huge concentration camps, and around 12,000 Cyrenaicans were executed. The camps were claimed to be 'oases of modern civilization, hygienic and efficiently run'. In practice, with limited sanitation, some 20,000 inmates, camels, and other animals all crowded into about one square kilometre; with just basic medical services, the camps were inhumane death-traps. The Soluch and Sisi Ahmed el Magrun concentration camps for instance had approximately 33,000 inmates and just one doctor. Typhus and other diseases spread quickly and in September 1933, when the camps closed, 40,000 of the 100,000 prisoners had died. Some senior Libyan figures were sent to concentration camps in Italy itself, and many died there. Facing such brutality and overwhelming military odds, by 1934, the indigenous resistance in Libya had been largely quashed.

Libya as a unified state

The Italian governor, Italo Balbo, now declared the new state of Italian Libya in place of the two regional states. The older name of Libya was resurrected for the new, unified colony but split into four administrative provinces: Tripoli, Misrata, Benghazi, and Derna, and the country was under military administration. In March 1937, there was a state visit to Libya by Mussolini who by now declared himself Protector of Islam, playing an Arab nationalist card in his pre-war efforts to confront both France and Britain. At home, he was settling Italian colonists into the main Libyan cities, particularly Tripoli. By 1939, there were over 100,000 Italian colonists who received land, buildings, and businesses.

Laws were passed in 1939 to allow Muslims to join the Italian National Fascist Party and Libyan military units were created with 30,000 native Muslim soldiers

French colonials fighting in Tunisia and Morocco, 1881.

French legions in Tunisia, 1881.

forming part of the Italian army. These forces took part in the Italian offensive against the British army in Egypt. However, by 1942, the tide had turned and the Axis forces in North Africa were defeated.

The British and other European powers had a long history of warfare in the North African deserts, such as in Sudan, 1884.

Omar al Mukhtar had held out against vastly superior Italian troops for nearly twenty years. Using his excellent knowledge and understanding of the regional topography and terrain, and with the support of local people, he was able to wage a long-term and highly successful guerrilla war. Libya provides an example of how desert and mountain conditions can combine to facilitate guerrilla resistance against technically and numerically superior forces. The end of the Libyan conflict with Italy was brought about by the wider conflicts of the Second World War.

The North Africa Campaign in the Second World War

Early in the 1940s, a combined Axis German-Italian army enjoyed considerable success across North Africa. With the control of access to oil wells and resources, and to the strategically significant Suez Canal, all open to a power grab, this was a key conflict in the Second World War. However, as already discussed, the arid lands of the north of Africa proved to be an unforgiving battlescape.

As we have seen, Italy had long had interests in Libya and North Africa and the Second World War came as an opportunity to consolidate those by military force. Since March 1941, the German-Italian army had swept through North Africa led and inspired by First World War veteran, Field Marshal Erwin Rommel, and his Panzer tank divisions. Rommel's astute and highly successful tactics gained him the nickname of the Desert Fox. By 1942, the German-led assault was focussed

Senior British military officers in North Africa, Second World War.

on the remote town of El Alamein on the Egyptian coast some seventy miles west of Alexandria. The prize was the Suez Canal, a vital connecting route between Britain and its Indian colonies, and as a supply line to the oilfields of Iraq and Iran. Strategically, El Alamein has the Mediterranean Sea to the north and the quicksand of the Sahara Desert, the Qattara Depression to the southwest. El Alamein was the hub of the conflict and in the first battle, from 1 to 27 July 1942, the Allies prevailed. However, by August, the Axis powers were once more in the ascendency.

The Allied army was led by General Bernard Montgomery with 190,000 men, 1,000 tanks, 900 artillery guns, and 1,400 anti-tank guns, a formidable force. Rommel had under his direct command around 116,000 troops, 540 tanks, 500 artillery guns, and 490 anti-tank weapons. However, strategic issues were taking effect and a significant weakness with Rommel's force was that they were running short on vital supplies. This meant the advantage was gradually shifting to the Allies, and their attack began on 23 October with a heavy artillery barrage and the clearing of a route through the German minefields. By 4 November, they achieved a key breakthrough and despite suffering heavy losses to German anti-tank weapons, the Allies drove the Axis force back through Libya and toward Tunisia.

This was a major turning point since El Alamein was the first significant defeat for the Axis powers in the West and the one that triggered the famous Churchill 1942 speech that 'this is not the end but it is perhaps the end of the beginning'. The battle probably turned on the British-made Crusader MKII tanks and the American-

Even before Hitler's invasion of Russia, Germans had experienced the rigours of warfare in the East European terrain. Here German and Russian troops are pictured at the Battle of Tannenberg, 1914.

made Sherman M4s. Supply problems also meant Rommel had to dig in and defend rather than use his favoured mobile tank warfare.

The desert environment presents an open field for battle but one with inherent problems and difficulties. Mobile tracked vehicles such as modern-day tanks are a part of the answer, but they demand a great deal of fuel and therefore supply chains are vital. Above all, that was perhaps Rommel's downfall. Understanding desert environments and adaptation to the extreme conditions are the key factors alongside the ability to maintain supply lines for fuel and ammunition particularly. Food and potable water are also essential for desert warfare.

Operation Barbarossa

Considering unforgiving landscapes, potential invading forces into Russia have always struggled with this expansive, almost unending countryside, and the inherent problems of establishing and maintaining supply lines. The other key factor, as Napoleon discovered, is the extreme weather of the region and the variation between winter and summer. Another problem for any invading force is the sheer scale of Russia and its vast tracts of countryside, much of it hot in summer and bitterly cold in winter.

The extensive flat steppes of southwest Russia provided ideal terrain for massed tank warfare. When Hitler launched Operation Barbarossa into the Soviet Union in June 1941, the aims were to seize control of land for future German peoples, so-called *lebensraum* or living space, to capture slaves as labour for the German war effort in Russia, and to occupy the important oilfields in the Urals. Following a rapid incursion into Russian territory the project stalled as the Germans got closer to Moscow. Indeed, the invasion along an 1,800-mile front apparently took the Soviet

German infantry in a hastily dug trench in Poland, First World War.

German motorcycle bogged down in Russia 1941.

leadership by surprise with the Red Army unprepared and partially demobilized. Cutting through the northern border, German tanks, employing their blitzkrieg tactic, sped fifty miles beyond the frontier on just the first day of the invasion. They had reached Minsk, 200 miles beyond it by 27 June. Almost 300,000 prisoners were

German transport struggling during the Russian muddy season, 1941.

captured in this first wave, though a significant part of the Russian force escaped eastward. Nevertheless, the swiftness of the German incursion was a terrible shock to the Russians.

The defence of Moscow

Soviet forces operated a strategic defence of the Moscow area with three defensive belts, newly raised reserve armies, and troops imported from Siberian and Far Eastern Military districts. Factory workers and students were enlisted into newly formed militias. There was even a unit made up of young female volunteers charged with halting the German 16th Tank division. Despite already horrendous losses of personnel, they were able to amass 1,250,000 men, 1,000 tanks, and 7,600 guns. Then, as the German offensives slowed, the Soviet strategic counterattack, and other smaller assaults, pushed them back to the cities of Oryol, Vyazma, and Vitebsk. In effect, the Soviets virtually surrounded the three German armies.

A further factor was the stubbornness with which the Russian troops fought and even held out in pockets of resistance behind what were now the German lines, as the Panzer divisions swept through. Then the weather kicked in and in mid-July 1941 brought a series of terrific rainstorms which turned the sand-covered Russian roads to

The German approach to Moscow 1941.

mud. This meant the German wheeled-transport vehicles following the tanks made slow progress and were left behind; the supply lines became increasingly stretched. The Germans were also seriously affected by the scorched-earth policy initially used by the retreating Russians. As they fell back, the Soviet armies had burnt crops, destroyed bridges, and evacuated factories. Amazingly, entire factories such as steel and munitions plants in western regions were disassembled, shipped eastwards by rail, and then re-built and put back into use. Most of their railway rolling stock, like railroad cars, was also either destroyed or relocated.

This stopped the Germans from using the Russian railway system because their own stock was the wrong gauge. By 15 November 1941, the cold wintry weather caused the ground to freeze, which at least solved the mud problem. The armoured Wehrmacht spearheads, now made up of fifty-one divisions, advanced to encircle Moscow, joining up east of the capital and close to the city of Noginsk. In response, the Russians struck back but the Wehrmacht withstood much of the Red Army's counterattack. Launched on 6 December, Marshal Georgi Zhukov's forces were successful in pushing back the Germans from the main approaches to Moscow. However, it was clear that they would be unable to follow Stalin's totally unrealistic demands to press back the opposition from their key positions along the battle front.

A German convoy stuck in the mud, Russia.

The result of trying to do this was that massive losses were inflicted on the Soviet army who were often slaughtered in impossible attacks. While the Russians were able to draw on vast numbers, many of their soldiers were poorly trained and equipped, certainly in comparison with the highly trained and disciplined Wehrmacht.

Nevertheless, Hitler, like Stalin, was unrealistic about the condition and capabilities of his armies. Most of all, he increasingly refused to accept unwelcome news from the front. Because he had anticipated a swift result from Barbarossa, the troops were not issued with winter uniforms or equipment, and they suffered badly when the bitter weather of the Russian winter closed in earlier than anticipated. Hitler also insisted that the German troops were to hold their ground in the face of the Soviet counteroffensives. This was even the case when tactical retreats were more sensible. The Russian generals understood that with massive losses by the Soviet army, the Battle of Moscow was indeed a Pyrrhic victory. They were losing around 500,000 men per month during the conflict, which was nearly six times more than the Wehrmacht and even with their vast human resources this was unacceptable.

However, the Soviet forces left abandoned and burnt-out settlements and farms as

A German staff car and motorcycle bogged down in Russia in the muddy season, 1941.

they retreated, and with supply chains stretched or non-existent, the German troops starved. With the Russian winter now setting in as well, the rain and snow turned roads and the wider landscape into trackless quagmires. The German tanks and other vehicles were now bogged down in the mud and the Soviets could more easily counterattack. By this time, with heavy losses, armoured vehicles struggling, and taking significant casualties, the Germans began a slow and very painful retreat. Nevertheless, despite the heavy German losses in the territories west of Moscow during the winter of 1941–42, Hitler still felt confident that the Germans and their allies could beat the Soviet Red Army. So, in spring 1942, despite Operation Barbarossa failing to decisively defeat the Soviet Union in a single campaign, the Wehrmacht had captured vast expanses of territory, including Ukraine, Belarus, and the Baltic republics. Hitler's strategy was now to focus on taking Stalingrad and the Caucasus oilfields, but this was to prove a critical error.

The move split the German forces in two, with one part heading south to the oilfields and the other moving on Stalingrad. The assault on Stalingrad began in earnest in August 1942, and Russian leader Joseph Stalin pronounced that the defenders would take 'not one step back'. However, with intensive bombing from the Luftwaffe much of the city was turned to rubble as the Germans advanced. By mid-September, the Soviet army was forced back to a narrow strip of the city along the bank of the Volga River and the street fighting that followed was some of the fiercest in the war. Then, in November 1942, the Soviet forces triggered a major two-pronged assault to the rear of the main German army and on the Hungarian and Romanian troops covering their back. This manoeuvre effectively encircled the German forces at Stalingrad, who under Hitler's orders to fight to the death, carried on until January

Military convoy on a wet, muddy road.

1943 when they finally surrendered. The Germans had tried and failed to break out from the Soviet encirclement and attempted to re-supply the force by air, without success. Thus ended the bloodiest battle ever witnessed in global warfare. There were around two million people, troops and civilians killed. The Axis forces lost around 800,000 dead and the Soviets something around 1,100,000.

Rat War

The Russians employed a tactic that the Germans described as *rattenkrieg* or 'rat war', which was essentially fighting for every building. If the Germans took a location, the Russians made every effort to gain it back. The conflict was unforgiving, and numbers cannot reflect the reality of the events. However, from 10,000 soldiers in the 13th Soviet Rifle Division for example, only 320, three per cent, survived.

An unforgiving landscape

The outcome of the German invasion into Soviet Russia had foundered on a combination of Russian tenacity and ability to accept huge losses, but also on the impacts of the flat steppe countryside, the extreme cold weather, and the consequent mud-bath conditions. With roads and wider landscapes turned into quagmires there were huge problems for vehicles becoming bogged down and of supply chains being maintained.

In this cataclysmic conflict, the Ural Mountains were a barrier to the advancing

German vehicles crossing a swollen river during the Russian muddy season, 1941

German transport completely bogged down in Russia.

German vehicles on a rutted road during the Russian muddy season, 1941.

Axis forces. Across this often bleak and inhospitable terrain, sheer distance combined with harsh winters to disrupt German supply lines. The German army logistics failed badly. By comparison, their access to extensive food-production areas meant the Soviet armies were kept well-fed. Furthermore, supplies shipped in from ports along the Arctic Sea also facilitated essential refuelling of Soviet transport. With roads and wider terrain turned to mud-baths even in the summer, and with the Germans short on appropriate clothing and essential supplies, the bitter winter weather was a deciding factor. The combination of hopelessly ambitious orders from remote commanders (on both sides), together with extreme weather, impossible conditions underfoot, and tenacious fighting meant a turning point in the whole war but with horrendous losses for both sides. The Russian pincer movement at Stalingrad that surrounded the German force and cut off their supplies was perhaps the death-knell for Barbarossa. On 23 January 1943, the German commander in the field in charge at Stalingrad, out of food and ammunition, requested permission to surrender. This was refused by Hitler and nine days later the Russians overran the German headquarters and took prisoner about 91,000 German soldiers. They were mostly sick, starving, wounded, and simply exhausted.

The Red Army was successful in pressing back the German forces across the plains and steppes of southern Russia. In March 1943, progress was then halted by

Whatever the terrain, supply lines are vital, in this case supplying the infantry in their First World War trench.

a German counteroffensive and a period of stalemate. However, the Germans were determined to press ahead with a further counterattack around the city of Kursk to a position where the Russian forces had advanced beyond their own frontline. But as they delayed the strike to bring in supplies, including new tanks, and reinforcements, they gave the Russians time to prepare for the assault. They were able to dig trenches, and bunkers, to lay mines, and to prepare tank traps. In July 1943, with about 800,000 men and 2,700 tanks, the German army advanced. Having travelled about twenty-two miles the Germans were faced down by the Russian forces and ended up fighting one of the largest tank battles ever.

Hitler's reasoning for the delay had been a desire to have the very latest Panther and Tiger tanks on the battlefield. These were both heavily armoured and very effective machines, but they had supply issues and the technology employed was now at its limits, so they frequently broke down. Additionally, the German army was generally short on fuel and these heavy tanks were fuel hungry. These tanks were deployed alongside the Panzer IV which was the latest and heavier variant of the standard German tank. However, the Russians, with 1.5 million troops and nearly 5,000 tanks, were using their well-armoured, reliable, and easy to manufacture T-34s. The battle ended with no decisive winner until news came through of the Allied

A tank dragging a captured heavy naval gun, First World War.

invasion of Sicily; Hitler withdrew his main armies and re-directed them to the Italian campaign.

Over the rolling croplands of Ukraine and Southern Russia, the role of the tank in such conflicts was well-established. Furthermore, the mobility of the T-34s was a key factor in their success although driver safety was not a consideration. Many tanks were simply rushed off production lines to the battlefields, some with basic components missing, yet able to function. Significant numbers of the tank crews died or were injured by damage inflicted simply from the machine itself.

Plains and deserts in warfare

Overall, open plains and extensive deserts bring advantage to certain types of warfare. From nomadic horsemen of the central European plains to the tank battles of North Africa and the Russian steppes, expansive, flat countryside can bring opportunities but also serious problems. Inability to cope with extreme weather such as rain, snow, and cold on the one hand, or driving, windblown sands on the other, has foiled many military actions. Furthermore, over-stretched supply lines can prove critical and over-ambitious leadership ignorant of the actual frontline conditions in the battlescape can be devastating.

French army training for a concealed battery, First World War.

The Charge of the Cuirassiers. Cavalry equipped with a cuirass, sword, and pistols, during the First World War.

Durham Light Infantry.

Chapter 10
Forests and Woods

In terms of strategy and tactics, military commanders view forests and urban areas as having a degree of similarity. They are both classified as 'close terrain' and the implications are close quarters fighting with potentially elevated levels of casualties. The opposite is 'open terrain' which mostly consists of farmland, grassland, desert, and similar landscapes. In forest or town, a conflict soon breaks down into uncoordinated fighting with lines of communication difficult to maintain and central command hard to achieve. Also, at close quarters, weapons can inflict more severe damage.

Of course, there are major differences between forests and towns and both examples of close terrain exhibit big variations. Scattered woodland, enclosed woods, forests, plantations, rainforest, jungle, and cold taiga, all have different characteristics, patterns, and occurrence. These necessitate different equipment and modified tactics.

British Rifle Brigade in woodland cover close to the German trenches, First World War.

Forests in the battlescape

Forests and wooded landscapes are key resources, providing vital raw materials and supplies for warfare and can also be places of cover and sanctuary. Dense forested lands provide shelter for those fleeing authority and for indigenous peoples threatened by insurgents. Forested countryside will be familiar to those living in and around it and can be used as cover for ambushes and counterattacks against invading forces. Around AD955 for instance, the Germanic forces of the Holy Roman Emperor Otto I were under assault from incoming Slavic tribes. On hearing that a 25,000-strong Magyar force was heading for Bavaria, Otto led his troops into the protection of the Rauherhorst Forest to avoid the open plans favoured by his opponents' horsemen. A part of the Magyar force harried the baggage train at the rear of the East Franks' column as it entered the forest, but the overall result was a catastrophic defeat for the Magyars against a numerically inferior Germanic force. This was compounded by the problems encountered by the defeated army as it retreated and was ambushed as it struggled to cross the swollen Isar River.

Up to the 1700s, across Europe in particular, the medieval and later Swiss troops were the only force effectively trained and experienced in forest combat. Most other professional soldiers were prepared for conflict in open country with generally accepted procedures and protocols to suit. Armies in general were ill-equipped

First World War German trenches with forest in the background.

for woodland conflicts and their officers had very limited experience of fighting in forested terrain. In this sense, many of the disciplined troops were not well prepared for forest conflicts and furthermore, such battles became more difficult the bigger the forest area. Over the period, there were four main approaches developed: 1) use of the forest for trained military units; 2) woodland as a base for attacks; 3) forests as refuges from attacking forces; 4) forest-based guerrillas or partisans. However, a general lack of maps or other topographic or geographic information beyond basic areas crudely marked, and major roads or settlements, made detailed planning based on sound knowledge of terrain very difficult. In these circumstances, good local knowledge can become invaluable. This was something utilized by European forces fighting in eighteenth-century North America, especially the French in Canada, where they took on local native-American scouts and guides with good knowledge of the extensive, forested landscape.

Various topographic features influence the tactical significance of forested countryside, including the shape and size of woodland, the age of its trees and the density of undergrowth from scrub to bracken. Whether forest ground is on wet or dry land, on upland or lowland, or on flat or rough terrain becomes significant. Swampy regions, or rocky ground, may have forest areas with edges that creep out on spurs or down valleys and morph into scrub or brushwood. Seasonal changes also

In the woods near Ypres to show the impact of warfare on a forest landscape, First World War.

Glencorse Wood with a German shell bursting and little of the treescape remaining, 1917.

Charcoal burning in a Sussex Wood to supply fuel for the trenches, First World War.

German soldiers sawing timber for larger constructional work, First World War.

German soldiers chopping wood for fuel.

affect woods and forests, particularly those with deciduous trees. This affects colours, light, visibility, and possible concealment.

Other factors are roadways and tracks, clearings, glades, and rides, all of which may offer space for infantry and possible routes for movement. These may aid movement of men and horses in historic conflicts, and personnel and vehicles in modern warfare. Forests have also been used in modern battles to conceal heavy armour on the move, such as tanks, or as transit and storage sites when tree canopies can hide the vehicles. Also relating to contemporary conflicts, tanks and other heavy armour can bulldoze smaller trees and shrubs but the fallen timber can then make travel through the area more difficult. Indeed, necessary clearance of such debris can reduce the personnel available for action.

Finally, for both defending and attacking armies, supply of food, fuel for vehicles and for heating and cooking, and in the past, hay for horses, and ammunition can become problematic. Evacuation of casualties from the area of conflict, and in some cases guarding any prisoners taken, can pose difficulties.

Even today, forests and other treescapes provide important raw materials for society. However, in past times, and especially before the Industrial Revolution, forests and woodlands were the source of essential products for both communities and for military purposes. They could be harvested for timber used in the construction of bridges, fences

Carrying 'Horses de Frise' which were portable defences made of small pieces of wood and branches, First World War.

Lining the German trenches with cut branches and coppice wood, First World War.

and barriers, props for trench systems, for building fortifications, and for things like waggons and other transport. The abatis was a barrier of cut timbers with sharpened ends, these were placed in the ground to face an oncoming enemy and was particularly used by infantry under attack from cavalry. Wood, which has a lesser diameter and is often from coppice woodlands, was used for smaller items. Cut wood was also needed for fuel for heating and cooking, and for making charcoal for a variety of functions including the manufacture of gunpowder. The impacts of warfare on forests and forest resources were often catastrophic.

Even though many battles have been fought in wooded or forested landscapes

Taking charcoal from the kilns in a French forest for the trenches, 1918.

in comparison with other settings for conflicts, there is a surprising dearth of critical information regarding terrain and tactical issues.

A partial explanation for this is that many conventional armies tried to avoid woodlands because they hid the enemy from view. Indeed, it may be fairly stated that military commanders dislike woodlands unless it is they that are using the benefits of the terrain. Trees conceal the enemy and associated hazards and provide ideal opportunities for ambushes and for combatants to attack enemy supply lines or the rear guard. Tree cover also helps conceal direct observation of an army's movements, numbers, and progress.

Forest or woodland, particularly if there is dense undergrowth, make life very difficult for an attacker even if they have superiority of numbers, training, and weapons. Soldiers easily lose sight of one another once they are inside woodland and can become disorientated even when only a hundred metres or so from the forest edge. Typical tactics employed in open country simply cannot be applied in a dense forest landscape. Lines are easily broken, and communication becomes increasingly difficult. Furthermore, sightlines and firing become problematic and perhaps worse still, whilst trees provide cover, the impact of projectiles striking trees can cause splintering to devastating effect. Vehicle use is only possible if there are effective tracks and forest roads but again, these bring their own hazards as obvious places to set booby-traps and ambushes. Horses may be more feasible but low-hanging

German infantry firing from cover, 1916.

branches and blocked tracks can be a problem.

Furthermore, if you are alien to a geographic area then the forest represents the unknown where partisans or other enemies can wait unseen. Densely forested countryside holds the threat of ambush, delay, and harassment. Commanders of troops on the move in foreign areas generally try to go around forests rather than through them. Today we can apply new technologies with remote sensing and geographical positioning systems, but despite this, forested landscapes and particularly those in difficult terrain, present major challenges. Even though modern weapons are increasingly devastating, the cover of wood or forest can tip the balance slightly toward irregular troops or partisans. Bands of defenders can encircle their enemy and ambush small groups of the attacking force effectively separating them from one another.

Military leaders in the field will try to avoid being led into forest conflicts and may attempt to use the locations of woodland to divert an opponent into combat in a more open landscape of their choosing. Defensive forces may similarly try to force the attackers into more favoured positions of their choosing. Despite the downsides of forest fighting for attackers, they hold advantages for defenders, particularly for irregular forces and small numbers of resistance fighters who can melt into the treescapes. Jungle fighting can be viewed as a particular type of forest conflict.

European forests and the Roman legions

View of a German First World War trench to show timber boarding.

The role of forest warfare for the Picts and Scots was discussed earlier and proved highly successful from the time of the Romans through into the medieval period. An early example of the importance of extensive dense forest was in the long-term conflicts between the Roman Empire and the Germanic tribes north of the Rhine River. By around 9BCE the Romans held much of the territory east of the Rhine and were warned of a revolt brewing in the region. Aided by a Germanic tribal leader, around 20,000 Roman troops were led deep into the region's forest. As the legions passed through to the area in question, they were constantly harried by Germanic tribes and stragglers were slaughtered. Because of the dense undergrowth the Romans were unable to pursue their assailants and the extended column was increasingly vulnerable. Worse was to come because the legionnaires discovered that their route was blocked, and they were trapped. The Roman leader Varus committed suicide and most of the troops were killed. The long-term outcome was that the empire rarely ventured so far north again, and the Rhine became the effective border.

The North American Colonies

Examples of forest warfare were discussed earlier with respect to the conflicts between the British and the breakaway United States during the American War of Independence or the American Revolutionary War (19 April 1775 – 3 September 1783). The typical British redcoats and their European mercenary forces were unprepared for conflict in forested terrain. Indeed, these conditions favoured the frontiersmen of the United States forces who were less formally trained in military tactics, but able to hide in the tree cover and snipe at the opposition from a distance. However, like many such conflicts this was an affair which was neither straightforward nor simple, and the forces involved, the terrain of the battles, and the tactics employed, all varied accordingly. Indeed, there have been three distinct types of warfare described:

1. Colonial conflict relating to both trade regulation and taxation by the British imperialist government policy.
2. Civil war throughout the thirteen states of that time, involving patriots, loyalists, and those neutral to the causes. Especially in the southern states the conflict was often between patriots and loyalists without any British involvement. This effectively morphed into the later American Civil War (12 April 1861 to 26 May 1865) after independence from Britain had been secured.
3. A part of the first global warfare, in this case between France, Spain, the Dutch Republic, and Britain, with North America being one of the theatres of operation.

These various scenarios each implied a different terrain, different participants, and hence variations in tactics. The French and Indian War was part of the global Seven Years' War which was settled by the 1763 Peace of Paris. This accord relieved France of its territories known as New France and consisting of extensive areas of eastern Canada, and effectively ended the threat to the British colonies of the French presence. In southern areas around Florida for instance, lands were occupied by Spain, which continued into the late 1700s. Having secured these lands in Atlantic Canada and West Florida, mostly with French or Spanish-speaking Catholic populations, the British government consolidated its hold by encouraging numbers of English-speaking settlers. To avoid an expensive military occupation, agreements also sought to limit conflict between white settlers and Native American tribes west of the Appalachian Mountains.

However, the conflict between Britain and pro-independence Americans spun out of control and became a major insurrection across the colony, ultimately leading to an independent United States of America. The conflict took place within two main campaign theatres in the then thirteen states, plus a lesser arena, but still strategically significant, west of the Appalachian Mountains. War started in the northern arena and was ongoing from 1775 to 1778. The patriot forces had key victories in the southern zone, and after a British force was defeated at Saratoga in October 1777, the French formally entered the war on the side of the patriots.

The territorial and political disputes within the three areas were inextricably linked. Indeed, from the perspective of the twenty-first century, an obvious question is why the US and Canada are not joined as one nation. However, at the time of the American Revolution, Canada had only been under British control for thirteen years. It was still mostly populated by French-speaking Catholics who did not trust the Americans. Indeed, the Quebec Act of 1774 protecting the rights of 'Canadiens' (French settlers) to keep the French language together with French civil law and Catholicism, was labelled by the Americans as being an 'Intolerable Act' which was in part a trigger for the Declaration of Independence. If the wider scope of North America is considered, excluding modern-day Alaska, then there were seventeen colonies of which four remained loyal to the British crown to form what broadly amounts to today's Canada. Thirteen colonies broke away to make up the nucleus of what evolved into the United States, but the Canadians were largely opposed to this. The Province of Ontario for example, was mostly established by those loyal to the British Crown and had moved from what was becoming the independent United States. They chose this situation rather than what was in their eyes a treasonous breakaway republic. Modern Canada developed significantly as a counter-response to the formation of the United States. Britain made the decision to allow Quebec to retain its French customs and culture rather than imposing forced anglicization or even deportation. This decision was one of numerous triggers for the American Revolution.

Forested terrain

Fighting across extensively forested mountain landscapes against firstly the French and their native American allies, and then against militias of independence-minded frontiersmen, Americans employed all the facets of conflicts in mountains and forests. Local knowledge of the terrain and of the natural resources of the region proved very important. In French Canada, the British military eventually won but this was just one part of a global conflict. In what became the United States, the American frontiersmen won the day. The conflict ebbed and flowed with varying alliances between Native American tribes and the British, and United States patriots and the French, sometimes with Native Americans too. Following military defeats, the retreating patriot forces applied the same strategy successfully used in campaigns around the world. As the patriot general, Horatio Gates, retreated in 1777, his soldiers blockaded roads, demolished bridges, dammed rivers, and streams, and took or destroyed food supplies. One example was at Saratoga, where the now-under-pressure British suffered heavy losses. By 11 October 1777, the British and their German mercenaries were pinned down and unable to escape. Heavy rain turned their Base camp into a 'squalid hell' of mud and starving cattle. With supplies dangerously low and the countryside largely stripped of resources by the patriots, they were in a dreadful state and had many wounded troops suffering. On 17 October, an estimated 6,222 British and German soldiers surrendered. This was just one example of a protracted and very difficult military campaign. Emerging from this, Canada and the United States became very different and separate countries. For the Native Americans, it seems that their cultures and communities in the northern forests remained more intact than that of their counterparts on the vast American plains, the prairies. Extensive mountains and forests provide sanctuary whereas on the open plain, where the white settlers pushed ever westward, the habitat was often converted to cattle ranching and breadbasket corn farming, and the once ubiquitous bison herds were driven close to extinction. The Native American cultures, as described previously, were inexorably squeezed out from the more easily accessible prairies but remained for decades in remote mountains and the wet forests of the Everglades. In the dense forests and high mountain regions of the northern US and of Canada, the Native Americans retain more possession than their southern counterparts.

The extensive forests of European Poland

Large areas of Poland are covered in forest and other areas include extensive peatbogs. The forest regions include Europe's last so-called primeval forest at Białowieża. Throughout history, sandwiched between great superpowers such as the emerging greater Germany and imperial Russia, then the Soviet Union, Poland has suffered incursions, counter-incursions, and conquests. The forests were prized as desirable resources, particularly as hunting grounds, with (now extinct) aurochs and European bison. These were the prey of Polish kings, Russian Tsars, Lithuanian grand dukes, German kaisers, and Nazi generals. So, the forests provided sanctuary for the indigenous people but also an incentive for powerful neighbours to capture this prestigious landscape and its unique resources for the sport of hunting.

On the one hand, the Polish forests were vast resources which lured Prussian poachers and the military forces of European powers noted above. On the other they were landscapes into which partisans might retreat and strike back. Invading armies as noted previously, would often seek to circumnavigate extensive forests because of the hazards they involved or hid. During the Napoleonic War (around 1812), most skirmishes and battles took place outside of the Forest but soldiers from both sides sought sanctuary within the cover it provided. These landscapes also provided cover for some of the appalling atrocities of modern warfare such as the murder and brutal disposal of Polish soldiers and resistance fighters during the Second World War.

As the German troops advanced through Poland into the Soviet Union in 1943, they located a mass grave in the Katyn Forest near Russian Smolensk. The grave contained around 4,500 bodies, many in Polish uniforms, some with hands tied behind their backs; they were stacked in layers twelve bodies deep. The burial pit was about ninety-two feet long and fifty-two feet wide. The executed victims had been shot in the back of the head. These victims reflected the multi-ethnic make-up of the Polish state that included ethnic Poles, Ukrainians, Belarusians, and Jews. Many had been captured when the Soviets invaded Poland on 17 September 1939. Thousands of Polish military and intelligentsia were captured and arrested with around 22,000 prisoners of war imprisoned in three camps in the Soviet Union: Kozelsk, Ostashkov, and Starobelsk. On 5 March 1940, Stalin signed a decree for the execution of these prisoners to be carried out in April and May 1940. It was the Polish prisoners of war at Kozelsk camp that were shot at the Katyn Forest site. Those at Ostashkov and Starobelsk were shot at the prisons of the NKVD (People's Commissariat for Internal Affairs, the Soviet Secret Police) at Kalinin and Kharkov.

Impacts of warfare on the forest

In Białowieża, a major impact of warfare was the harvesting of tall trees as timber for ships' masts, something that dramatically reduced with the coming of the ironclad warships. Furthermore, because of the known hunting interest, much of the forest was strictly protected from unfettered taking of timber or poaching of animals. Conflict however threatened such stability. For instance, the impact of the German invasion in the First World War was marked by their occupation of the forest from 1915 to 1918; during that time they harvested approximately 2.6 million cubic metres of timber. With uncontrolled exploitation and hunting, this period wrought a devastating impact on this unique forest landscape. Fortunately, much of the core area was left unscathed. However, in the first few years, the population of the globally unique European bison was reduced from 727 to 160 animals. Despite orders for protection, German soldiers, Soviet insurgents, and poachers, still hunted with impunity in the forest until February 1919 when the Polish army re-captured the region. The last bison was shot just one month previously, and thousands of deer and wild boar had been slaughtered.

The Second World War had a similarly brutal impact on the great forest. In 1939, following the Soviet invasion, the local inhabitants of Polish ethnicity, including the forest rangers, were deported to remote areas of the Soviet Union. Their place was taken by imported Soviet forest workers who, in 1941, were displaced by the invading Germans. Hermann Göring aimed to turn the forest into the largest hunting reserve in the world. However, from July 1941 onward, the forest was a sanctuary for partisans both Polish and Soviet. In a vicious crackdown, the Nazi authorities set in

US military tractor sinking in the swamp in the Philippines, Second World War.

motion mass executions. The Russians had left around 800 to 1,000 soldiers in the forest to continually harass the German army. There are graves of people murdered by the Gestapo when, between 1942 and 1944, Göring ordered Luftwaffe security battalions in the Białowieża Forest to stop these anti-partisan activities. Thousands of Jews and Polish civilians were killed as a result. Then, in July 1944, the forest was overrun by the Soviet Red Army; as the Wehrmacht soldiers retreated, they destroyed the historic Białowieża hunting lodge. After the war ended, the remaining forest was split between Soviet Belarusia and Poland. The forest clearly impacted on major conflicts but was itself significantly altered by warfare.

Jungle warfare

Fighting in tropical rainforest, or jungle, can be regarded as a particular version of forest warfare, and very specific and extreme conditions may apply. The issues and factors noted earlier apply here but with the impacts considerably magnified by inherently hot and humid conditions, and there can be serious health implications from diseases to skins infections, and unpleasant parasites. In modern times, there have been extensive conflicts in the tropical regions of the Pacific and around the Indian Ocean, from Burma to Malaysia, and from Vietnam to Indonesia. A big challenge for military commanders has been the sheer scale of these landscapes, their

American vehicles completely stuck in mud in the Philippines, Second World War.

impenetrable nature, and that conflicts may occur across and within entire regions. Jungles often vastly exceed anything in Europe or even in North America in terms of woodland cover. These landscapes favour indigenous guerrillas and local insurgents familiar with the terrain, the soldiers most likely to operate from dense, wet, tropical forests. Aircraft can fly over extensive woodlands and tracked vehicles such as tanks could be used, but local knowledge and adaptation become key facets to any jungle conflict. In the Pacific regions warfare, such as that fought in the Second World War, often involved mountains, dense forests, and islands or archipelagos.

Jungle warfare is a description of specific conditions and thus requires techniques for a military force to survive and be combatant. In this respect, the jungle brings various peculiarities and has a variety of effects on military operations. As in any close forest, dense vegetation restricts lines of sight. At the same time, this cover provides opportunities for camouflage and abundant materials for constructing defensive structures. The terrain is frequently without useable roadways, and those that do exist are often not accessible by vehicles. This means that transit, logistical supply lines, and general transport become problematic. Furthermore, in jungle terrain it is difficult to deploy modern armoured troops and vehicles effectively. In modern warfare, indeed since the 1960s, this has led to reliance on access and supply by air or sometimes river. These transportation difficulties place emphasis on engineering

Japanese transport stuck in the mud, Second World War.

solutions to improve roads, construct bridges and airfields, and to provide potable water. However, once constructed, such infrastructures are targets for guerrilla counter offensives and booby traps. Success in jungle conflicts is often achieved by small units trained for these conditions with tactics and leadership tailored to these situations.

As already noted, the jungle environment is an inherently unhealthy place, especially for non-indigenous people. There are numerous tropical diseases and unpleasant parasites that will require medical treatment.

Burma, Malaya, and the Pacific

The Second World War brought jungle combat to the fore in several battlescapes, particularly Burma, Malaya, Indonesia, and the Pacific more widely. When war in the Pacific began in the Far East, following the late 1941 attack on Pearl Harbor, the Japanese Imperial Forces soon advanced on all fronts. In truth there had already been longstanding conflicts between Japan, China, and other nations in the region,

The impact of intensive warfare on a wooded landscape, Polygon Wood, Belgium, 1917.

but it was the airborne assault on the Americans that brought these tensions into the Second World War. The Japanese had some experience of fighting in these conditions and terrain, and in the Malayan Campaign for example, they moved through the jungle to bypass static positions such as defensive roadblocks held by the British and their allies. The Japanese thus used the terrain to their advantage, being able to sever British supply lines and attack defensive positions from every side. This tactic was also used during early 1942, at the start of the Burma Campaign, and led to one of British military history's longest retreats. Indeed, the unstoppable nature of the Japanese forces in jungle conflicts, and their soldiers' abilities to survive with minimal supplies, became the stuff of legend among many of the British Indian Army in Burma. It was said that the Japanese troops were trained as jungle fighters but that was not the case. However, their doctrine involved very resolute purpose and their military training emphasized the significance of night fighting. This contrasted with the British and Australians who, in 1942, were not trained to operate in darkness. So, while the Japanese had some prior experience of fighting in tropical forests, it was their training in night fighting that was important.

There are indeed basic challenges when fighting in dense, wet jungle. For instance, an attacking force may easily become disorientated and get lost. If the forest is in mountainous country, often with mist and heavy rain, these problems are compounded

The shattered Remus Wood, on the French-Belgium border, 1917.

with movement slowed due to restricted visibility. Sub-units of a military force cannot see each other therefore coordination of fire and movement becomes very difficult. Defenders, perhaps in foxholes or trenches, are unable to direct fire on clear targets because of dense foliage. The fighting in these conditions becomes an infantryman's battle or skirmish with the enemy often unseen until just a few metres away. Weapons, designed to fire accurately for hundreds of metres, become far less effective with sightlines down to twenty metres. The lessons learned by the British fighting in Burma included how to fight in jungle terrain and the importance of air transport in moving troops and supplies. These lessons underpinned tactics and strategies for future large-scale jungle conflicts. But the impacts and psychology of jungle warfare, especially at night, are hard to imagine. The total blackness, with the unfamiliar night-time noises of the forest all around, must have been desperately troubling and disorientating.

The problems and hazards are not merely related to the enemy, but also, as noted above, to disease. For example, in New Guinea, both the Australians and the Japanese suffered more casualties to disease than fighting. All-pervading fungal infections can affect eighty per cent of body skin cover, and shred clothing; there are other parasites too. Contaminated water is a big problem and for the soldiers two major issues were malaria and dysentery, but there were other debilitating and potentially fatal infections like dengue fever and scrub typhus.

The response from the British, Australians and Americans, to the fall of Malaya and the conflicts in New Guinea, Borneo, Burma and elsewhere in the Pacific and tropical Asia, was to establish and train special units to fight in this most difficult terrain. Some of these special units were highly successful, though in some cases their merit and effectiveness has been debated. The largest of all the Allied special units of the Second World War was the Chindits (the Burmese word for lions), established and led by Major-General Orde Wingate DSO. In 1943 and 1944 these specially trained troops fought behind enemy lines in northern Burma. This unit was a special force of 3,000 men; in February 1942, they undertook a deep penetration raid, code-named Operation Longcloth, into Japanese-occupied territory in Burma. The operation was on foot with mules carrying supplies; while militarily it was not a success, it provided much-needed propaganda. Essentially, it demonstrated how Allied troops could move and fight in jungle terrain, away from roads. To follow this 'success', resources were provided to increase the force to divisional size with American Air Force support by the 1st Air Commando Group. Use of air transport transformed the operations and in February 1944, they launched Operation Thursday. American air support allowed for the establishment of bases well behind Japanese lines. From these, combat patrols intercepted Japanese supply lines and attacked their support forces. One result was the Japanese withdrawing frontline troops from fighting against the Allied force advancing into northern Burma. Furthermore, if Japanese troops with artillery managed to get through to one of these base units, it could be speedily abandoned and removed to a new remote position. Air transport was the key to success.

This approach continued into late 1943 when the Japanese launched a counter offensive and overran and cut off the British Allied headquarters. However, as the Allies fell back to their defensive positions, the response was to hold firm and counter the manoeuvre with resupply and relocation facilitated by aerial support. Both sides sought to outflank and out-manoeuvre each other in the jungle terrain, but the Allied aerial tactics won the day, and the Japanese army was now in retreat. These lessons, learned from warfare in Burma, of how to fight in the jungle and how to use air transport to move troops and supplies, informed tactics for future large-scale jungle conflicts.

A similar pattern had occurred following the 1942 fall of Malaya and Singapore. In this case, British officers who escaped the Japanese invasion took to the central Malaysian jungle. Here, they were involved in organizing and training groups of

Tropical rainforest from a nineteenth century print: dense, humid, hot, and with poor visibility.

lightly-armed local ethnic Chinese communists in guerrilla tactics to fight the Japanese invaders. This approach was in part the inspiration for the tactics described earlier. In this context, British and Australian troops helped develop the unconventional, low-intensity, guerrilla-style of warfare suitable for jungle combat. Further support was gradually provided by the so-called V Force and Force 136, British special operations units for the Far East. These were small groups of soldiers and irregulars, with small arms and explosives, but trained in guerrilla warfare tactics, including close-quarters combat, fighting behind Japanese lines. In Burma there were also American-led Kachin guerrillas, a regional ethnic group, armed and coordinated by the US forces. In the South West Pacific theatre there was a further special force, the Australian-led Z Special Unit. This was established as a joint Allied special forces unit operating behind Japanese lines consisting mainly of Australians, but with British, Dutch, New Zealand, Timorese, and Indonesian soldiers too. The unit was a reconnaissance and sabotage group that undertook eighty-one covert missions in the jungle and elsewhere.

Jungle tactics

The tactics of infantry fighting jungle warfare were based on fire and movement.

French soldiers in Vietnam with amphibious armoured vehicle 1960s.

When attacking an enemy position, a group moves to close with the opponent as their comrades fire to pin down the enemy. In tactical terms, the first group, armed with rifles, submachine guns, and grenades, was called the rifle group. The second group, with at least one light machine gun, was known as the gun group. When fighting over a relatively open battlefield, the gun group would be a company of about a hundred men armed with mortars or medium machine guns. As they laid down a barrage on the enemy position, the rifle group advanced toward the same. However, such a tactic was not possible in dense forest due to limited visibility made worse with fog and rain. Often, the defensive position, perhaps a camouflaged fighting pit or trench, was hidden up to the point that the leading attack scout was shot at by the enemy. Even if the scout or scouts survived, they might still have little idea of where exactly it came from. The gun group behind the rifle group was even more disadvantaged with little idea of where to direct their supporting fire.

The tactical response was often to fight in a section of two small groups, six-man rifle groups and four-man gun group, with the former crawling close to the enemy to lob grenades into their pit or trench. This inherently slow process carries on with soldiers crawling and utilizing what cover they can find and enduring

Cypress peat-swamp in Louisiana, US, to show the sorts of conditions faced in tropical and subtropical forests.

long periods when they cannot see the enemy and the latter cannot see them. A further problem in jungle combat is the difficulty of issuing or receiving commands, as thick jungle with often steep slopes, few if any tracks, and potentially deep treacherous streams and swamps, limit communications. A company commander might be able to see very few of his own men, and platoon commanders would often be uncertain of their location relative to their leader, to other platoons, and even to each other. An additional complication is that unlike in an open field, dense forest hides combatants, so you not only don't know where the enemy is, you also don't know how large the force is. One response to these difficulties was to send out patrols with the unenviable task of scouting for information on enemy positions and numbers, while the main force waits behind for this intelligence. Of course, both sides may be carrying out similar operations in the same area of terrain.

The Chindits' long-distance, remote action, Operation Longcloth, was intended to be part of a greater offensive in Burma which at the time did not happen. A result was that the main columns were left to make their way back however best they could. By late April 1943, after a three-month operation in Burma, most surviving Chindits, having marched nearly a thousand miles in atrocious jungle conditions, were instructed to return. From around 3,000 troops almost a third (818 men) were dead from fighting or disease, or had been taken prisoner. Of 2,182 returning soldiers, six hundred were unable to return to active service due to wounds or disease. Some of these survivors were air-lifted out, part of one column ended up in China, and another group made it to the far north of Burma. Militarily the venture was something of a disaster, but it achieved two things. One was that it helped develop successful jungle-fighting tactics, and the other was that it provided much-needed morale-boosting propaganda.

The First Vietnam War or First Indochina War

French troops on elephant transport, Laos, 1950.

Often forgotten because of the greater American conflict, the First Vietnam War or the First Indochina War took place from 1946 to 1954. It was a revolution led by the Vietnamese nationalist group the Viet Minh under Ho Chi Minh against French imperial rule. Following eight years of guerrilla warfare in mountain and jungle, the conflict came to a finale at Dien Bien Phu, a small hilltop town in northwest Vietnam close to the border with Laos. Revolutionary forces had crossed into Laos and the French aim was to cut off their supply lines by setting up a major camp at Dien Bien Phu. The topography of the site is described as a rice bowl, with the French at the bottom and the sides comprising a ring of forest-covered steep mountain slopes. For some mistaken reason the French military felt this was a good defensive position and that the jungle-covered slopes afforded them protection. However, they badly misjudged the determination of the revolutionary fighters and the latter's knowledge of the local terrain and conditions. The Viet Minh forces were motivated, for instance, to do what the French had thought unthinkable, and haul heavy artillery through the jungle and up the mountain slopes. Furthermore, they tunnelled through the rock to provide better access to the centre of the rice bowl. This was clearly a recipe for a disaster.

The French had brought in around 10,000 paratroopers and created a landing strip close to the camp: their only means of supply. The Viet Minh general, Vã Nguyên Giáp, having dragged artillery guns over the mountains and through the forests, assembled his forces overlooking the French camp. Additionally, he brought in five more Viet Minh Divisions to assemble a force totalling about 50,000 men. With guns and men in position on 13 March 1954 they began artillery bombardments of the French camp. Within a day the airstrip was damaged beyond repair. Then, on 30 March, the Viet Minh unleashed infantry assaults against the French defences

Viet Cong soldiers near Saigon, 1960s.

which held out an astonishingly long time, until 7 May. This defeat for the French effectively marked the end of the First Indochina War and French control over Indochina terminated on 31 July. At this point, Vietnam officially split into two with the communist north and the south supported by its Western allies. The Vietnam War with America followed.

Warfare in tropical forests and mountains

Dien Bien Phu really emphasizes some key points about warfare in both mountains and jungles. Good local knowledge of terrain and conditions can be a huge advantage and misjudging these can be catastrophic. The Viet Minh were able to manoeuvre artillery and men into key positions to fire into the French camp with tremendous accuracy and little chance of effective return fire. The French could not see where the Viet Minh forces were. The whole episode had begun badly when the French landed with a parachute drop near Dien Bien Phu and then relied on in-coming aircraft to resupply their base. They assumed the opposition had little artillery and no anti-aircraft weapons; on both counts they were badly misinformed. The French were surrounded, cut-off, outgunned, and outmanoeuvred. From their initial force of around 10,000 they lost about 1,500 dead, 4,000 wounded, and something like 1,600 missing, leaving around 2,900 survivors.

With Vietnam under French colonial rule since the nineteenth century, the First Indochina War ended a long period of enforced subjugation.

The Vietnam War and the Tet Offensive

However, the north-south split between communist and non-communist regimes, was untenable to the northern power base which sought to unify the country under

Village near Saigon, 1960s.

a single communist regime. Elections were promised but didn't happen as northern communists and their southern sympathizers (Vietcong) drew the country into a guerrilla war. The US intervened and sent hundreds of thousands of conscripted soldiers to fight another anti-communist war. The outcome was an abject failure on the part of the US and the South Vietnamese government of the day.

Many of the same issues and problems arose as in the First Indochina War; these included the tremendous difficulties of fighting against indigenous peoples. They know the terrain and are fighting for their homes and livelihoods, and for their independent identity in wet mountainous jungle areas, and coastal or riverine wetlands. Aside from problems of disease and overstretched supply lines, these are very difficult places in which to fight, and technology does not necessarily level the imbalances. Furthermore, for the imported soldiers they often cannot differentiate friend from foe.

The Vietnamese celebrate the lunar New Year, falling usually in late January or early February, as the most important holiday; during the war this was often declared an unofficial truce. However, in 1968, instead of a ceasefire on 30 January, the Vietcong and the North Vietnamese launched a blistering series of attacks against South Vietnamese troops and American forces in over a hundred towns, cities, and military outposts countrywide. The intention of the Tet Offensive was to

Vietnam War. US soldiers on the Mekong River, 1960s.

kick-start the conflict out of a grinding stalemate, engender rebellion in the south, and encourage the US to reduce its commitment in Vietnam. There was widespread fighting in the southern capital Saigon, and very fierce conflict in Hue City south of the border between the north and south. A Vietcong platoon even managed to enter the American Embassy compound, though they were all killed. In Hue City, the North Vietnamese captured the city for around three weeks, though American and South Vietnamese forces retook it. Despite enduring very heavy casualties the North Vietnamese achieved many of their objectives. American public opinion was shocked into increasingly strong anti-war sentiment, and from this point onward there was a general move toward American withdrawal.

Fighting in a foreign land and in horribly difficult terrain is problematic. Imperfect knowledge of topography and infrastructure can cause huge problems and headaches. A further example is when a US tank column headed north toward a strategic goal to rescue infantry under attack from the Vietcong. This was only to find that the bridge over a key river crossing was not wide enough for the tanks to cross. They had to retrace their steps; laden with the bodies of dead and injured soldiers, and under constant guerrilla attack from forest on either side of the highway, their task was nearly impossible.

Forest landscapes in Second World War Europe

Returning to the Second World War, in the autumn of 1944, the Allied invasion of Europe was well underway. However, it was meeting fierce resistance from German troops and was slowed significantly when the Germans launched an unexpected counterattack through the densely forested Ardennes region of Belgium. Since this was inherently difficult terrain the Allies had left it relatively lightly protected, assuming this was not an option for any German response. With a front of around six hundred miles, forces had to be selectively positioned and the terrain in this area was considered sufficient defence. Germany's objective was to cut between the British and American forces in a surprise offensive, separating the two. The British might then be surrounded, isolated, and hopefully overwhelmed so that Hitler might negotiate a peace settlement from a position of strength.

The Battle of the Bulge

The American forces were indeed surprised, and the Germans managed to drive a wedge or 'bulge' between them and the British forces further north. At this point the balance shifted; the Americans were able to hold key strategic positions which bought time, and the British moved to reinforce the American positions. At the same time, the American General George Patton drove his Third Army north from southern France. He was able to relieve the US troops at Bastogne and thus halt the German advance. The American 289th Infantry Regiment marched through the snow-bound Ardennes Forest to cut off a key road through Belgium and successfully slow the advance of the Sixth Panzer Army. Then, between 8 and 15 January 1945, the Allies made a push to retake 'The Bulge' leading the German army to make a speedy withdrawal from the area. Both Allied and Axis forces took serious losses, but Germany especially lost much of their remaining equipment and stores. The battle effectively ended German resistance on the Western Front. The German use of the forest cover, the nature of this cover to conceal troops, and the element of surprise could have meant a very different outcome. Furthermore, the higher ground provided drier terrain than the lowlands of Flanders, which was more suitable for the use of heavy German tanks. The dense tree canopy also provided concealment from Allied bombers. Another tactic was that the Germans waited for weather that would aid their campaign: mist, rain and even snow, which reduced visibility even further. Poor weather also helped the German cause by limiting the effectiveness of the Allies' superior air power. There was also a problem for troops in dense forests both here and elsewhere across northern Europe, for example into Poland. If the opposition simply shelled the forest, catastrophic damage was caused to the soldiers by flying timber and wood splinters. Another challenge was the rapid march through topographically difficult terrain that was exhausting for the German troops, compounded by lack of supplies including fuel and ammunition. Many of the German soldiers at this time were inexperienced and untrained.

Despite the efforts put into the assault by the German forces, the result was a victory for the Allies, but the German commanders demonstrated a canny knowledge of the terrain and topography, and of the weather conditions. In the end, this was to no avail.

Forested countryside as a battlescape

Forested or wooded countryside whether hot, humid tropical landscapes or cold northern alpine forests, brings distinctive qualities and factors to the battlescape. A dense forest can provide refuge and sanctuary for partisans, defensive positions, and resistance movements. They hinder machinery and vehicles, and in medieval conflicts could be problematic for cavalry. Large armies on the move will tend to avoid or skirt extensive treescapes, whereas indigenous fighters, knowing their terrain, take full advantage of the cover provided.

German bomber on the First World War frontline.

Chapter 11
Airfields

Examples of the interactions between conflicts, nature, and landscapes can be especially informative and provide a chance to consider more deeply some of the underlying issues and complexities. Such insights can be informative in terms of the core questions of tactics and strategies. Topography and terrain also interact with military infrastructure and the militarization of landscapes, and a relevant example is the use of countryside areas as bases for aircraft. With a few minor exceptions, such as the use of balloons in sieges, air power in conflicts began with aeroplanes and grew rapidly during the First World War. Many of the complex issues arising from aerial power and conflict are largely omitted from this account because, like naval battles, they add a further dimension to warfare that cannot be done justice in this short volume. However, some matters have wider relevance and are considered here. Finding suitable landscapes for airbases raises issues of terrain and topography

The capacity to fly added a new element to warfare. Here a seaplane lands on Lake Tanganyika, January 1917.

of the chosen sites but also of the immediate surroundings and the hazards these may present. Furthermore, there may be associated difficulties caused by weather conditions and patterns and these are especially significant in a period pre-radar or radio. Then, of course there is the matter of avoiding collisions between incoming and outgoing aircraft in busy airspace and sometimes at night. Such problems are exacerbated by numerous airfields in the same geographic area. Other issues may differ between airfields for bomber crews and those for fighters despatched to head-off income enemy bombers, and there is also the need to protect and sometimes to camouflage airbases in case of enemy attack. These factors combine to create a very complex battlescape which in the case study emerged during the period of the two World Wars and as the technologies of flying and ground support rapidly evolved.

First, during the First World War the Zeppelin air raids from Germany into Britain opened a whole new aspect of conflict. Residential civilian communities a long distance from the frontline were suddenly open to assault and were proved to be vulnerable. The fact that the British government was caught totally unaware and unprepared was a national scandal. What pilots and planes Britain had, were already in and around the Western Front and the idea of the war crossing the sea to our shores had been unthinkable.

The search for air bases

The response was to rapidly expand and recruit to the air services, the predecessor of

Top right: Italian First World War biplane bomber.

Centre right: Italian First World War triplane bomber.

the RAF, the Royal Flying Corps, and to begin an urgent search for suitable locations from which to launch and land the biplanes of the time. This is perhaps where the connection between landscape and war become very acute. There were specific requirements for sites geographically positioned where they were needed. But they also needed to be safe and free from hazards from which primitive planes could operate without modern radar and high-powered lighting and guidance. Locations would need to be level and long enough for an airstrip. Furthermore, they had to be free from obvious hazards in the nearby terrain such as hills and preferably in countryside not too prone to fog and mist. However, most English sites in both World Wars needed to be in the eastern flatlands as they were either for fighters to intercept incoming attacks or else to launch Allied bombers and fighters heading eastwards into Europe. Essentially, most locations were along the eastern seaboards of Yorkshire, Lincolnshire and into East Anglia, and many of these areas whilst climatically dry do have a tendency for low-lying mist and fog.

Additionally, a location would need to have basic services such as access,

Westland Wallace general purpose military biplane used for training in the Second World War.

Halifax Bomber about to take off.

power, and drainage, or else had the potential for these to be speedily provided. Those tasked with the job of finding these places were given what amounted to a tick-list and were sent out to scour the countryside. The Royal Air Force Archives provide valuable insight into this process.

The English example of York and its military airfields

By the outbreak of the Second World War the power and potential of aerial military forces, both offensive and defensive, was clear. When conflict broke out there was an even greater impetus to find and secure suitable locations. This can be further examined by considering the eastern region of England and the wartime airfields around the historically strategic city of York.

The first military airfields around York were sited during the First World War on some of the extensive flatlands of the Vale of York. There is relatively little known about these early sites but far more about those which followed in the Second World War. The area around York during the Second World War was described as a huge aircraft carrier providing essential bases for planes departing and returning, for training pilots and crews, and for maintaining, supplying, and repairing the craft themselves. The sites were home to the flying crews, the ground crews, and all the necessary support services and personnel.

In the 1940s, the skies over York must have echoed with the noise of heavy bombers climbing high prior to heading east and over the North Sea to Germany. At sometimes very short notice, large parcels of countryside were requisitioned by the Air Ministry to construct the necessary airfields and sometimes dummy airfields

Curtiss P40 American-built pursuit and fighter plane.

Laying a steel mesh runway over grassland in the Yorkshire Wolds, Second World War.

were established to lure enemy bombers away from their more vulnerable targets. Around the airstrips were living quarters and all the necessary infrastructure for the flying and ground crews from across the country, and indeed from around the world. Today many of these often-short-term airfields are forgotten and many have returned to their original farmland uses. Some are still active, whilst others were allowed to

Escape of a British aviator from the Germans.

revert to nature. Other bases ended up with industrial uses which often included former wartime buildings. Landscape, nature, and topography all combined with basic geographic location, to influence site suitability. Indeed, because of landscape conditions a bad choice of site could prove fatal to air crews.

Acaster Malbis Airfield

Acaster Malbis Airfield was a very poor choice for a site because of its proximity to the Ouse River and its low-lying floodplain flatlands prone to mists and fogs. The conditions were frequently impossible or at least very dangerous for flying operations without radar and with minimal ground lighting. The site was established in 1942 as part of No. 12 Group, Fighter Command, and a satellite to RAF Church Fenton. The first planes to arrive were Airacobras with No. 601 Unit, a plane that was one of the main American fighters when the United States entered the war. However, the aircraft was unpopular and had technical problems. This, combined with frequently poor weather, including bad visibility around the site, caused numerous accidents. As with many airfields there was a regular turnover of both personnel and planes. No. 601 Unit gave way to No. 21 Group, Flying Training Command, and then No. 15 Advanced Flying Unit with Airspeed Oxfords. Nevertheless, the poor visibility inherent in this location took its toll for both combat and training flights. The airfield

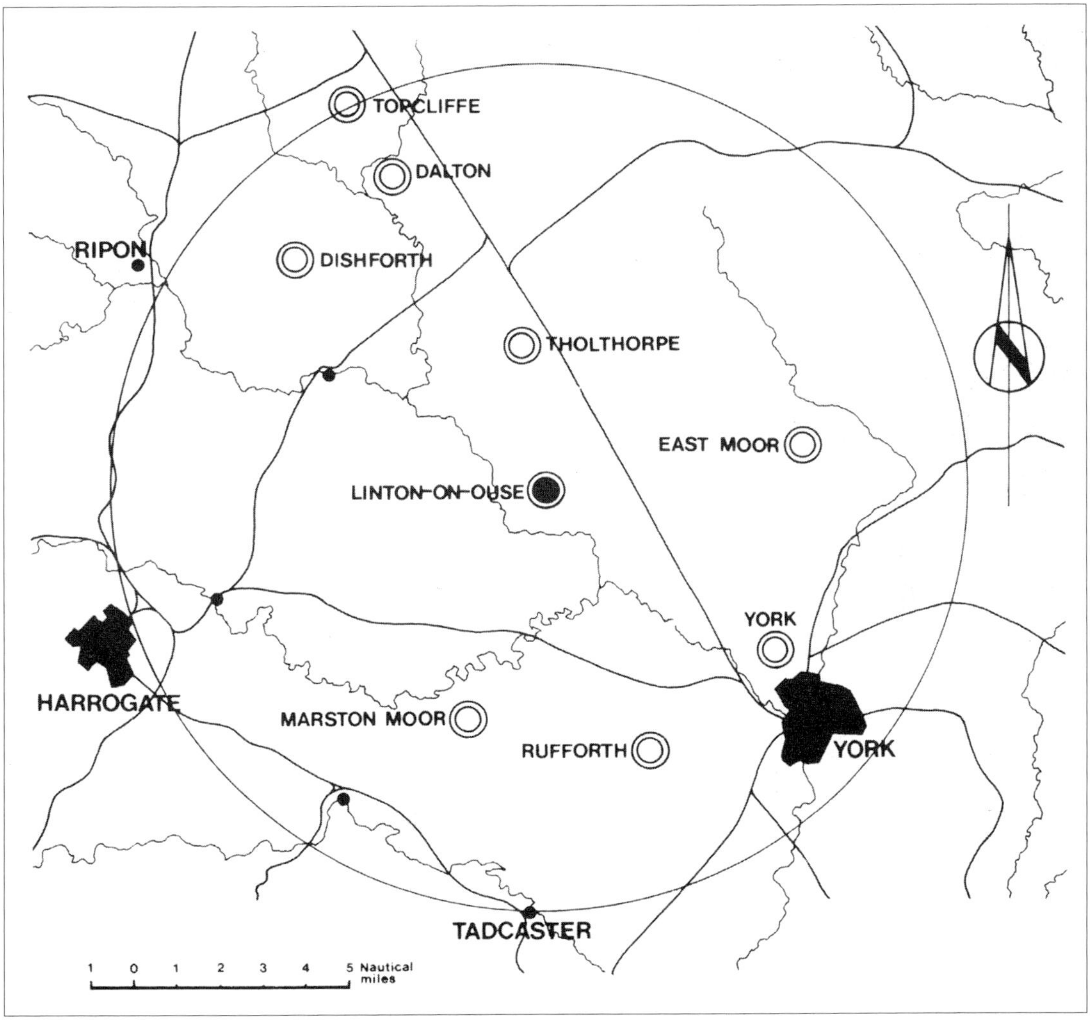

A map to show the airfields close to Linton and York during the Second World War.

was eventually considered unsuitable for the latter.

In 1943, the airfield was temporarily closed and reopened as a heavy bomber station for part of No. 4 Group, Bomber Command. This later period involved the construction of concrete runways, new hangars, and fresh accommodation blocks. With its recurring problems, the airfield was only used for circuit training by flying crews; active flights were eventually abandoned. The site became a bomb storage depot and finally closed in 1946. The best interpretation of the history of this airfield is one of tenacity in the face of continuing failure combined with a totally unsuitable location. According to the online enthusiasts' guides, the site is interesting because it still has its control tower and some of the domestic quarters. Like many wartime sites the runways survived long after active service but were eventually broken up and the land was returned to farming.

Marston Moor Airfield

Close to the famous battlefield described earlier, Marston Moor Airfield (RAF Tockwith) opened in 1941 as a heavy bomber conversion training station; part of No. 4 Group, Bomber Command, with conversion units equipped with Halifax Mk Is. However, there seems to have been numerous crashes here as well. These included a Stirling bomber crashing into Tockwith village northeast of the site; along with the crew the village postmaster was also killed. Fragments from the crash scene are still to be found in local gardens. Decommissioned in 1945, the site is now an industrial estate though much of the original base remains as one of the best-preserved examples of a Second World War Yorkshire airfield. Again, located in the naturally wet landscape of Marston Moor, the base was inherently prone to fog and other poor weather that made flying and especially landing potentially difficult.

Linton-on-Ouse Airfield

Linton-on-Ouse Airfield was a site chosen during the airfields expansion of the 1930s, with buildings constructed for longer-term use, unlike some sites built at short notice responding to expediency. Formally commissioned in 1937, Linton housed No. 4 Group, Headquarters which in 1940 moved to Heslington Hall in York. Linton retained operational functions and in 1940 received four-engine Halifax bombers of 35 Squadron from Leeming. The airfield sites around York were obvious targets for German counter bombing, and despite the extensive use of decoys and camouflage, remained vulnerable. Consequently, in May 1941, Linton was hit by a German bombing raid and suffered significant damage, with casualties including the Station Commander. During 1942, Linton passed to the Canadian Group and in 1943 transferred to No. 6 Group Royal Canadian Air Force (RCAF). It then became No. 62 (Beaver) Base Station with sub-stations at East Moor and Tholthorpe. The first group to arrive was the No. 426 'Thunderbird' Squadron which began conversion to the Lancaster Mk II with Hercules engines. In August 1943 No. 426 Squadron was joined by No. 408 'Goose' Squadron from Leeming. By the close of the war in Europe, No. 408 Squadron had moved to the Tiger Force for deployment in the Far East. They never reached Japan as the war ended and they returned to Canada with their Lancaster Mk Xs. They disbanded at Greenwood, Nova Scotia, in September 1945, by now a long way from York. The nature of the

Hawker Hart ,1920s and 1930s.

aircraft and crews, plus ground staff, was often one of mobility and flexibility.

No. 426 Squadron remained closer to home, moving to No. 47 Squadron, Group Transport Command at Driffield in East Yorkshire in May 1945. Linton returned to the RAF and for a short while was part of No. 4 Group Transport Command. However, in 1946 it became part of Fighter Command. Subsequently, it was home to various fighter aircraft and squadrons until 1957; by then it was clearly unsuitable for the newer, high-performance jet fighters coming into service. Briefly mothballed Linton re-opened as part of Flying Training Command with No. 1 Flying Training School which moved from Syerston. The base trained students from both the RAF and the Fleet Air Arm until 1969 when the latter transferred to Church Fenton. Linton remains active as the training base for future RAF pilots, and as a working site, many original Second World War buildings remain. This is an example of a good geographic location with suitable landscape as both topography and terrain suited its military purpose. Furthermore, local weather conditions were acceptable too.

Skipwith Common Airfield

Riccall Airfield, RAF Riccall, or Skipwith Common Airfield was built in 1942 with three concrete and asphalt runways and various specification hangars (six T2 and one B1). It opened in December the same year as a secondary site associated with RAF Marston Moor. On coming into operational service, it already had Halifax conversion units of No. 76 Squadron and No. 78 Squadron that arrived in September. By October 1942, they merged to become the 1658 Heavy Conversion Unit (HCU) with 158 Conversion Unit arriving in November to form 'C' Flight 1658. This meant a total of thirty-two Halifax bombers based at the airfield. Riccall became the training base for many aircrew personnel flying Halifax squadrons. However, there was a heavy price to pay with seventy-two planes lost during a period when Bomber Command frequently suffered catastrophic losses of pilots and crews. There is a story of human suffering and dedication associated with these militarized landscapes even today. This was not an issue for the landscape of choice but simply the horrendous risk for those flying these particular nighttime missions. This airfield location demonstrates the benefits of flat, level topography in a suitable landscape setting for take-off and landing. However, despite the landscape suitability, the active flights from Riccall suffered terrible losses.

The 1658 Heavy Conversion Unit disbanded near the end of the war in Europe, and Riccall became home to 1332 Transport Conversion Unit with Avro Yorks and Short Stirlings converted for transportation. When this ended on 7 November 1945, Riccall was mothballed until final closure in February 1957. The land returned to agriculture or developed as birchwood and heath. The former bomb dump remains within Skipwith Common Nature Reserve.

Pocklington

The Pocklington airbase developed during the 1930s expansion plans for military airfields perhaps in anticipation of potential conflict to come. However, it was not until 1941 that it opened for No. 4 Squadron of Group Bomber Command. Sometime after opening, No. 405 Squadron RCAF, with Wellington bombers, arrived from Driffield to convert crews to Halifax bombers. Indeed, the Halifax B Mk IIs became operational soon afterward becoming the first Canadian unit to fly them in action. In April 1942, No. 405 Squadron switched with No. 102 Squadron who moved to Pocklington from Topcliffe. Then, during 1944, the latter changed from Halifax B Mk II bombers to Mark IIIs in preparation for them to support the Normandy D-Day landings. Finally, in 1945, No. 102 Squadron changed to transport duties with Liberators and departed Pocklington in September. The base closed in 1946 and mostly returned to agriculture though its hangars remain in a nearby industrial estate. One original runway remains in use by Pocklington Gliding Club, and again, this exemplifies where location and topography combine to be a suitable site for its military purpose, essentially flat, dry, and close to the east coast.

Church Fenton Airbase

Wreckage from a crash near Beverley, First World War.

Anti-aircraft gun to combat airships, 1914.

Church Fenton Airbase was also planned before the war, designated as a fighter station during the pre-war expansion. Part of No. 12 Group, Fighter Command, the site opened in 1937 with a grass airstrip and accommodated No. 72 Squadron with Gloster Gladiators and No. 213 Squadron with Gloster Gauntlets. With the outbreak of war, the site was home to No. 13 Group, Fighter Command with No. 72 Squadron converted to the Spitfire Mk I. The latter moved to Leconfield and was replaced with part of No. 245 Squadron from Leconfield, followed by the reformed No. 242 Squadron of Hurricane fighters.

Both geographic location and topography were significant factors in choosing Church Fenton. This is because the primary role of the base during the early war was protecting the English East Coast and nearby towns. During the Battle of Britain, squadrons were also despatched to Church Fenton for relief and re-equipping. One special claim to fame was the award of the Victoria Cross to Flight Lieutenant J.B. Nicholson, the only such award to Fighter Command during the war. He was based at Church Fenton from 1937 to 1940. Nicolson was 23 years old and a flight lieutenant in No. 249 Squadron during the Second World War when he was awarded the Victoria Cross. On 16 August 1940, having taken off from RAF Boscombe Down near Salisbury, Nicolson's Hawker Hurricane was almost certainly fired on by the Messerschmitt Bf 109 of Heinz Bretnutz of II./JG 53, who returned to base with claims for two Hurricane kills following this action. Nicolson's engine was damaged, and the petrol tank set alight. As he struggled to leave the blazing machine he saw another Messerschmitt, and managing to get back into the bucket seat, pressed the firing button and continued firing until the enemy plane dived away to destruction. Not until then did he bail out and was able to open his parachute

Seaplane stationed at Hornsea and Bridlington from 1914 to counter Zeppelin raids.

An early British aircraft carrier. Good for taking off but not suitable for coming back in and landing.

in time to land safely in a field. On his descent, he was fired on by members of the Home Guard, who ignored his cry of being a RAF pilot. As squadron leader and commanding officer of No. 27 Squadron, he flew Bristol Beaufighters over Burma. During this time he was awarded the Distinguished Flying Cross, but died when flying as an observer in an RAF B-24 Liberator from No. 355 Squadron that caught fire and crashed into the Bay of Bengal.

Church Fenton remained a fighter station until in 1959, when it transferred to Flying Training Command. The suitability of the site is obvious in its continued use

War Graves to the fallen aviators of the Second World War. All Saints Church, Holme-on-Spalding Moor.

Extreme weather at Hornsea, with heavy snow, 1940s.

Farnborough Royal Army Aircraft Factory.

for flying. In 1962, No. 7 Flying Training School was established with Jet Provost planes and today is the base for Grob Tutor aircraft of the University Air Squadron and is Leeds East Airport Church Fenton.

The wider provision

Similar accounts could be written about a selection of airfield sites not only across Britain but around the world. In England, numerous flying sites were constructed throughout Lincolnshire, Cambridgeshire, Norfolk, and Suffolk. Some survive, but many were built with immediacy in mind, and following their use reverted to their pre-military landscapes.

There were other factors affecting the suitability of sites, such as seasonal and topographic influences. In seasonally cold climates like Finland, planes might land and take off from frozen lakes in wintertime to add a level of unpredictability. Of course, in some cases, planes were designed to take off and land on either lakes or on the sea. Whilst Church Fenton was noted for its coastal defence duties, another forgotten 'airstrip' was on the English East Coast at Hornsea Mere, a freshwater lake adjacent to the North Sea, where seaplanes took off and landed.

The short-lived Coal Aston Airfield just south of Sheffield was a First World War site chosen for topographic reasons. Here they converted Sopwith Camels to naval use by fitting them with wooden flotation devices. The basic problem for naval flying was that you could take off from the suitably designed deck of a ship but couldn't land on return. The pilots had to bail out into the sea and be rescued with the planes specially fitted with wooden floats then retrieved later and returned to the ship. Of interest here is the process of selection of suitable sites to be militarized. Coal Aston, while aiding the wider war effort, stood in defence of a major industrial city.

For most of these locations the key factor was suitable geographic positioning for a specific purpose which differed depending on whether it primarily served outgoing bomber raids or a protection function from incoming bombers. In some cases, localized weather conditions could tip the balance from a site being good and viable, to not making the grade. Sites needed to be flat, free from major topographic hazards, preferably with good access and services, and preferably not vulnerable to overly bad weather such as low-lying fogs.

Reading accounts of the airfields around York and across the East Riding of Yorkshire, it is clear that the hazards associated with all flying, and not just the bomber missions, were manifold. Wet terrain and a tendency to low, hanging fogs, was inherently risky, but other extreme weather such as heavy snowfalls could increase the hazards too. Furthermore, from the time of the First World War, many of the pilots were young and trainees, and accidents happened. An additional problem, particularly in the days before effective radar and radio communications, was posed by the sheer numbers of airfields and planes operating in this flat battlescape. Crashes were bound to happen and even more so when fog descended.

Many chosen sites were heaths, moors, commons, or drained bogs and fens, and this leads us to Chapter 12 and the roles of peatlands in warfare.

Turf barges in Worpswede Germany, 1930s.

Chapter 12
Peatlands in the European theatre of war

Wetlands and specifically peatlands such as bogs, fens, and wet moors, have been important as both places for conflicts and as sources of important natural resources such as fuel during times of warfare.

The role of wetlands in wars, specifically peatlands such as fens and bogs, is often overlooked. Like woods and forests, and sometimes co-existing as wet woods and wet forests, peatlands have had varied impacts on conflict. Some of these aspects are outlined below. In summary the roles in conflicts include the following:

1. Peatlands influence war and conflict through topography and nature, often being of critical significance to strategy and outcome.
2. Heaths and moors were often used as military training grounds, from early times up to the present day.

Brussels battle scene with cavalry, 1917.

3. Peatlands were used as wartime bases especially during the Second World War when they were brought into use as airfields and similar facilities.
4. Bogs and moors especially, had unplanned and passive roles in warfare such being the last resting places for stricken or lost bombers and their crews from both sides during the Second World War.
5. Peatlands, especially bogs and fens, provided materials of immense value to wartime efforts such as supplying horse litter, sphagnum moss, alder buckthorn and peat fuel.
6. Conflicts, socio-economic stresses, or extreme weather all influenced fuel use and competition and therefore peat exploitation.
7. Fens and bogs were places of sanctuary, of non-conformism, and independence.

Peat-dominated landscapes were important in many countries around the world, especially across northwest Europe. This was particularly so in Germany, Holland, and the other Low Countries, as well as further east into Poland, and beyond that in Russia and Ukraine. The French situation makes an interesting case study. In 1869, France exported 321,000 tonnes of peat at 10 francs 20 cents per tonne. Significant fuel usage and resources were noted at the turn of the nineteenth century, but by 1914, the amount was insignificant. Then in the early 1940s, there was renewed

As warfare grew in scale and longevity, supply lines and transport became increasingly important, as with these war horses carrying shells to the frontline, First World War.

Fuel in wartime may be critical, and people turn to the peat bogs to source it as here with French extraction of peat turf at Rivery-des-Amiens, 1916.

German soldiers at the peat ruckles, Trondheim, Norway, 1941.

German soldiers transporting peat turf by barge, near Essen camp, 1941.

A Mark IV tank struggling in the mud Flanders, 1917.

interest in the industrial exploitation of peat as fuel and for chemical extracts due to the Second World War.

This focus on peat turf as fuel during times of shortage or of adversity was noted for regions such as Scotland, Canada, and the US. The situation in wartime France was a similar response to crisis. An inventory of French peat resources at the time suggested around 1,200,000 hectares available for exploitation including valley peats, marine peats, and lowland plains peats. The report in *La Nature* (1941) concluded that in its peat reserves France had a resource to be exploited to help reinvigorate its economy. Exploitation continued after the war, and by 1980 France's annual peat production was 50,000 tons per year for fuel and 100,000 tons per year for horticulture, half that of the UK (Bord Na Mona, 1985).

A major role of peat bogs and wet landscapes was in the actual warfare and the strategy of the battlefield. This ranges from the importance of a line of massive peat bogs that separated Holland from its aggressive neighbour, Germany, to the Allies' strategic flooding of worked peat-cuts and polders to slow the German advance in the Second World War. In retaliation German forces broke the dykes to flood and destroy Dutch food production and cause punitive starvation.

Dragging a field gun through the mud, Western Front, First World War.

Particularly in the Great War, bogs, marshes, fens, mud, and peat, were immensely important. The Somme, Flanders, and other major battlefields were in generally flat or rolling landscapes dominated by bogs, rivers, marshes, and farmland, which quickly degenerated into fields of mud as the conflict developed.

One impact of conflicts on peatlands was the migration of skilled workers and application of prisoners of war, to the reclamation of bog and fen. In the 1600s, as described in the *Lost Fens* and in *Yorkshire's Forgotten Fenlands*, Huguenots and Walloons escaping Catholic persecution came to England's fenlands and helped in their drainage. Prisoners of war from Dutch and Scottish conflicts with the English were also put to work on this task; many of them died in the process, often of marsh malaria, and were buried in the soft, peaty soils by the drains they had dug. An indirect impact of major conflicts was the transformation of the English Fens drained and converted to agriculture by wartime migrants and prisoners.

In terms of peat and peatlands in warfare, there is a further remarkable story well known in Holland but hardly so elsewhere. This was the recapture from the Spanish, of Breda in the Netherlands during the Eighty-Year War, which used a Trojan Horse-type plan. However, in this case, a turf barge in which seventy soldiers

Hurrying up the coal mines, US and Canada November 1906.

were concealed replaced the wooden horse and on 25 February 1590, was left for the Spanish to take inside the fortress. The ruse was successful as the soldiers escaped and opened the walled city's gates. The vital fortress of Breda fell to Maurice of Nassau, Prince of Orange. The Dutch recall the victory as the *Turfschip van Breda* but one has to wonder, had the defenders never heard of the Trojan horse?

German attack on the Allied trenches near Soissons, First World War.

Chapter 13
Key issues of terrain and natural resources

Key facets of terrain and resources in conflicts

According to the United States military field manual, weather and terrain have greater impacts on battles than any other physical factor. They include in this statement equipment, supplies, and weaponry. The guidance goes on to state that most battles have been won by the side that used terrain to both protect itself and to facilitate firepower sufficient to destroy the enemy. This means that to take maximum advantage of potential landscape benefits, commanders of a military force need to have a good understanding of topography and terrain, their characteristics and potential, and the possibilities of reinforcing such natural assets. Such understanding connects intimately to the view that military combat is very much a matter of mobility, concealment, movement, and either shooting at or carrying out a direct assault on an enemy position. This view can be distilled down to three major facets of offence: 1) force combined with 2) protection or defence, and 3) mobility. Connected to these are the key aspects of terrain which can be described as 1) routes for approach, 2) positions of observation, 3) zones of potential fire, and 4) cover for concealment. Ease of mobility over or through a landscape for personnel and machines is also important. In essence, a big consideration is the ability or potential to shoot – or at least shoot at – the enemy without falling victim to incoming fire. Lines and distance of sight together with range become central issues to such assessments.

Advantage to the holder

The key terrain in the theatre of war, and on a battlefield, is that which lends advantage to the holder. Clearly, this varies with landscape, the overall objectives of those holding the place, and those seeking to oust them. There are also the influences of weaponry, other equipment, and numbers of personnel available and deployed. For various reasons the same territory might be highly attractive to one side but not to the other. In the 1960s and 1970s Vietnam War, the open, grassy hilltops of the central highlands were ideal for the airborne American assault troops and thus were avoided by the Vietcong. This meant the opposite of the usual situation with defenders holding high ground to force an assault from below. The American attacks began with hilltop landings and the fight was carried downhill to where the scrub and other cover were vital for the guerrillas.

However, in general terms for defence in the field of battle, the high ground is advantageous to whichever side occupies it. For your opponent to have to climb uphill, often exposed to hostile fire, is a great benefit to you and has been so since time immemorial. Among other things, the high position provides distant views and commanding positions from which to launch weapons or to fire rifles, or in the past, arrows and spears. In all these circumstances, height brings advantage. This is one major reason why so many prehistoric cultures defended hillforts and similar positions. Even today this advantage holds; with longer-range missiles and artillery, any enemy position that can be seen can be effectively engaged, and therefore most likely destroyed.

Cover and concealment then become especially significant for infantry forces, so terrain and topography hold the key to survival and success. Cover may also be important for heavy combat materiel such as helicopters, to avoid ground to air missiles, and for tanks, to avoid anti-tank weapons at ground level and aircraft fire from above.

Survival in the terrain

In extreme environments such as deserts, arctic zones, and high mountains, a key

An abandoned medieval fortress in Scotland, Dunnottar Castle, near Stonehaven, pictured in the 1980s and clearly showing how terrain can favour the holder.

The British army in a mountain skirmish with the Jacobites in the Highlands in 1719; the terrain can aid a mobile guerrilla force able to strike, retreat, and hide.

In difficult terrain, information and intelligence can be the key. British soldiers searching for wire-tappers, or German spies, 1914.

factor associated with any possible military success is merely survival. In such circumstances, the control of key geographic and landscape features or resources may be vital and become a primary objective. In desert landscapes access to oases or wadis will be essential for potable water, and in bitterly cold environments, shelter from the elements may be vital to hopes of survival. Contestation of space with these resources becomes a focus of conflicts.

Transit through the land

In conflicts and military campaigns, access to and control of vital routes for movement and supply of personnel, resources, and equipment are important considerations for commanders. Movement through and around the theatre of battle is essential; so passes through mountains or deserts assume great significance. Bridges, key junctions of routeways, and similar strategic positions become the focus of both offence and defence. In the modern conflict, locations such as airfields, harbours, and railway stations are also vital. Throughout the history of warfare, towns and cities that effectively control important infrastructure have been essential targets for conflicts and control.

Defensive lines and tactics

The history of tactics, strategies and ploys of combatants varies considerably between formally trained and regimental troops, and combatants in partisan or guerrilla warfare. For the former, the primary means of deployment are the line, the column, and the square; decision-making is based on these basic concepts and whether to redeploy from one to another. A line generates the longest fighting deployment and is hard to outflank. The approach can be a defensive ploy which is reinforced by structures such as wires, walls, trenches, bunkers, various obstacles and redoubts, or other fortifications. Modern warfare with highly trained soldiers has perhaps moved more toward the styles adopted by guerrilla forces in the past.

British infantry attacking a fortified village on the Western Front, First World War.

A German convoy stuck in the mud, 1942, when German supply lines and transport became a major problem during the Second World War.

German motor-drawn gun with caterpillar feet.

Towing a big gun ashore at Cape Helles Gallipoli. The effective placement and movement of troops and equipment on the battlescape is essential.

Advancing in line on the offensive involves concentration of firepower and resources in critical positions to gain traction. A defensive line will be set within the context of the landscape and its geographic features, such as marshes, bogs, lakes, rivers, forests, hills, mountains, even man-made structures such as buildings or settlements may form the endpoints of such a deployment.

The weakness of a defensive line may be its lack of depth and therefore susceptibility to penetration by assailants. Lack of mobility may also be a problem as an attack line could be hard to maintain as combatants advance. For a defensive tactic the line may fragment and allow piecemeal breakthrough by assault troops who then become disorientated and vulnerable to being picked off in small groups. Connection

Worcestershire Regiment marching to the Somme trenches, First World War.

A French soldier observing the enemy from a ruined building, 1915.

A French soldier carrying a trench observation periscope, 1915.

to physical features as endpoints of the line can be difficult to maintain and may also mean the line is relatively immobile.

If a line is turned to face an end, then the result is a column, and this sacrifices length for increased mobility. However, both attacking and defensive columns are vulnerable to assault along their flanks and the tactic is one applied to move troops rapidly over a distance. Master tactician, Napoleon, famously stated that the strength of an army is like that of a moving body in mechanics and is the result of mass multiplied by velocity; the column provides velocity. Generals like Sherman, Napoleon I, and Genghis Khan took armies forward in multiple columns to reduce risk, to increase uncertainty in their opponents, and to facilitate maximum impact and force at the weakest point of the enemy.

The most defensive position for a formal military force to adopt is a square which is achieved by a column wheeled so that its front meets up with the tail. This is a very immobile deployment but there is no single weakness exposed to the assailants. Each face presents a front to the enemy and the soldiers can fight back-to-back. However, whatever the landscape context, a square is static, and it lacks access to supplies of resources, or if necessary, for retreat. Various leaders throughout history, such as King Richard I and the Duke of Wellington, employed mobile squares of foot soldiers to direct their forces safely through the terrain.

Deployment

Beyond the basic formations of troops is the decision to attack or not, and if so, how to deploy forces to this end. For this there are three main options available, the first being a direct frontal attack on the opposition force. Second, assailants may seek to outflank the opponent to facilitate an attack from the flanks or the rear. The third and final ploy is to focus efforts on a perceived point of weakness and try to drive a wedge into the defensive line. This opens a chink in a defensive line to help concentrate force to maximum effect. These tactics can be combined in various forms along with movements such as feints, counterattacks, and effective use of terrain to support the ploys. Successful moves on the rear of a column can cut off lines of supply and potential retreat.

Many of the ploys, rules and tactics that apply to a formally trained and organized military force do not apply to informal organizations such as guerrilla forces and partisans. Flanking attacks are opportunities to take a fight to a superior army, especially in suitable terrain; smaller forces can strike with an ambush and then retreat into a place of sanctuary. If landscape provides concealment close enough to a route of advance, sufficient to hide a force able to ambush troops on the move, then that force can be vulnerable to hit-and-run strikes by a numerically inferior group. A small number of determined partisans or guerrillas can hide in terrain or vegetation to allow both close assault and speedy retreat into the landscape. While on the move, a military force can be especially vulnerable and landscape, through its properties of topography and vegetation, has a major impact on the risk and the outcomes.

An army with greater resources, superior weaponry, advantage in numbers, better training and enhanced aggression may find victory in a full-frontal attack. Nevertheless, if there is equality in these factors, as in the trenches of the First World War, then the result of direct frontal attack may be absolute carnage for both attacker and defender.

Observing the enemy and directing firepower becomes very important; a French observation tower, First World War.

The objective of a frontal attack may be to focus the defender's resources and responses while hooking around the flanks or rear of their position. Indeed, outflanking the enemy position might result from superior numbers or force applied to the head of a column or other defensive positions. A further ploy is to feign a direct assault to the front which might then be followed by a retreat to draw out the defenders who may break ranks and pursue. A little like the Normans with King Harold II at Hastings. This makes the defending force vulnerable as they break formation, especially if a twin pincer movement along the flanks is carried out to attack both sides simultaneously.

Lines and squares are essentially defensive formations that can be static or mobile. Whatever the situation regarding mobility and defence, those holding the ground against assault can choose where to make their stand. This can be a considerable advantage. The defenders can pick a location that provides cover for their own force

Communication is essential: a Japanese field telephone, Russo-Japanese War, March 1905.

where attackers may find the going difficult when it comes to a fight. Whoever chooses the ground can turn landscape to their advantage. Lines of assault can be skilfully directed by the defence to create killing grounds where defenders can wreak havoc among assailants.

Those choosing and defending a location may utilize the advantages of terrain and topography such as marshes, woods, bogs, wetlands, deserts, and mountains to their advantage. Additionally, if the defensive formation is long-lived or static, then those holding it may construct fortifications or other structures to enhance topographical features. Such defensive structures in the landscape may be long, static lines as in the First World War, the Great Wall of China, or on the boundaries of the Roman Empire. These may seek to hold back an invading force along a defensive frontline or to break up an overall assault by holding key locations. In many cases though, such major lines are more symbolic statements than strategically defensive positions, and when need be, can often be overrun or gone around.

Mobility and weaponry

Partisans and guerrillas may utilize mobility to avoid direct conflict. Indeed, mobile defensive strategy is often adopted by such forces to overcome superior numbers in soldiers and weaponry. Stealth, speed, and surprise can be employed by partisans and guerrillas as they make use of terrain to provide cover and concealment. The tactic may lead to the assailant's superior forces being spread thinly and worn down by continual skirmishes. The terrain slows the opposition and direct frontal conflict is avoided, the archetypal guerrilla strategy.

While Western military initiatives were hugely significant in the period from the 1500s to the mid-1800s, it cannot be forgotten that elsewhere in the world,

Possibly Russo-Japanese War showing light cavalry encountering barbed wire making the terrain difficult and hazardous.

such as in China and Japan, there were major and sometimes on-going conflicts. Warfare in these other regions of the globe frequently involved different tactics and types of weaponry. Furthermore, smaller, and more localized tribal disputes also occurred very widely and many morphed into conflicts with expanding Western superpowers. Though firearms were initially invented in the East, it was in Europe that they swiftly emerged as game changers in warfare. Military deployment from 1700 to the 1800s developed with soldiers armed with guns but with socket bayonets for close quarters fighting. The troops were then deployed in ranks of infantry generally three deep that could fire with each line in succession, allowing the time required for re-loading and aiming. This organization changed with the advent of breech-loading rifles and an associated increase in firing distance to around five-hundred metres from a mere hundred and fifty. The ranks of foot-soldiers were supported from the rear by horse-drawn artillery and on the flanks by cavalry. This evolved into the standard approach to battle formations in Europe at that time.

However, there was a massive requirement for soldiers and for equipment with around 20,000 men required to hold just one mile of such a front. With improving performance in rifles there were opportunities for skirmishing lines for the attack, and a need to dig in for defenders. By 1870, the estimated requirement for frontline troops was around 12,000 per mile of defensive position. By 1917, with magazine-fed rifles, machine guns, smokeless gunpowder, and heavy artillery behind the lines, 2,500 troops were needed per mile.

In terms of wider military strategy, the development of nation states with increasingly rapid transportation and communication systems was to transform wars and their battles. Railways, roads, and motor vehicles combined with the telegraph to

German guns bogged down at the Westwall bunker gun position on the Siegrfried Line 1940.

change the pace of conflict, deployment, and outcomes. These changes all impacted on the First World War when massive artillery defence and offence combined with machine guns to dominate a stalemate from the North Sea coast to the Alps. However, improvements to weapons such as light machine guns, hand grenades, portable mortars, and ultimately armoured vehicles, especially tanks, transformed battlefield tactics and wider strategy to place much greater emphasis on mobility. The changes soon morphed into the Second World War approach of rapid movement and decentralization of command systems as manifested in German *blitzkrieg* tactics. This ploy was first demonstrated in 1918, with the idea of taking light artillery and machine guns forward with assault troops to penetrate defensive positions, getting behind the lines to cause havoc. This method developed into a fluid use of mobile armour to break through enemy positions with infantry support to flow around and over defensive points and locations of resistance.

Aerial support also developed from the First World War onward and became a key element of *blitzkrieg* tactics as exemplified by German and Russian forces with mobile attacks over a broad geographic front. An overall strategic plan, commanded from military headquarters, was implemented on the ground by highly trained, devolved, decision makers at a tactical level. Weak points were identified and then targeted by bombers, especially dive-bombers, with mobile artillery on the ground and the rapid deployment of tanks. Infantry could then mop up and hold the areas overcome.

Russian soldiers on the Second World War front.

Of course, with any new tactic countermeasures evolve to challenge it. For *blitzkrieg* the first significant and successful response was around 1941–1942 with the German invasion of Russia. It seemed that *blitzkrieg* was a fair-weather strategy which began to founder in the Russian autumn and winter. The northerly region of the Russian plains is both forested and boggy, and the German heavy armour was unprepared for off-road deployment in these conditions. With the Russian Red Army mobilizing through landscapes of forest and marsh, the German forces were made to fight an unfavourable infantry war in a unfamiliar landscape. The tough Russian forces were on home turf and were probably better at close-quarters fighting. Combined with the use of weapons such as Molotov cocktails (invented by the Spanish republicans in the 1930s) and the so-called satchel charge (a remotely detonated explosive carried in a satchel) to destroy tanks and defensive structures, the Russian strategy was very successful. This was amplified when they received American bazookas. The Russian losses were catastrophic, but they absorbed them and won through.

Similar tactics could be adapted for urban areas such as towns and cities; in Stalingrad the Russians fought hand to hand and block to block. A defensive network could be set up with key buildings and strong points. The idea in both urban and rural situations was pockets of resistance and penetration of the German offensive lines, with networks of defensive forces able to grind away at the opposition. Another tactic employed was for the Russian troops to engage the Germans at close quarters

Schloss Stolzenfels am Rhein rebuilt on the site of a major medieval fortification in a significant topographic situation overlooking the River Rhine, the original castle being destroyed in 1689.

and so to limit the effectiveness of aerial support by the Luftwaffe.

Another modern-day example of successfully deployed infantry was in the Second World War landscapes of central Italy such as the Tuscan hills and the bocage field countryside of Normandy, with scattered small settlements, intimate fields, narrow lanes, and high hedge-banks. These landscapes offer terrain and topography very unsuitable for deployment of tank warfare.

When the Allies invaded, they too required an overwhelming infantry presence on the ground because the movement of heavy armour was inherently difficult. The outcomes of the relationships between evolving technology and tactics are often eventually settled by topography, terrain, and weather.

Landscape, seasons, and extreme conditions

As noted, landscape, climate and seasonality, weather, and patterns of human settlement vary dramatically around the world. These have a major bearing on strategy and tactics and on potential success or disaster. Understanding and preparing for both terrain and climate are critically important considerations, made even more so if wars are conducted in extreme and inhospitable conditions. Misjudgement, from inception and planning to execution, can be disastrous. Furthermore, underestimating the advantage given to indigenous forces by local terrain can be problematic, especially when such forces have access to advanced weaponry; it can prove a great leveller. This applies for instance in modern warfare where the use of rapid transport such as a helicopter can bring great benefits of speedy access or retreat in mountainous country. However, if the indigenous resistance gains access to ground-to-air missiles such as Stingers, as was the case with Afghan resistance to the

Russian artillery negotiating a shallow ford during the Russo-Japanese War, early 1900s.

Soviets in the late 1900s, the advantage is lost. Similarly, a numerically superior force seeking to engage local fighters in mountains, with limited narrow passes or steep knife-edge ridges and only narrow winding roads, will be unable to bring their advantage to bear. Vehicles may be limited to single file convoy, which is inherently vulnerable and in terms of infantry, the terrain favours lightly armed personnel capable of manoeuvring in such topography. This has been the case throughout history from the Soviet tanks in Afghanistan to Austrian heavily armoured knights in medieval Switzerland; it remains so

Street fighting in Malines in Belgium with a cavalry charge under rifle fire from the infantry defenders, First World War.

A Russian column in retreat, Russo-Japanese War. With bad weather and unfriendly terrain such a movement of troops renders them very vulnerable.

today. Just a small number of determined partisans can hold off a far superior force of highly trained soldiers for a very long time. The use of booby-traps and landmines can make progress through such regions desperately difficult.

Deserts, both hot and cold, are inherently inhospitable places that lack basic resources, they can offer little cover and may present shifting landscapes where navigation is problematic. Indeed, true deserts with shifting sands can be hugely difficult for vehicles to negotiate for tracked and wheeled machines as well as foot soldiers. Furthermore, as the late twentieth-century American forces discovered in Iran, unless specialized machinery is available, sand can simply clog up or otherwise damage the mechanics of vehicles, helicopters, and planes. Sand erodes tank track sprockets, causes rapid wear of helicopter blades, and triggers tremendous damage to jet engines. In hot deserts, the metal of armoured vehicles becomes too hot to touch, and electronic circuitry may simply melt. Another complication is that while a vast desert may superficially appear like a great ocean through which people and vehicles can manoeuvre freely, the reality is different, and it is perhaps more like a swamp: open but impenetrable. In later twentieth-century conflicts such as between Israel

US Marines crossing sand dunes on the Pohang battlefront, Korea 1950.

and Egypt, the actual battles were generally centred on specific roadways, junctions, or passes.

While in some situations, huge sand dunes restrict visibility and lines of sight, in open level desert tanks can engage in battle over distances of a mile or more. There are few trees, shrubs, or other features to obscure vision and to provide cover. Seasonality and weather also become very important to combatants in these extreme terrains, where winds can generate terrific sandstorms to change topography and obscure vision.

The other areas of desert-like conditions are the polar snow-caps but generally these have not yet become theatres for warfare. In Alpine, Scandinavian, and other seasonally ice-bound or snow-bound territories, specialist forces have operated since the two World Wars. With mobility adapted to the conditions, troops are trained to ski though the landscape or may use snow-adapted vehicles. In both hot sandy desert and snowy terrain, appropriate camouflage equipment and clothing are part of the adaptation. Winter snowfields can be a further complication, especially in landscapes where summers are hot but winters bitterly cold. In some situations, conflicts pause

until spring comes and in others, such as the Alpine zone in the First World War, combatants utilized snow and ice drifts as part of their military strategy. German troops bombarded ice and snow on slopes above the Italians to trigger massive avalanches to sweep away and bury the enemy under huge amounts of snow. The poorly equipped and often untrained Italian infantry were mostly unprepared for winter conditions and with nighttime temperatures falling well below zero, many simply froze at their posts overnight.

Extreme cold, like extreme heat,

brings many challenges to military actions both for personnel and equipment. Mobility may be improved as vehicles, soldiers, and even aircraft can utilize frozen lakes and rivers for example, but deep accumulations of snow can block routes and restrict vehicles to roadways. Again, infantry with light packs and manoeuvrability with skis or snow mobiles may have a battlefield advantage. Changes between seasons can also bring specific problems. So, while frozen winter tundra allows for easy transit, as spring warmth brings a thaw, the layer above the permafrost becomes a boggy quagmire that is almost impassable.

Opposite page top: US Marines in Korean snow, 1950.
Opposite page bottom: British Lancers or Light Dragoons, 1800s.

Stretcher bearers in the mud, Western Front, First World War.

Chapter 14
Disease, landscape, and conflict

Infectious diseases have long been a part of humanity's ecological space and increasingly so once the twin processes of urbanization and globalization spread. As these phenomena accelerated so did infections and their potentially catastrophic impacts. Historically, diseases have been major causes of death, both during wartime and peacetime. However, until the late nineteenth century, our understanding of the causes of bacterial diseases was very limited indeed. Viral causation of diseases was not recognized until the twentieth century, and in both cases, any effective treatments followed some way behind recognition. Furthermore, establishing the connection between for instance, wet countryside, hygiene, and sanitation was late to emerge and until this was more fully understood, the consequences were truly dire.

Rampant disease often accompanies warfare. Both civilian and military populations may suffer severe stress, especially lack of food and of sanitation, this is compounded by injury and accident. A major factor is the mass movement of people around the world, the often-cramped conditions they have in both transit and at their destination, and the placement of individuals into situations where they have limited acquired immunity. Moreover, the selective impacts of disease may be crucial in determining the outcomes of conflicts. As examined in *Ecological Imperialism* it was often disease to which one side or the other was immune that frequently carried the day. Along with people, during periods of mass migration or of international warfare, ships bring with them a host of disease-carrying vermin.

The landscape or environment in which conflict takes place has a major influence on any likely diseases or epidemics. Warm and moist climates favour diseases, parasites, and vectors such as malarial mosquitoes, but extreme cold can also be hazardous. Wet landscapes, particularly with standing water can be especially dangerous with foul water and parasites from microorganisms to insects and other invertebrates, and a risk of toxic algae.

Furthermore, environmental catastrophes, floods, droughts, and earthquakes, may trigger both civil disruption and unrest leading to conflicts, and even war. Major environmental disruptions, such as the massive earthquakes and associated land subsidence in China in the 1300s, one of several disasters across that region, which combined to trigger the global pandemic of Black Death or Bubonic Plague. This situation was compounded by warfare, for example in the Mediterranean region, and the disease itself impacted directly on conflicts.

Diseases may be especially virulent when people are exposed to new or particularly aggressive infections. It seems that the emergence of endemic diseases in human populations began with farming settlements, domestication of animals, and subsequent urbanization. People in close communities bring problems of sanitation, of potable water, and of transfer between individuals. Furthermore, when communities live close to domesticated livestock and other animals, diseases spread between species, and the combination of these factors triggers the onset of the diseases of civilizations. In the few accounts describing the earliest times, such as biblical scriptures, these problems are generally regarded as pestilences or plagues and are put down to 'acts of God'. Some of these were undoubtedly caused by malaria, but others may have been any one of several infections such as bubonic plague or smallpox. Beginning in the late Neolithic period 7,000 years ago, migration and its associated spread of diseases emerged and grew throughout history to the present day. Diseases spread between old worlds and new, particularly during the period of medieval commerce and conquest, and then the 1500s' expansion of European cultures; in each case they became terrible epidemics or pandemics. Until the early modern period, with

A native American sees the Spanish fleet arriving off the coast of Mexico, 1518.

Aztec temple to the god of war where captives were sacrificed, 1500s.

the emergence of modern medicine, it is often very difficult to be clear which disease was responsible at any one time.

A well-documented example of the impacts on native people subject to invasion was the case of the southern tip of Africa in 1713, when smallpox arrived with British and Dutch settlers and soldiers. The disease swept through the community to devastating effect. The local indigenous people were annihilated and, quite rightly, blamed the foreigners.

The problems of remote communities

Any society remote from a population centre and urbanisation, may be prone to debilitating diseases because of a lack of resistance to the new disease or a novel strain of an old infection. Resistance decreases with distance from the core population, the relative size of the community under threat, and the frequency of contact with the core population from where traders or invaders are coming. The medieval Viking settlers of Iceland,

Greenland, and North America are good examples. The Icelandic population was viable and indeed populated the island with people and sheep and was in close and regular contact with its Scandinavian origins. The Greenland settlement was less successful and relatively short-lived, and the mainland Vikings in Vinland, North America were even less so. When the main European explorers arrived in North America in the 1500s, their diseases (particularly smallpox) had a devastating effect on the indigenous people and settlements, and swept across the landscape in the next two to three hundred years. Conquest was then inevitable. For the Vikings in Greenland and Vinland, where their numbers were low, they were just as isolated from their European homeland and source of disease immunity, as the Native Americans were. There was no immunity, no advantage, and therefore no conquest.

Smallpox and the Aztecs

A particularly famous, but especially unpleasant example of the impact of disease in warfare, was the destruction of the Aztec city of Tenochtitlán, and the eradication of the Aztec civilization by the Spanish. The Aztec Empire was relatively late in emerging and came about as a result of the alliance of three city-states in Central America in 1428. In search of treasure, the Spanish conquistadores arrived with a force of just 600 in 1519 led by Hernán Cortés. They overran the Tenochtitlán city where they had been welcomed and took the Aztec leader, Emperor Moctezuma II, as a hostage. The Spanish remained in control of the city until a revolt broke out and they had to flee.

However, within a short time the Spanish returned with their own troops supported by recruits from non-Aztec tribes from the surrounding regions. Despite vastly inferior weaponry – reed shields and padded cotton armour against crossbows, swords, and cannon, the defensive city walls and numerical superiority enabled the Aztecs to hold out for a long time. Then, after a siege lasting seventy-nine days, the city fell and the Spanish looted and pillaged at will. Ultimately, the conflict was vastly swayed by what was for the Aztecs a new disease, smallpox, and for which they had little or no immunity. By the time the Spanish entered the vast city, its inhabitants had been effectively annihilated by disease and were thus unable to mount effective resistance to the invaders. The city was a massive metropolis of over 200,000 people. Furthermore, it was defended by high city walls located on a large lake, Texcoco, with connections to the shore by just three main causeways, the water acting as a moat. Nevertheless, a combination of superior technology and a nasty invasive microbe caused their downfall. The Peruvian Incas fell shortly afterwards.

Execution of Inca ruler, Atahualpa, by the Spanish in 1533, though he was garroted not burned.

Slaughter of the Spanish by the Aztecs, 1 July 1520.

The Black Death

Bubonic plague evolved around modern-day China two millennia ago. From this base where it is endemic in rodents, it spread globally as several deadly pandemics, with the first documented in Europe being a contributory factor in the fall of the Roaman Empire. This struck during the reign of Emperor Justinian from around AD541 to 549. Justinian I, known as Justinian the Great, was emperor of the Eastern Roman Empire from AD527 to 565 and his domain stretched from Constantinople to North Africa, and across parts of southern Europe as he recovered areas lost by the Western Empire following the so-called fall of Rome around AD476. Indeed,

The Black Death of 1349 killed between a third and two thirds of the European population.

the capitulation of Rome at that time did not necessarily mean the end but merely a major setback for Rome and the Western Empire. It is also surmised that the collapse of the Western Empire under pressure from Goths and Vandals, was also in part due to disease, in this case malaria. However, in AD542, bubonic plague arrived to plunge the classical world into crisis; and it was from this shock that medieval and modern Europe emerged. At the peak of the plague, about five thousand people died every day in Constantinople, and cities across the region became depopulated. This was the first documented global pandemic, with over twenty-five million people dead by its end, a huge impact on people and the landscape was felt.

This first pandemic of bubonic plague ran its course from AD542 in Constantinople and it is suggested that by the middle AD600s it had hit Britain too. This was a period of mass migration from Germanic countries to post-Roman Britain, with all the associated risks that entailed, and the carriage of disease was just one. As noted, a key issue is that island communities are relatively isolated from their mainland and are therefore inherently vulnerable. They simply don't have the built-in immunity acquired through wider contact. In Britain for example, as a collection of islands, the first documented 'crowd disease' arrived across the sea around AD664 and was described as devastating. This was 'a sudden pestilence first depopulated the southern parts of Britain and afterwards attacked the Kingdom of Northumbria, raging

Crusaders catapulting severed heads of Muslim soldiers over the city walls at Nicaea, 1098.

far and wide and laying low a vast number of people'. This was probably Black Death which became rife in the Mediterranean, effectively ending the so-called golden age of the Roman Empire under Emperor Justinian. The epidemic was one of the first major documented examples of bubonic plague influencing military outcomes, with impacts on the Roman Empire but also on communities and countries from the Mediterranean to northern and western Europe.

The plague bacterium moved along different routes over both land and sea into new terrain. Then, in medieval times known as the Black Death, the disease once more erupted in the east and progressed through Asia, Europe, and Africa between 1347 and 1351, a pandemic which began deep in the heartlands of medieval China. Droughts, followed by floods caused by a massive earthquake in 1333, killed around four hundred thousand people. It was said that the great mountain of Tsincheou had fallen in, to create 'great chasms in the earth'. In 1334 a drought in Houkouang and Honan was followed by swarms of locusts, and consequent famine and disease. The catastrophes were ongoing until around 1345 including an earthquake in the Ki-Ming-Chan mountains that created a lake with a circumference of over 300 miles. With many homes now under water, the result was a death toll of over five million and no remaining structure or organization to clear the bodies. Endemic in the rodents which now proliferated, the Black Death spread to devastating effect into the human population that remained. Carried by Chinese travellers with the explorer Zheng He, it travelled into West Asia along the Silk Road and into Africa around 1409 and 1433. It is estimated to have depleted the world's human population from 450 million to perhaps 350 million, with approximately half China's population dying.

The first use of biological warfare

Another major topic but one for which space here only allows a light touch, is that of the deliberate use of disease as a weapon of war. It has been suggested that the crusaders in the siege of Nicaea (1098) pelted the city with diseased, severed heads catapulted over the battlements. This was probably not the case, but it was a ploy to simply horrify those within the city walls as the heads of their dead soldiers came flying over to land amongst them. The Christians also paraded the severed heads on spikes in view of the guards on the walls and towers of the heavily fortified city. However, the first recorded example of biological warfare was the medieval use of plague victims to spread infection. Bubonic plague or Black Death, endemic in rodent populations in regions in and around China. The disease caused by the bacterium *Yersinia pestis* is transferred to people by rodents through either fleabites or in droplets of fluid. It occurs in two forms, pneumonic plague, and bubonic plague. The former affects the respiratory tracts, especially the lungs, and the latter the lymphatic system, particularly the underarms and groin. Death can be sudden, violent, unpleasant, and most distressing.

Rumours of a growing catastrophe began to arrive in India and then in Europe. At the time it was believed that the disease or pestilence was carried in foul air on the southerly winds. By 1346, the plague was becoming established in Asia Minor, then under the control of the Tartars. Genoese traders occupied a local city in the Crimea at that time, and following a street brawl during which a local Muslim was killed, pursued by the Tartars, the Genoese left, escaping to their fortified base at Caffa (now Feodosia) where the Tartar army then laid siege. The scene was set for a drawn-out conflict as the army used its huge catapults to bombard the walls of the fortified settlement. However, there was a twist as the recently arrived plague was especially virulent. Consequently, the Tartar force was cut down 'fatigued, stupefied, and amazed'. Those inside the city watched with amazement as their assailants collapsed before their eyes. However, as the Tartars abandoned the siege, before they retreated, they turned to lobbing the rapidly decomposing and putrefying corpses of their peers over the walls into the city with the great catapults. As the bodies flew over the walls the Genoese carried them to a point where they could drop them into the sea, but it was to no avail. The plague spread rapidly though the walled city and those Genoese that survived took to their ships. From Caffa they sailed out from the Black Sea and across the Mediterranean, carrying the plague with them. Bubonic plague was back in Europe, and with it the first documented account of biological warfare. Around 85,000 people died of bubonic plague in Crimea alone. In terms of the corpses thrown over the walls, it has been questioned as to whether they could carry infection or not. However, I see no reason why they shouldn't.

Europe's numbers fell by about one third or more, and Africa's by an eighth. In Asia the spread followed natural disaster, in Europe the disease arrived in a landscape

Malaria as the spectre of the swamp in the 1800s.

already torn by ongoing wars and furthermore, with a population that now exceeded the carrying capacity of its agricultural system and a rapidly deteriorating climate. This was a perfect scenario for a terrible catastrophe, 'The Black Death'.

Malaria and other mosquito-borne infections

The spread of nasty infections was not merely a one-way exchange; alongside invaders carrying disease to remote corners of the world, they also contracted some horrible infections while on their travels. Some of these simply killed the travellers who lacked immunity but the diseases, such as Yellow Fever, is a mosquito-borne acute viral haemorrhagic disease of wet tropical areas, the 'yellow' referring to the associated jaundice. The virus is endemic in tropical areas of Africa, and Central and South America, and formerly across Asia; for some victims death occurs within a week or two. This was an affliction that affected seafarers, but generally didn't travel back home.

However, malaria, that other terrible killer, did travel and establish as the troops brought back the plasmodium and the mosquito vector. It seems that Greek and Roman soldiers contracted malaria in North Africa and brought it back to Europe. In Rome especially, with the famous aqueducts and water piped into many houses and courtyards, the mosquitoes flourished as did the disease; this may have been one of the factors that helped end the glory days of old Rome. Furthermore, the Roman legionaries brought malaria to Britain where it flourished in the still undrained countryside, as 'marsh malaria' or 'ague'. This continued in Britain and lingered until the early 1900s in East Anglia, with a slight upsurge in the 1920s and 1940s when it was brought back by soldiers who contracted it in France and Italy. The disease was plasmodium malaria transmitted by anopheline mosquitoes breeding in stagnant pools and ditches. The marsh ague was the tertian fever which recurred with severe fits twice in a three-day period.

This disease had a big impact on history, and probably on conflicts too, as many famous and influential leaders suffered and died. One significant English king during the Wars of the Roses was King Edward IV; his reign ended in 1483 when he died of various complications, including malarial fever. Another example was King James I of England who died of it in 1625 having become increasingly frail and often ill. When he became sick with ague fever it was clear that this was the issue but physicians at the time had no idea of the cause and little insight into effective treatments. In 1658 Oliver Cromwell, a fenman by birth, also died of ague fever. Following the death of Cromwell and the Restoration, King Charles II came to the throne and he too suffered, with recorded bouts of tertian fever in 1678 and 1679; he was cured using quinine, known as Talbor's remedy. However, he took ill once more and, on 2 February 1685, suffered a sudden apoplectic fit and died aged fifty-four. There are various theories on the cause of his sudden death, but it is likely that complications with malaria played a big part.

Leprosy

One especially unpleasant disease sometimes contracted during long military campaigns was leprosy, and one sufferer was indeed King Robert the Bruce of Scotland. The disease was probably contracted due to poor diet, poor sleeping and living quarters, and especially, poor hygiene during campaigns, and appeared to spread north and westwards from the hot climates of the Mediterranean where it first appeared endemic. Causing serious debilitation and disfigurement leprosy was feared and stigmatised by all the communities where it became prevalent. Like many diseases during times of trauma and conflict, leprosy spread through stress and squalor, and may have been exacerbated in hotter climates where bodies were less covered by clothing and more naked skin exposed, thus allowing skin-to-skin transmission. Foreign wars also meant long-distance travel, exposure to novel diseases, and the opportunity for international transmission of infections and vectors.

Disease and conflicts

Diseases and infections have influenced specific conflicts from wars to individual

Purification of a medieval Christian knight suffering from leprosy.

battles. Since the earliest times, military campaigns over distances were fraught with the threat of contracting debilitating disease, even though sufferers and their leaders had little idea of the causes. Sometimes, such as in the case of malarial infections, it was recognised that wetlands and especially stagnant waters were in some way the source of disease. However, since there was no understanding of microbes and transmission, it was assumed that the problems somehow seemed out of the waterscape as a poisonous 'miasma'.

Alexander the Great

One major example that perhaps transformed history, was when Macedonian general Alexander the Great died of malaria. He was at the peak of his powers when, allied with Greek states, he conquered the Persians and took over the entire eastern Mediterranean coastline, including Syria, Phoenicia, Arabia, and Egypt. His armies pressed on to defeat the tribes of northern India, thus completing the conquest of almost the entire known world at that time. With the ambition of subjugating the world, as they knew it, he was ready to depart with his army in early June 323BCE but developed a fever and the enterprise was delayed. It was assumed that at thirty-three years this was a trifling matter. However, Alexander's health deteriorated as he passed into a coma and subsequently died. The cause was malaria contracted during his campaigns; with Alexander's death the course of history was changed forever. If he had survived to continue his military conquests, he might well have joined east and west to combine Greeks and Asians into a unified nation. Yet, with Alexander dead, the emerging empire collapsed, and his undefeated army fell apart. So, malaria was pivotal in the ending of Alexander's conquests but also, as noted earlier, it was a key factor in the demise of Greek civilization because, brought back to Greece by returning armies, it spread to become endemic with devastating effect on people, causing the depopulation of large swathes of the countryside.

Another military example was that of Emperor Otto I, the AD936 East Frankish king and Holy Roman Emperor from AD962 until his death in AD973. To suppress an uprising he took his army to attack Rome in AD964 but almost all his men died

Alexander the Great as the heroic leader, celebrated by Hindu tribesmen.

of malaria. Those surviving were described as only daring to hope to survive from one evening to the following morning. At that time Rome was surrounded by the extensive Pontine marshland, an ideal breeding ground for malarial mosquitoes. Ten years later, on 7 December AD983, his eldest son Otto II, also died of malaria; just twenty-eight years old, medicine proved ineffective.

Warfare and disease have gone together down the centuries as large numbers of people come together from across countries and continents, and many of them carry different strains of infections. Furthermore, forced proximity in living quarters combine with lack of sanitation, often poor diet, and many other stresses, to trigger outbreaks of sicknesses. Alongside the inevitable exposure to death, the dying and the injured, the scene is set for battlescape catastrophe beyond the actual conflict.

The army of Charles V at Naples in 1528.

An example was in 1528, when the French army was laying siege to Naples defended by the army of Charles V of Naples (and King of Spain) but the latter had been laid low by bubonic plague and near starvation. The French army under Francis I seemed poised for a significant victory when 30,000 of their soldiers died of typhus in a single month. In disarray, the French army withdrew, and Charles was victorious. This was a disease that seemed to be carried by the troops and was closely associated with the battlefields presumably due to lack of sanitation, absence of clean, potable water, and marshy conditions with limited drainage.

The history of warfare and military campaigns is full of similar accounts of great armies brought to their knees by disease. Carried from Europe, malaria spread throughout North America during the War of Independence. Entire British garrisons are described as succumbing to the scourge, and the final British surrender at Yorktown was probably in part associated with a major epidemic fever. Indeed, the importance of malaria in the conflict was reflected on in 1775 by one of the first military expenditures of the Continental Congress. They spent 300 US dollars on the purchase of quinine to protect General Washington's soldiers.

An ideal breeding ground for mosquitoes and other pests around the tracks and shell holes in the Zonnebeke marshes, Western Front, Flanders.

The pattern continued as malaria became the most significant health hazard for US troops in the South Pacific conflict of the Second World War, with around half a million infected. It was suggested that sixty thousand American soldiers were killed by malaria during the African and South Pacific campaigns.

Another dramatic use of biological warfare was by Napoleon with malaria during the British Walcheren Expedition to the Low Countries. On 30 July 1809 a British army of about 39,000 men landed at Walcheren to support the Austrians in their campaign against Napoleon and attack the French navy moored at Flushing. Napoleon's hold on Europe was strengthened by his defeat of the Austrians at Wagram earlier that month. Stating, 'We must oppose the English with nothing but fever, which will soon devour them all', Napoleon's tactic was to flood the Dutch countryside with shallow water to trigger the rampant spread of malaria. The result was that the British Army expeditionary force was so badly affected from August to October 1809, that they could not continue. Early in August seven hundred men were ill, but by 3 September more than eight thousand were hospitalized. This number rose to

Florence Nightingale during the Crimean War started the movement toward modern hospital treatment and nursing care for the sick and wounded.

A waterlogged trench near Westhoek, Flanders, 1917.

nine thousand by late October and with the appalling conditions, hospitals were established in houses, churches, and warehouses. Treatment was basic and largely ineffective with laxatives and emetics plus venesection (bloodletting), blistering, dousing with cold water, and some relief through alcohol and tobacco. When the expedition ended in February 1810, malaria had killed sixty officers and 3,900 troops. Nearly half the army had been affected and six months later eleven thousand men were still listed as sick. The losses in actual combat were a mere hundred.

One of the issues of course, was the

Early English settlements in North America suffered badly from disease and starvation, such as at Jamestown in the early 1600s where the wetland triggered typhoid, malaria and other problems.

limited scope of medical practice and the dire treatment of increasingly complex battlefield injuries, compounded by increasingly varied diseases and exposure to unhygienic conditions and contamination. The move towards more modern hospitalisation and organisation was pioneered by Florence Nightingale during the Crimean War of the mid-1800s.

Dealing with the sick and the battlefield injuries meant finding, collecting, and then treating the casualties in often inhospitable terrain, with limited supplies of basic necessities, and frequently under enemy fire.

Epworth Church in North Lincolnshire and the Northern Fen, the birthplace of Methodism.

Chapter 15
Dissention and non-conformity

Both territory and culture play major roles in wars and conflicts, with many disputes or persecutions being linked to territorial gain, ambitions, and cultural separations. The latter are frequently due to landscape and geography. The invasion of land frequently takes place because of economic and material motivations, but also because of cultural or religious differences. Similarly, within a particular country or territory, minority groups are often persecuted, and their lands eroded. Indeed, this process of attrition has occurred throughout history and continues today with the deliberate genocide of indigenous people in the Amazon, Indonesia, and elsewhere. It seems that the underlying reasons are difference, independence, in fact and in thought, and perhaps vulnerability.

Remote and protective terrain and topography may protect cultures and cultural differences, but they also provide refuges to which people can retreat from invaders and those seeking to persecute them. Groups of islands, dense forest, hills, and mountains, deserts, and wetlands all provide the possibility of sanctuary. Additionally, survival in such situations often requires adaptation and development to suit the conditions and this naturally moves the culture into a new and distinctive area and identity.

Associated with refuge, such landscapes may engender independence of thought and of behaviour; tendencies which may trigger alarm for ruling elites and the like. As we have seen in some examples of battlescapes throughout the ages, the response is often to suppress independence and, in some cases such as wetlands or forests, to remove the natural protection.

King Charles I of England whose dispute with Parliament triggered the English Civil War, perhaps sparked by fenland drainage and loss of traditional rights.

Culture, separation, and non-conformism

During the long history of humanity, those apart from the social and political mainstream have been subject to persecution and to violent assault from their neighbours. An example was the siege of the fortified Jewish city of Jotapata by the Romans in AD67 and the slaughter of many of the Jewish population. The topographical setting was a major reason for the Jewish rebels retreating to the fortified settlement. Positioned on an isolated hill hidden between high peaks, it was surrounded on three sides by steep ravines and only accessible with ease from the saddle on the hill to the north. The defenders held out against overwhelming military odds for around forty-seven days. Ultimately, as so often the case, the Romans won out.

Important, in the context of this volume, landscape, geographic location, topography, and terrain have played major roles in the issues of identity, isolation, and independence. These in turn have triggered and influenced wars, battles, and conflicts, and have determined the outcomes of disputes over natural resources. The results are seen in historical events such as the highland clearances in Scotland

A typical wetland scene in the English Fens and a place of non-conformism, independent thinking, and resistance to externally imposed change.

following the battle of Culloden, and in the parliamentary enclosures of the English commons. The fenland drainage of the 1600s in England led to riots, running battles, and deaths across South Yorkshire, Lincolnshire, and Cambridgeshire, the latter being pivotal in triggering the English Civil War.

With the Jacobite rebellions, the Scots ultimately panicked once they were deep into English territory and their response was to retreat deep into their heartland in the remote and rugged Highlands of Scotland. Ultimately this was in vain, and they lost the battle, the war, and for many, their lands.

Contrary to the often-held belief, this drainage and 'improvement' was not totally about agricultural production *per se*, but rather the twin motivations of a land-grab for control and production, and the attempted removal of opportunities for independent thought and religion. For centrally controlled church and state, the independence and separateness of the fenland communities was a problem, and for the bigger landowners, the self-sufficiency of the peasantry was an issue. Additionally, the extent and geographical isolation of the fens, and the relative independence of its peoples, provided refuge for those fleeing the central state or the law. This applied from the time of the Norman conquest with leaders such as Hereward the Wake, through until the great drainage and enclosures that started in the 1600s, terminating only in

Crowland Abbey in South Lincolnshire and the burial place of Earl Waltheof, one of the last leaders of Saxon resistance to the eleventh-century Norman invasion.

the nineteenth century. The vast and often remote areas of English fens proved to be a hotbed of independent thought and action at a time in history when neither church nor state tolerated such transgressions. Henry VIII described Lincolnshire as 'that despicable shire' on account of the populace disagreeing with many of his imposed changes to religion and social order.

Religious beliefs and non-conformism have been major triggers for persecution, for conflict, and for warfare around the world and throughout history. This has frequently triggered other impacts, conflicts, and changes. So, for example, the persecution of the Protestant Walloons and Huguenots in France and the Low Countries, by Catholic overlords, led to mass emigration to England including to the wetlands of the English Fens during the 1600s. One consequence was that these people, often skilled in water management and drainage, were responsible for much of the subsequent removal of the fenland waterscapes in a conflict between the social strata in rural England. The persecution of one community inadvertently was in part responsible for the extinction of the widespread common rights of another.

Religion and beliefs were often at the core of 'difference' between peoples. In the 1600–1700s, the Quakers, or Society of Friends, was evolving in northern England and became active in the emerging industrial towns and also rural areas such as the fens. However, they were considered a radical, dangerous, and treasonous movement, and punishments were severe.

Similarly, Methodism, a Christian doctrine that originated within the Church of England in the 1700s, came to be equally frowned upon. The two main proponents, John Wesley (1703–1791) and his younger brother Charles (1707–1788), were born in their father's parish at Epworth in North Lincolnshire. John was the fifteenth child and second son of Reverend Samuel Wesley, Anglican Rector of Epworth and his wife, Susanna. Epworth is on the Isle of Axholme, so-called because until the 'Great Drainage' around 1627–1629, it was an island in an inland 'lake' surrounded by rivers, streams, bogs, and meres. Topographically and socially, this was an isolated place. The Methodist movement occurred in the early eighteenth century within the Church of England and was founded by a small group of Oxford University students, including the Wesley brothers. From this modest beginning Methodism grew to become one of the largest churches on the planet. Methodism grew in England, particularly in the industrial centres of the north and the rural areas in Devon, Cornwall, and Wales. By the late nineteenth century, other 'Reformed Christians', such as Presbyterians and Congregationalists, were labelled 'Nonconformists' or 'Free Church', along with Baptists, Brethren, Methodists, and Quakers. These were broad groups of Protestant Christians that did not 'conform' to the governance and practices of the established Church of England. Across many rural areas, including the fenlands, non-conformism with church and government ran deep.

Time and again, a reason for invasion and oppression concerns beliefs and suppression of independent thought. We see this process with modern Chinese oppression of Tibet, a peaceful Buddhist culture with few resources to pillage, but strongly held beliefs and culture. The Chinese also have a problem with the Moslem Uyghurs. Distinct from the Han Chinese, these are a Turkic ethnic group native to Xinjiang and are the second largest predominantly Muslim ethnic group in China with around ten million Uyghur speakers. The government pursues policies of ethnic cleansing and re-education against them. Such distinct and oppressed groups often seek refuge in remote places away from the mainstream. Even so, history suggests that such strategies ultimately fail to protect communities.

These types of policies are not new: throughout history centralized, conquering, invading and dominant cultures have sought to displace, dispossess, and subjugate, or exterminate, indigenous people. We only need consider North America, Central

America, Australia, and Africa under the cosh of European settlement. Similar fates befell the remaining non-Christian societies across northern Europe as the Sami and other communities were forcibly converted to Christianity. Many battles, conflicts, and wars relate to these drivers, with topography, terrain, and geographical location central to the theme.

The resistance and survival of minority, indigenous, and culturally independent peoples have often depended on landscape and the isolation it can provide. This might be remote mountains, dense forest, high latitude, expansive desert, or extensive wetlands. Terrain and topography may provide a location to survive or offer protection from outside intrusion. It is an effective barrier – an impenetrable habitat – that cuts off a land and its people from the outside world. Today, such locations are few and far between.

In Northern Europe, the last non-Christian group to be converted and repressed was the nomadic Sami, an aboriginal culture. In many cases, they were forcibly converted but also their lands were taken, as the Swedes for example, colonised the northern parts of Lapland to bring them into mainstream forestry and farming culture. This began in earnest in the 1600s and was paralleled in neighbouring countries such as Norway and Russia. The Sami cultures survived so long because they were geographically remote, and in a landscape where the terrain and the climate mitigated against incoming colonisers. Furthermore, in terms of productive countryside the northern zone of Sweden lacks obvious resources. Ultimately, the Swedish government provided incentives for southern farmers and foresters to settle and produced booklets of instructions on how to farm and to manage the forest for economic benefit. Most of the Sami who survived became settled and some continued to try and live their traditional, nomadic lives but increasingly at odds with the modern world.

The barrier that allows survival might be a physical presence such as a mountain range, wetland, or forest, or it might be associated challenges that make incursions into a locale difficult, as earlier chapters have described. Too much or too little water for example, are problematic. Landscapes that are very hot or very cold, are difficult, and those with parasites and nasty diseases are especially challenging for non-indigenous people. Indeed, long-term survival in these conditions comes at a cost but also triggers benefits such as tolerance or immunity to many of the disease and similar problems and to which the incomer has little defence. This was the case in the English Fenlands, where the local indigenous communities were largely immune to endemic 'ague' or marsh malaria, whereas incomers or travellers might succumb rather quickly.

On the march at Strensall Common near York.

Chapter 16
Review and contemporary issues

Nature, consisting of landscape (topography, terrain), and geography (natural resources, soils, water, habitats, diseases, and ecology), and climate (seasonal changes and weather) has influenced human settlement patterns throughout history. Similarly, these factors impact on disputes and conflicts over those resources and geographic spaces. Earlier chapters considered key environments or habitats with case-study examples to examine how various landscapes and countryside influence or affect conflicts with perspectives of assailants and defenders, indigenous people, and invaders, and from the earliest recorded histories to modern day. Landscape may facilitate invasions and assaults or provide obstacles that favour defenders. Indeed, as the case-studies demonstrate, landscape and nature can be great levellers that allow outnumbered forces, with inferior technology, to hold out or even win through. Furthermore, landscapes, with differing topography and terrain, influence

Remains of the French Maginot Line, 1970s.

strategies and tactics of military forces and their leaders.

Wetlands like peat bogs, fenlands, rivers, marshes, and wet forests have all played significant roles in conflicts large and small. Similarly, deserts and plains (hot and cold), provided sanctuary for indigenous tribes, while allowing distinct styles of military combat. Historically this could mean armoured cavalry, and in the modern era, armoured tanks.

Mountains and hills are major obstacles and barriers to advancing armies but sanctuary for partisans or guerrillas. Similarly forests and woodlands can be ideal hideaways for resistance forces and are avoided and by-passed by more formal troops. Dense trees make navigation difficult, limit line of sight, and allow opponents to approach close enough to strike without being seen. Recognizing broad, basic factors, and responding with appropriate tactics, may be the key to success.

Landscapes and countryside present challenges for supply chains and communication, and misjudgement and poor decision making may prove very costly. The case-studies show how seasonality, through impacts on weather and on terrain or ground conditions, can be pivotal in both individual battles and in longer wars or campaigns. Connected in many and varied ways to all these matters, are potential impacts of diseases and infections on military personnel and on civilian populations.

Combatants have fought within, through and beyond these landscapes with geographic

Yorkshire troops at the Battle of Broodseinde, October 1917, fought on 4 October 1917 near Ypres in Belgium and at the east end of the Gheluvelt plateau. The British Second and Fifth Armies against the German 4th Army used bite-and-hold tactics limited to what could be held against German counterattacks and proved devastating. This triggered a crisis among the German command and severe loss of morale. The battle was the most successful Allied attack of the Third Battle of Ypres.

context often being the difference between life and death, as soldiers battled enemies and also the environment. A good general heeded the landscape and the climate.

The impacts of warfare

While some tribal wars might have limited long-term impacts on countryside, those of modern wars can endure. The tipping point in this was probably the industrialization of warfare, especially long-term, static trench-based conflicts with entire landscapes erased and re-constructed, with potential for massive pollution legacies too, ranging from radiation to heavy metal contamination

Disease

The long-term persistence of disease propagules like Anthrax with spores deliberately developed for biological warfare surviving harsh conditions in soils, for decades or even centuries, means they are now found on all continents. The various forms of infection have mortality if untreated ranging from twenty-five to eighty per cent or higher. Infection is usually through contact with carcases of infected dead animals,

German transport wagons mounted on sledges necessary in a cold climate.

but developed as a biological warfare weapon, this remains a terrible problem in some areas. Experimental usage left test areas, such as uninhabited islands, contaminated death-traps for centuries.

Impacts on the countryside

Military impacts on landscapes include extensive training grounds like Salisbury Plain and Sherwood Forest in England, army camps and bases, and airfields and supporting military infrastructure. They also include historic defensive structures from walls, castles, moats, ditches, and twentieth-century pillboxes and anti-tank blocks. Many military features date back to the medieval period and beyond to prehistoric structures such as

Snowshoe drill of Prussian infantry, March 1894. Training for extreme weather and terrain are vital for military success.

Military training event on Hampstead Heath in August 1860. Such activities were well publicized and became major public entertainments.

the great dykes. Around the world, evidence of military occupation is marked by evidence of encampments and trenches or other features. Some of these in England for instance, were practice trenches for trainees who would later be sent to the Western Front to dig for real; others were dug by civil defence units in case of invasion. Great territorial and defensive markers such as Hadrian's Wall, Offa's Dyke, and the Great Wall of China are evidence of vast militarized landscapes. Across much of Europe there are still huge structures built by the Nazis on the one hand, and by the French on the other. The Siegfried Line built during the 1930s and known in German as the Westwall, was a German defensive line. This was placed opposite the massive French Maginot Line with its concrete forts and bunkers. The German line ran over 630 km from Kleve on the border with the Netherlands, along the western border of Nazi Germany, to the town of Weil am Rhein on the border with Switzerland. The French Maginot Line was named after the French Minister of War André Maginot. It was a defensive line of concrete fortifications, obstacles, and weapon installations built by France in the 1930s. The idea was to deter any German invasion and slow any assault long enough for the French military to mobilize. Indeed, the Maginot Line was impervious to most forms of attack but in 1940, passing it to the north of the line, the

Soldiers at Strensall Common Camp near York.

Germans invaded through the Low Countries. The original plan had been to extend the defences further west to avoid being by-passed, but this was scaled back because the Belgians felt they might be sacrificed on the wrong side of any invasion. Massive concrete defences, long abandoned, will mark these landscapes for centuries to come.

With the increasing industrialization of battlescapes throughout the nineteenth and twentieth centuries, the idea of a specific 'battlefield' became at best fuzzy and at worst meaningless. At one time a battle was limited spatially to a relatively discrete area that only morphed into a wider landscape when defeat became a rout and defeated soldiers fled into the wider countryside. By the late 1800s, many battles extended to take in hamlets and villages, fields, orchards, woods, and forests. Battlescapes on this scale meant displacement of civilians and communities, and often displacement of farmers and farmland. Some of these changes were long-term and even permanent. Furthermore, the militarization of battlescapes might mean starvation or bankruptcy for local farmers and the peasantry.

Militarized landscapes

We see the impacts of militarization on landscape and communities as far back, and even beyond the Romans in Britain. Hadrian's Wall created a major barrier

French machine guns in action defending a route.

A French fortification held by the Allies, 1939.

Underground in a French fortification held by the Allies, 1939.

and a striking feature etched across the landscape. It also brought fortresses and camps, and then trading posts and small townships with communities and economic activity along this length. The troops required food, equipment, homes, animals, and entertainment. All these were provided locally, and the necessary settlements grew up in the militarized zone. Take a visit to pre-Roman Dorset around Maiden Castle and the view is of multiple hilltops with enclosures and fortifications. Again, this is a prehistoric militarized landscape, as are large areas of, for example, England's Peak District moorlands.

Some battlefields, camps, prisons, and other features around the world have been preserved as monuments. The mass graveyards from the Second World War in France and Belgium, and the battlefields and cemeteries from the American Civil War, are set aside as sanctuaries and shrines to commemorate the fallen. Other battlefields and structures have been dismantled and restored to farmland or simply allowed to change gradually as nature reclaims its own.

Military occupation of the countryside

The British army controls around 38,000 hectares of land on Salisbury Plain, plus sites such as Castlemartin (Pembrokeshire, Wales), and Otterburn (Northumberland) and other firing ranges and camps. Even though many areas have passed back to

A massed German attack in front of Arras.

A concealed heavy gun captured by the Highlanders, First World War.

Aerial view of Maiden Castle, Dorset.

civilian use, the army still controls about 241,000 hectares or one per cent of the country's land area. Similar situations are found around the world with ten million hectares in the US, around 260,000 hectares in France, and three million hectares in Australia. There are numerous airfield and airbase sites such as Royal Navy Air Station Culdrose at Helston in Cornwall, one of Europe's largest helicopter bases. Indeed, many landscapes are dotted with wartime features such as battlefields, plus infrastructures from both training and active service today and historically. These military structures include bunkers, early warning stations, silos, fortifications, testing sites for weapons, camps and training areas, factories to supply all of these,

Training New Zealand troops to face a gas attack, October 1917.

and of course cemeteries. There are also all the extraction sites and processing areas for modern, industrialized warfare.

Throughout history military training has often taken place in landscapes offering the sorts of conditions likely to be faced on real-time battlefields. Medieval soldiers fought mock battles on heaths and commons, and the London Trained Bands of the Parliamentarian forces, during the English Civil War, assembled and trained on the great fields and commons just outside the city. Similar accounts exist of military training on heaths and moors across the country, such as Exmoor and Dartmoor in the southwest, and Hampstead Heath near London. Cannock Chase, a heathland in Staffordshire had extensive military use and major encampments until the twentieth century and the archaeological evidence remains. Frimley Fuel Allotments in Surrey was a site extensively used for training infantry soldiers in the First World War. This use of the Allotments for military training resulted in the digging of several miles of trenches and the removal of around 1,000 trees. The aim was to give the troops an impression of a French battlefield. The overall impact joined with that of a prisoner-of-war camp which had no sanitation and generated foul smells across the area. When the war ended the military compensated the landowner (the local

Military manoeuvres at Cannock Chase, Staffordshire, 1873.

council) for its losses and started a programme of re-planting the trees. However, the Second World War triggered fresh military training, and further damage to this one-time peatland landscape. Earlier chapters noted the importance of York as a miliary base over many centuries, up to and including the twentieth century. Nearby Strensall Common was used for military camps, parades, and training, and evidence of this former use remains on the ground.

Warfare and the preparation for active conflict mostly takes place outdoors, although today much can be done with computer-aided virtual environments. Even so, in the absence of artificial intelligence and virtual experiential conflicts, the militarization of the environment is one impact of use or infrastructure on the place or setting. It includes the consequences of deployment, training, and use of these areas. Impacts may be short-lived and transient or long-lived and even permanent. Furthermore, these processes of militarization impact on societies, cultures, economies, and on politics both directly and through either constancy or change in the landscape or countryside. Such changes may be rapid and dramatic such as the First World War transformation of rural farming landscapes in France and Belgium, into battlescapes of semi-permanent trenches, fortifications, barriers, and other military infrastructure.

Military practice on Dartmoor, 1870.

Farms, villages, copses, orchards, fields, and woods were swept away to become a sea of dereliction, destruction, trenches, barbed wire, mud, and gore. Less widely recognized, though often more permanent in duration than actual battlefields, are the supporting infrastructures of camps, firing ranges, training sites and hospitals. In both peacetime and conflict, these may have major impacts on civilians, local towns, and the countryside. Military occupation of land means an absence of civilian development, such as housing, so large tracts of land, like Salisbury Plain, may remain 'green' today. Indeed, promoted

The repair of a destroyed bridge, such as in the East African Campaign of 1917, would fall to the sappers or engineers.

by military conservation groups many British army and air force bases and training areas have become nature conservation sites of some significance. Indeed, when it comes to the sort of disturbance caused by military training, nature can be surprisingly resilient. The military in these areas has acquired what has been described as 'companion' species of birds, butterflies, mammals, and reptiles and indeed they use their presence to help justify peacetime military occupation of large tracts of land. The militarization of nature is often so all-pervasive and deep-seated that sometimes we don't even see it.

Culloden in the Highlands of Scotland, 1746.

Conflict and society: engineers and map makers

Warfare and conflicts have also impacted on society through the emergence of new technologies and innovations, such as surgeons and civil engineers, and even map makers. The concept of the civil engineer is a contrast with military engineers that existed as far back as the Romans. When the English fenlands were being drained in the 1600s, there weren't any formally trained engineers as such, except for those who trained with and worked for the military. The Dutch drainage engineers who arrived to begin the Great Drainage of England were men steeped in military training who had applied their skills to the Dutch wetlands. From the 1700s into the 1800s, these men became the engineers who created new roads, railways, towns and cities, and a host of other essential infrastructure. All this was originally triggered and nurtured on the battlescape. Indeed, modern engineering as opposed to the work of stone masons who built great buildings, emerged from those charged with undermining castle walls, ramparts, and keeps, and constructing other structures specifically for the battlefield.

These engineers also built military roads and bridges and were responsible for necessary surveys and map making. One of the most well-known of these was William Roy, the Scottish surveyor responsible for mapping much of the Highlands after the Scots defeat at Culloden. It was deemed necessary to have better and up-to-date maps of the region and to improve roads to ensure easy military access, even to remote areas. This was an issue discussed earlier in terms of the problems of holding a conquered country rather than merely defeating its army on the battlefield. The Scottish Highlands were an extensive, isolated, and unconquerable landscape since the time of the Romans, but engineering would change this forever.

Born in Miltonhead, William Roy (1726–1790) was the son of an estate factor and attended the local grammar school at Lanark. It may be that Roy developed his skills in surveying and mapping working for the Edinburgh Post Office as a surveyor of roads. He also worked as a draughtsman for the Board of Ordnance when there was a shortage of engineers, with only four for the whole of Scotland in the 1740s. It is believed that Roy took on the surveys around Fort Augustus and the surrounding countryside, mostly single-handed. Then, from 1748, he set about the mapping of the Highlands supported by six surveying parties each of which had six men. The task was mostly finished by 1752, and was followed by southern Scotland, south of the Forth-Clyde line, which they completed three years later. The road improvements that followed the surveys and mapping would bring the wild, untameable Highlands within the sphere of national governance. Other actions were also taken, including the forcible removal of many of the clans and their crofts (mostly by Scottish lairds), the suppression of spoken Gaelic, and the banning of the wearing of tartan. Many of the peasanty simply left, either to the big towns and cities, or to emigrate in search of better lives.

Understanding and recording the landscape: the emergence of the Ordnance Survey

Conflicts and the threat of warfare provide impetus for the making of maps and especially ones that accurately portray terrain and topography. Many early maps in England for instance had scales that were not linear but that reflected the importance of a particular landowner. Indeed, pre-Ordnance Survey maps might miss out entire settlements because there was simply nobody of 'worth' residing there. However, such inaccuracies render these maps useless in terms of a military campaign. In Britian and Europe throughout the 1700s and 1800s, the widespread political uncertainty combined with expansionist, imperial powerplays to make the possession of good maps increasingly important. Furthermore, along with the Anglo-Scottish turmoil the revolution in France triggered events across the Continent and around the world. When Napoleon took command of the French army in 1795, he began his military campaigns which he planned would give him mastery over much of Europe. So, these cataclysmic forces provided an urgent incentive to develop reliable and portable surveying equipment, and the consequent production of reliable, accurate maps. This

Surveying party in the Highlands of Scotland in the late 1740s.

was exemplified by the British army in Scotland and the maps produced by Roy and his contemporaries.

With a real threat of invasion from continental Europe the British government commissioned a military survey of the vulnerable English south coast. There was already a good map of the island of Jersey commissioned shortly after an attempted French invasion in 1781. Not widely available, this was restricted to government use only. It was apparent that from a perspective of national security that new and improved maps were required and these were to be published at a scale of one inch to the mile. Previous proposals to map the whole country had failed to gain support from key landowners. This was probably because they didn't want details of their estates surveying and the results being used for taxation purposes. However, now that it was clear that national security was at stake and the threat was imminent, the business of surveying the landscape assumed greater urgency.

The task of this landmark survey was given to the Board of Ordnance, from which the Ordnance Survey takes its name. The Board was set up by the government under the Tudors to manage supplies of stores and armaments primarily for the army. Based in the Tower of London, it was also responsible for maintaining national defences. The Board's trained military engineers and draftsmen set about a full survey of the countryside using a system of triangulation. From the surveys the necessary military maps could be produced. The surveyors used a theodolite to measure the angles of a remote point from each end of a steel chain. From the triangle made by the known length of the chain and the two sight lines, the distance of the far point could be calculated precisely by trigonometry. The technology that enabled the work was a theodolite, specially built by Jesse Ramsden. A theodolite is a precision instrument incorporating a level, able to rotate in both planes, and used to measure angles in the horizontal and the vertical. Almost a metre in diameter and weighing over ninety kilogrammes, Ramsden's machine was a formidable instrument and required a four-wheeled sprung carriage pulled by two horses to carry it from site to site. The first survey by the Ordnance Board was of Kent on the English south coast and clearly vulnerable to invasion from France. Directed by the Board's chief draftsman William Gardner, work began in 1795.

Being a survey by the Ordnance Board and for primarily military use, the engineers focused on features such as critically important communication routes especially roads, rivers, and bridges. Such significant infrastructure was to be shown clearly and accurately. Furthermore, and important in the context of the battlescapes described in this book, topographic features such as woods, forests, and hills that might provide cover for enemy forces, partisans, and ambush. On these early OS maps, elaborate shading was used to depict such things as the contours of terrain that might offer cover and therefore hazard, or perhaps tactical advantage in the battlescape. Since that time the mapping has moved to remote sensing, satellite imagery, and drones, but it began as an urgent response to perceived threat of war and invasion. Whether on home turf with an invading force or as a conquering army abroad, good information on terrain, topography, and on settlements and infrastructure like routes and river crossings etc, may tip the balance between success and failure. In Britian the coverage of the Ordnance Survey was completed in 1874, transformed from a military necessity to an enduring legacy central to modern living.

The development of cartography demonstrates the evolution in approach from the two-dimensional maps used by explorers in the 1500s and 1600s, to the three-dimensional topographic maps of the 1700s and 1800s. The latter reflected the need for military maps showing terrain and topographic features and thus identifying landscape that might be of use or else a hazard. It is worthwhile too, considering the awareness of landscape and local terrain held by indigenous cultures. In terms of landscapes of defence and of battlescapes, such mental maps, passed down by tradition and oral history between generations, may be a huge advantage to a community under invasion by an external force of oppression.

German medical orderlies searching along a destroyed railway line during the Second World War.

Battlescapes

Some battles were terrible bloody affairs, but they were often short-lived, maybe just a few days from start to end, and were focused in a relatively defined area. Other battlescapes are long-term scars and the countryside has been altered forever. In many areas, if allowed to do so, nature will return, and landscapes heal to a degree. At the same time, some sites are preserved to honour the dead and to be a tangible reminder of the awful tragedy for people and for nature.

Even when a landscape has greened over and apparently recovered, you will see the stark reminders of bomb craters, trench systems, machine-gun posts, and even fragments of shrapnel and the occasional unexploded shell or bomb. In the high moors and bogs of the English Peak District, you can visit the crash sites of bombers, both Allied and German, where the planes and their crews came to rest. The landscape is still physically and chemically scarred and in many cases the names of the crews are known; many were only in their teens.

Some militarized landscapes were drained of their wetlands, other areas were deliberately flooded. Some impacts were long-term as floodwaters deposited thick layers of intractable mud and silt that made future farming impossible.

Diseases and invasive species

The side-effects of conflicts though diseases as discussed, were probably as significant in history as the battles and wars themselves. However, other impacts of long-distance campaigns were movement and transfer of animals and plants around the world. Species always moved with people, so the Celts from Central Europe for instance, brought the brown hare to Britain. The Romans brought animals like fallow deer, but also herbal and culinary plants, and of course vines. The Normans brought similar new species including the now ubiquitous rabbit. The medieval Christian crusades had major effects on our ecology through animals and plants brought back to Britain from the Mediterranean. Along with monastic introductions, these events continue to have big impacts on the fauna and flora of our countryside.

Technologies and countryside

Warfare and conflicts trigger technical innovations and developments such as the Second World War 'land improvement' by drainage and farming in the English fenlands. A breakthrough in land reclamation was the importation of North American farming technology with heavy-duty tractors and tracked vehicles able to deal with clay soils and fen. These vehicles were direct descendants from the First World War tank innovations, transferred to the American prairie farms and then shipped across the Atlantic to British farms, and especially to the fens. Other innovations driven by conflict include aeroplanes, radar, rockets, and jet-propulsion.

Emigration and immigration

Pressures following wars and subjugation led to many communities with skills and experience in working the land leaving the British Isles in the 1700s and 1800s. The Scottish, Irish, Welsh and Cornish especially, emigrated. These massive demographic shifts were brought about through wars (Scotland and Ireland), the Clearances (Scottish Highlands), the enclosures (all areas), and impoverishment and starvation. Clearance, enclosures, and the resulting consequences may not have been military endeavours, but they were undoubtedly social conflicts on a major scale. From all these scenarios, the mass exodus of farmers, crofters and others around the world had significant impacts on the countries and landscapes in which they settled. In many cases, the conflicts over lands, nature, and resources transferred to new continents, where the migrants became the oppressors and displaced indigenous peoples.

In the 1620s, the hope of draining the English fens proved problematic because of a lack of willing local labour. However, migrant workers from the European Low Countries were French Protestant Huguenots from Picardy, and Walloons

A British trench excavator. The idea developed from the stalemate of First World War trench warfare. It was intended to avoid the repeat of such problems. Known as NLE Tractors, or Nellie, it was a massive, heavy vehicle, lightly armoured and without weapons, designed to advance on enemy positions mostly below ground level via a trench that it excavated. When at the enemy's frontline Nellie would act as a ramp for assault troops and tanks. It never saw active service; blitzkrieg changed the nature of warfare from the static stalemate of the First World War.

from Flanders, all arriving in England to escape religious persecution from Catholic overlords. They came ready-skilled with knowledge of living in and draining a wet landscape. Of course, importing labour, when the local fenmen opposed the drainage, was itself an issue that led to violent and long-running conflicts over possession of land and resources.

The later attempt to drain the Cambridgeshire fens from around 1650, was undertaken with Scottish prisoners of war taken at the Battle of Dunbar, on 3 September 1650. This battle was part of the Third English

Testing a Crossley car for war service, January 1918.

Dragon teeth, the Siegfried Line, Wissembourg, France, near the German border, 1940s.

Civil War where Oliver Cromwell's English Parliamentarian forces defeated a Scottish army commanded by David Leslie, loyal to the future King Charles II. From several thousand prisoners following the battle, a thousand were put to work north of the Bedford River in the fens. Many worked until they died of disease, mainly malaria.

Once the supply of Scottish prisoners of war dried up following English victory in 1652, a fresh influx was provided through Dutch prisoners of war, many of whom were skilled in drainage. Five hundred new prisoners were brought back to England and immediately set to labour on the drainage of the Great Level in Cambridgeshire. These movements of people related directly to wars, influencing people, communities, and countryside in the countries both populated and de-populated. Exported skills helped to transform landscapes in the countries to which people migrated or were sent as prisoners.

Wars depopulate towns, villages, and countryside, sometimes permanently and indigenous peoples are removed, and cultural landscapes are abandoned or transformed. This has happened across the world from Europe to North America, Central and South America, to Australia, and Africa, where indigenous and aboriginal people are displaced and frequently exterminated. The Scottish Highlands were turned from a populated countryside with deeply cultural origins, to a landscape largely depopulated and now incorrectly perceived as wilderness. The English lowlands were mostly depopulated through parliamentary enclosures, to become modern farmland. In England's uplands, enclosures removed peasant commoners and replaced them with private grouse moors, and sheep-walk. Public access by the descendants of those commoners, to land formerly theirs by right, was only regained in 2000, nearly sixty years after the infamous Battle of Kinder Scout in 1932.

Long-term conflicts over access to land and natural resources have transformed the ecological landscapes and triggered the de-population of human spaces.

Battlescapes in a countryside past

British Light Dragoons, 1800s.

There are significant problems in interpreting and understanding the roles of landscape in conflicts, because the modern countryside differs from when battles were fought. Landscapes have changed and been transformed, sometimes influenced by a conflict, but even more so because of modernization and industrialization of farming and countryside. Even when battlescapes remain relatively intact spatially, the nature of that countryside is radically different. A major factor influencing many battlescapes and their modern interpretation is that they have mostly been drained. Very often, to realistically interpret a battlescape, it is necessary to reimagine the landscape with its wetlands, bogs, marshes, fens, and wet woodlands. Only then is it possible to effectively and realistically reconstruct tactics and strategy.

The context for warfare is generally topographic and climatic, whereas that for individual battles and skirmishes is a matter of local and regional terrain, and of weather. However, overall impacts of interactions between conflicts, communities, nature, and landscapes have often been transformational. Furthermore, in many situations, the influences of nature and landscape on wars, battles, and skirmishes, have been pivotal for the outcomes.

Bibliography and recommended readings

Adkin, M. (2013) *The Western Front Companion: The Complete Guide to How the Armies Fought for Four Devastating Years, 1914-1918*. Aurum Press Ltd, London.

Anon. (1893) Exploitation de la Tourbe. *La Nature*, 1071, 17-18.

Anon. (1918) *British Trench Warfare 1917-1918. A Reference Manual*. General Staff, War Office, London.

Anon. (1918) *Summary Report of the Mines Branch of the Department of Mines for the Calendar Year Ending December 31, 1917*. Sessional Paper No. 26a, Printed by Order of Parliament, Ottawa.

Anon. (1918) Nos resources locales dans la zone des armées: La Tourbe. *L'Illustration*, 16 February 1918, 167-168.

Anon. (1918) Find many uses for peat: War-torn Industry Gives Promise of Great development. *The New York Times*, undated and unpaginated extract.

Anon. (1940) Sea Floods Holland. Nazi demolitions and allied bombs blast dikes that guard lowlands. Unknown magazine extract, p34-36.

Anon. (1940) The Low Countries' Traditional Defence; strategic inundations. *The Illustrated London News*, 18 May 1940, 647.

Anon. (1940) Holland opens the dykes: floods which confronted the Nazis. *The Illustrated London News*, 18 May 1940, 648.

Anon. (1944) Mud bogs Nazis Fleeing Holland: British in Breda. *The Stars and Stripes*, Volume 1, No. 101, 30 October 1944 p1.

Anrep, A. (1918) *Investigation of Peat Bogs*. In: anon. (1918) *Summary Report of the Mines Branch of the Department of Mines for the Calendar Year Ending December 31, 1917*. Sessional Paper No. 26a, Printed by Order of Parliament, Ottawa.

Anrep, A.v. (1914) *Investigation of the Peat Bogs and Peat Industry of Canada 1911-12*. Canada Department of Mines, Ottowa.

Anrep, A.v. (1915) *Investigation of the Peat Bogs and Peat Industry of Canada 1913-14*. Canada Department of Mines, Ottowa.

Ayres, P.G. (2015) *Britain's Green Allies: Medicinal Plants in Wartime*. Matador, Market Harborough.

Bell, S. (2013) *The effect of marsh, bog and moor environments on the execution of warfare with particular reference to the Early Modern period in Britain and Europe*. In: Rotherham, I.D., & Handley, C. (eds) (2013) *War & Peat*. Wildtrack Publishing, Sheffield, 139-142.

Berthelot, Ch. (1941) La Tourbe. *La Nature*, 3066, 35-41.

Berthelot, Ch. (1942) Organisation et Avenir de la Tourbière Française. *L'Illustration*, 5187, 101-103.

Bevan, B. (2013) *Burbage and Houndkirk in the Second World War: defending Sheffield and training the liberators*. In: Rotherham, I.D., & Handley, C. (eds) (2013) *War & Peat*. Wildtrack Publishing, Sheffield, 23-236.

Blizard, J. (1917) *The Value of Peat Fuel for the Generation of Steam*. Government Printing Bureau, Ottowa.

Burgess, C. (2013) *In to the bog: 'silently and in good order. German fashion....'* In: Rotherham,

I.D., & Handley, C. (eds) (2013) *War & Peat*. Wildtrack Publishing, Sheffield, 135-138.

Cana, F.R. (1920) *The Great War in Europe. A Record of the Struggle against Germany*. (In 8 volumes), Virtue & Company, London.

Cantor, N.F. (2001) *In the Wake of the Plague*. Simon & Schuster UK Ltd, London.

Clayton, A. (2012) *Warfare in Woods and Forests*. Indiana University Press, Bloomington & Indianapolis.

Cornish, V. (1916) *Naval and Military Geography of the British Empire (Considered in Relation to the War with Germany)*. Hugh Rees, Ltd, London.

Cornish, V. (1922) *A Geography of Imperial Defence*. Sifton, Praed & Co, Ltd, London.

Crosby, A.W. (1986) *Ecological Imperialism. The Biological Expansion of Europe, 900-1900*. Cambridge University Press, Cambridge.

De Vries, J. (1974) *The Dutch Rural Economy in the Golden Age, 1500-1700*. Yale University Press, New Haven and London.

De Zeeuw, J.W. (1978) Peat and the Dutch Golden Age – The historical meaning of energy-attainability. *A.A.G. BIJDRAGEN*, 21, 3-31.

Dean, S. (2013) *Cannock Chase: conserving the military heritage*. In: Rotherham, I.D., & Handley, C. (eds) (2013) *War & Peat*. Wildtrack Publishing, Sheffield, 79-90.

Frøland, S.S. (2022) *Duel Without End. Mankind's Battle with Microbes*. Reaktion Books, London.

Gerding, M. (2013) *Bogs as defence in the seventeenth century Dutch Republic*. In: Rotherham, I.D., & Handley, C. (eds) (2013) *War & Peat*. Wildtrack Publishing, Sheffield, 105-114.

Griffiths, T., Rotherham, I.D., & Handley, C. (2013) *Sphagnum: the healing harvest*. In: Rotherham, I.D., & Handley, C. (eds) (2013) *War & Peat*. Wildtrack Publishing, Sheffield, 201-220.

Grunwald, M. (2006) *The Swamp: The Everglades, Florida, and the Politics of Paradise*. Simon & Schuster, New York

Haanel, B.F. (1912) *Report on the Utilization of Peat Fuel*. Canada Department of Mines, Ottowa.

Haanel, E. (1918) *Peat as a Source of fuel*. Commission of Conservation, Canada, Ottowa.

Halpenny, B.B. (1982) *Action Stations 4. Military airfields of Yorkshire*. Patrick Stephens Limited, Cambridge.

Hempel, S. (2018) *The Atlas of Disease*. White Lion Publishing, London.

Home, A. (1985) *The Diary of a World War I Cavalry Officer*. D.J. Costello (Publishers) Ltd, Tunbridge Wells.

Howard, T. (2013) *The moorland access campaigns – (with some military interludes)*. In: Rotherham, I.D., & Handley, C. (eds) (2013) War & Peat. Wildtrack Publishing, Sheffield, 257-272.

Johnson, D.W. (1921) *Battlefields of the World War. Western and Southern Fronts. A Study in Military Geography*. American Geographical Society Research Series No. 3.

Kiple, K.F. (ed.) *Plague, Pox & Pestilence. Disease in History*. Weindenfeld & Nicolson, London.

Laffin, J. (1987) *Battlefield Archaeology*. Ian Allan Ltd, London.

McNeil, W.H. (1976) *Plagues and People*. Anchor Press, New York

Mitchel, T.J., & Smith, G.M. (1922) *History of the Great War based on official documents. Medical Services. Casualties and Medical statistics of the Great War*. HMSO, London.

Nikiforuk, A. (1992) *The Fourth Horseman. A Short History of Epidemics, Plagues and Other Scourges*. Fourth Estate Limited, London.

Nyström, E. & Anrep, S.A. (1909) *Bulletin No. 1. Investigation of the Peat Bogs and Peat Industry of Canada, During the Season 1908-9.* Canada Department of Mines, Ottowa.

O'Sullivan, P. (1991) *Terrain and Tactics.* Greenwood Press, New York.

Parker, P., Grant, R.G., & Humphreys, A. (2018) *Battles That Changed History. Epic conflicts explored and explained.* Dorling Kindersley Ltd, London.

Pearson, C. (2012) *Mobilizing nature. The environmental history of war and militarization in Modern France.* Manchester University Press, Manchester.

Pearson, C., Coates, P., & Cole, T. (eds) (2010) *Militarized Landscapes. From Gettysburg to Salisbury Plain.* Continuum International Publishing Group, London.

Peckham, S.F. (ed.) (1874) *Peat for Domestic Fuel. The Geological and Natural History survey of Minnesota.* Tribune Publishing Company, Minneapolis.

Rotherham, I.D. (2010) *Yorkshire's Forgotten Fenlands.* Pen & Sword Books Limited, Barnsley.

Rotherham, I.D. (2013) *The Lost Fens: England's Greatest Ecological Disaster.* The History Press, Stroud.

Rotherham, I.D. (2013) *War & Peat: exploring interactions between people, human conflict, peatlands, and ecology.* In: Rotherham, I.D., & Handley, C. (eds) (2013) *War & Peat.* Wildtrack Publishing, Sheffield, 7-44.

Rotherham, I.D. (2013) *Sherwood Forest and the Dukeries. A Companion to the Land of Robin Hood.* Amberley, Stroud.

Rotherham, I.D. (2017) *York's Military Legacy.* Pen & Sword, Barnsley. Rotherham, I.D., & Handley, C. (eds) (2013) *War & Peat.* Wildtrack Publishing, Sheffield.

Rotherham, I.D. & McCallam, D. (2008) *Peat Bogs, Marshes and Fen as disputed Landscapes in Late Eighteenth-Century France and England.* Lyle, L. & McCallam, D. (eds.) *Histoires de la Terre: Earth Sciences and French Culture 1740-1940.* Rodopi B.V., Amsterdam & New York, 75-90.

Santarelli, E., Rochat, G., Rainero, R., & Goglia, L. (1986) *Omar al-Mukhtar. The Italian Reconquest of Libya.* [Translated by John Gilbert] Darf Publishers Ltd., London.

Shaler, N.S. (1895) *Origin, Distribution, and Commercial Value of Peat Deposits.* Government Printing Office, Washington D.C.

Soper, E.K. & Osbon, C.C. (1922) *The occurrence and uses of peat in the United States.* Government Printing Office, Washington D.C.

Smurthwaite, D. (1984) *The Complete Guide to the Battlefields of Britain.* Web and Bower, Exeter.

Storey, N.R. (2014) *Animals in the First World War.* Shire Publications Ltd., Oxford.

Tanner, S. (2000) *Epic Retreats. From 1776 to the Evacuation of Saigon.* Greenhill Books, London.

TeBrake, W.H. (1985) *Medieval Frontier. Culture and Ecology in Rinjland.* A.&M. University Press, Texas.

Tucker, R.P., & Russell, E. (eds) (2004) *Natural Enemy, Natural Ally. Toward an Environmental History of Warfare.* Oregon State University Pres, Corvallis.

Turp, J.S. (1916) *Peat in 1915.* Government Printing Office, Washington D.C.

Weir, W. (2011) *Secrets of Warfare. Exposing the Myths and Hidden History of Weapons and Battles.* New Page Books, Pompton Plains, NJ.

Wellard, G. (1995) *200 Years of Frimley's History. The Story of the Frimley Fuel Allotments Charity and Pine Ridge Golf Centre.* Pine Ridge Golf Centre and Frimley Fuel Allotments Charity, Camberley, Surrey.

Winters, H.A., Galloway, G.E. Jnr, Reynolds, W.J., & Rhyne, D.W. (1998) *Battling the Elements. Weather and Terrain in the Conduct of War.* The John Hopkins University Press, Baltimore and London.

Wolff, L. (1960) *In Flanders Fields. The 1917 Campaign*. Longmans, Green & Co., London.

Woodward, R. (2013) *Military pastoral and the military sublime in British army training landscapes.* In: Rotherham, I.D., & Handley, C. (eds) (2013) *War & Peat.* Wildtrack Publishing, Sheffield.

Woolley, B. (2004) *The Herbalist.* HarperCollins Publishers, London.

Virtanen, P. (2013) *War and Forest.* In: Rotherham, I.D., & Handley, C. (eds) (2013) *War & Peat.* Wildtrack Publishing, Sheffield, 195-200.

Yorke, T. (2014) *The Trench. Life and Death on the Western Front 1914 – 1918.* Countryside Books, Newbury, Berkshire.

Ziegler, P. (1969) *The Black Death.* Collins, London.

Zinsser, H. (1935) *Rats, Lice and History. A Chronicle of Pestilence and Plagues.* Little Brown and Company Inc., Boston.

Index